CURRENT ISSUES IN FINANCIAL AND MONETARY ECONOMICS

CURRENT ISSUES IN ECONOMICS

General Editor: David Greenaway, University of Nottingham

Current Issues in Microeconomics
Edited by John D. Hey

Current Issues in Macroeconomics
Edited by David Greenaway

Current Issues in Labour Economics
Edited by David Sapsford
and Zafiris Tzannatos

Current Issues in International Monetary Economics
Edited by David T. Llewellyn and Chris Milner

Current Issues in Development Economics
Edited by V. N. Balasubramanyam
and Sanjaya Lall

Current Issues in Financial and Monetary Economics
Edited by Kevin Dowd and Mervyn K. Lewis

Forthcoming

Current Issues in Public Sector Economics
Edited by Peter Jackson

Current Issues in Industrial Economics
Edited by John Cable

Current Issues in Welfare Economics
Edited by Nicholas Barr and David Whynes

Current Issues in Agricultural Economics
Edited by A. J. Rayner and David R. Colman

CURRENT ISSUES IN FINANCIAL AND MONETARY ECONOMICS

Edited by

Kevin Dowd and Mervyn K. Lewis

Department of Economics
University of Nottingham

M
MACMILLAN

First published 1992 by
MACMILLAN EDUCATION LTD
Houndmills, Basingstoke, Hampshire RG21 2XS
and London
Companies and representatives
throughout the world

ISBN 0–333–51639–7 hardcover
ISBN 0–333–51640–0 paperback

A catalogue record for this book is available
from the British Library.

Printed in Hong Kong

Contents

List of Tables

List of Figures

Series Editor's Preface

The *Current Issues* series has slightly unusual origins. *Current Issues in International Trade*, which was published in 1987, and which turned out to be the pilot for the series was in fact 'conceived' in the Horton Hospital, Banbury and 'delivered' (in the sense of completed) in the Hilton International in Nicosia! The reader may be struck by the thought that a more worthwhile and enjoyable production process would start and finish the other way around. I agree! Be that as it may, that is how the series started.

As I said in the Preface to *Current Issues in International Trade* the reason for its creation was the difficulty of finding suitable references on 'frontier' subjects for undergraduate students. Many of the issues which excite professional economists and which dominate the journal literature take quite a time to percolate down into texts, hence the need for a volume of *Current Issues*. The reception which *Current Issues in International Trade* received persuaded me that it may be worth doing something similar for the other subject areas we teach. Thus each volume in this series is intended to take readers to the 'frontier' of the particular subject area. Each volume contains nine or ten essays, one of which provides a general overview while the remainder are devoted to current issues.

As series editor the main challenge I faced was finding suitable editors for each of the volumes – the best people are generally the busiest! I believe, however, that I have been fortunate in having such an impressive and experienced team of editors with the necessary skills and reputation to persuade first-class authors to participate. I would like to thank all of them for their cooperation and assistance in the development of the series. Like me, all of them will, I am sure, hope that this series provides a useful service to undergraduate and graduate students as well as faculty.

Current Issues in Financial and Monetary Economics is the sixth in the series. This has been an area of profound change over the last decade or so. Fundamental institutional change and a number of financial crises have guaranteed that the subject matter will remain high on the policy agenda for some time to come. The editors of this volume are to be commended on their choice of topics and authors. As they say in their introduction, they consciously avoided 'long running sagas' such as the demand for money and the tactics of monetary control. Instead they selected topics which are genuinely 'current issues' – topics like financial intermediation, the operation of financial markets, the impact of deregulation and the credibility of policy. In so doing they have provided us with a rich blend of theory, empirics and policy analysis. The authors they persuaded to contribute are from four different countries giving the volume an international perspective and enriching it as a result. In turn the authors are to be congratulated on producing such excellent essays. Many of the issues addressed have barely emerged from the leading journals and are of great complexity. Despite this we still have a very accessible volume. I have enjoyed reading these essays and have certainly learned something in the process. I hope others have a similar experience.

University of Nottingham DAVID GREENAWAY

Notes on the Contributors

Keith Blackburn is a Lecturer in Economics at the University of Southampton.

Robin C. Bladen-Hovell is a Lecturer in Economics at the University of Manchester.

John Chant is Professor of Economics at Simon Fraser University.

Alec Chrystal is Professor of Personal Finance at the City University Business School.

Kevin T. Davis is Professor of Finance at the University of Melbourne.

Kevin Dowd is a Lecturer in Economics at the University of Nottingham.

Charles A. E. Goodhart is Norman Sosnow Professor of Money and Banking at the London School of Economics.

Mervyn K. Lewis is Midland Bank Professor of Money and Banking at the University of Nottingham.

Gerald P. O'Driscoll, Jr, is Vice-President and Associate Director of Research at the Federal Reserve Bank of Dallas.

Courteney C. Stone is a Professor of Economics at Ball State University in Muncie, Indiana.

Daniel L. Thornton is a Senior Economist at the Federal Reserve Bank of St Louis.

List of Abbreviations

ARM(s)	adjustable rate mortgage(s)
ATM	automatic teller machine
ATS	automatic transfer service
BIS	Bank for International Settlements
CARS	Collateralised Automobile Receivables
CARDS	Certificates of Amortising Revolving Debts
CAT	Certificate of Treasury Securities
CD(s)	certificate of deposit(s)
CMO(s)	collateralised mortgage obligation(s)
DM	Deutschemark
EMS	European Monetary System
EMU	Economic and Monetary Union
EOM	early ownership mortgage
ERM	Exchange Rate Mechanism
ESCB	European System of Central Banks
FDIC	Federal Deposit Insurance Corporation
FHLBB	Federal Home Loan Bank Board
FIRREA	Financial Institutions Reform, Recovery and Enforcement Act, 1989 (USA)
FSLIC	Federal Saving and Loans Insurance Corporation
GDP	gross domestic product
IRA(s)	individual retirement account(s)
LIBOR	London Inter Bank Offer Rate
LYONS	Lehman investment opportunity notes
MMDA	money market deposit account
MMMF	money market mutual funds
MSB	mutual savings bank
NOW	notice of withdrawal
NYSE	New York Stock Exchange
OCD	other chequeable accounts
PIKS	pay-in-kind bonds
PIN	portfolio income notes

REMIC	real estate mortgage investment conduit
ROL	reduction option loans
SAM	shared appreciation mortgage
S&L	savings and loan association
STRIPS	separate trading of registered principal of securities
TIGR	Treasury Investment Growth Receipts
YCAN	yield curve adjustable notes

1 Introduction: Current Issues in Financial and Monetary Economics

KEVIN DOWD and MERVYN K. LEWIS

In common with the other volumes in the *Current Issues* series, this book contains essays that review recent developments in an important field of economics. As in the rest of the series, the authors are chosen for their ability to crystallise the issues authoritatively for students of economics and readers who are not specialists in the field. The essays here cover major new issues which have interested monetary and financial economists in recent years. In selecting them we have deliberately stayed away from long-running sagas such as the demand and supply of money, and the tactics of monetary policy to focus upon those issues which have come into prominence in the 1980s. The ten authors – four from the UK, three from the USA, two Australians and one Canadian – bring an international perspective to the issues selected.

The choice of a monetary standard underpins a country's monetary system and the workings of its financial institutions and markets, and there is a very real sense in which the issues examined in this book can be traced to the decision of the major countries to adopt fiat money standards when the Bretton Woods system of fixed but adjustable exchange rates broke down in the early 1970s. Erratic, expansionary monetary policies followed the change in regime, leading to substantial inflation, high and variable interest rates, and wide fluctuations in nominal and real exchange rates. Milton Friedman,[1] for one, sees much of the wave of financial innovation and deregulation in the 1980s as induced responses to the unstable monetary environment. In combination, these developments sowed the seeds for much of the savings and loan crisis in the USA and increased bank failures and difficulties there and in other countries later in the decade. Such financial stresses have focused economists' attention upon the operation of banks and other financial intermediaries and on ways in which banking markets and regulatory structures might be reformed. At the same time, the variability of interest rates and exchange rates in the new environment has led to an examination of how well financial markets work, and how added credibility can be lent to policy actions including ways in which monetary policies might be coordinated internationally to influence market outcomes. Charles Goodhart's essay on monetary standards thus provides an appropriate setting for the other chapters.

ALTERNATIVE MONETARY STANDARDS

Monetary authorities can seek control of prices and incomes by means of external stabilisation – maintaining the domestic currency in a nearly-fixed relation to some external standard (e.g. gold, commodities, another currency) – or by means of internal stabilisation – varying the domestic currency to control incomes directly. In the immediate aftermath of Bretton Woods, most of the major countries sought internal price stabilisation by means of monetary growth targets. During the 1980s, however, various factors combined to produce a de-emphasis in monetary targets, and there has been some drift back towards fixed exchange rates. In the UK, for example, less attention began to be given to monetary targets in the mid-1980s, and the UK authorities began increasingly to target the £/DM exchange rate; a policy which eventually culminated in the UK's entry in 1990 to the European Exchange Rate Mechanism (ERM). This decision, of course, in no way settles the question of the monetary standard but transfers it from the individual country level to the level of the Community as a whole: the European countries must engage (as they are now doing) in a process of determining how Community-wide monetary policy is to operate.

The roots of the monetary standards debate go far back in history, and Professor Goodhart provides a detailed account of the evolution of financial intermediation and modern *central banking* and the development of modern fiat money from the gold-backed currency that preceded it. That history shows that the main threat to the maintenance of convertibility and price stability has come when governments felt obliged to resort to the printing press and print money to finance their activities, most often under the stimulus of financing a war. The pressure to inflate has also been compounded by other political factors – pressure to boost the economy, for example – and the difficulty of establishing an adequate means of monetary control. Professor Goodhart then discusses the main options currently facing monetary authorities: an exchange rate link like that operating in Europe; tying the currency to a basket of 'real' goods and services of some sort, and, perhaps, abolishing the central bank outright (i.e. establishing free banking on a convertible standard); adopting an 'independent' monetary policy by targeting nominal national income; monetary targets or rules of the traditional type; or discretionary monetary management. In the case of the UK authorities he concludes that the best course of action is to continue with the ERM as they are currently doing, and thus by implication to seek a European-wide solution to the monetary standard in which the influence of low-inflation countries such as Germany, Holland and France will presumably be paramount.

FINANCIAL INTERMEDIATION

It is readily observable that financial intermediaries – banks, savings institutions, finance companies, life insurance houses, mutual funds and trusts – play a central role in the process of financing. Yet economic theory has long treated them in an ambivalent fashion. Much of the pure theory of finance simply assumes them away with the perfect markets paradigm: consumers who live forever and can plan their spending with full knowledge of all future events have little need for the services of financial intermediaries. At the other extreme, many traditional accounts of financial intermediation have been descriptive ones that took the existence and form of financial intermediation more or less for granted. The shortcomings of this gap bewteen the two approaches have become increasinly obvious over the past few years, for economic theory cannot adequately explain what intermediaries actually do, and consequently cannot tell us how their activities are influenced by government policies and regulation.

These deficiencies provided the impetus for the development of new theory that gives a rigorous micro-foundation for the analysis of financial intermediation, and John Chant provides an overview of this literature in Chapter 3 which makes some valuable contributions in its own right. The new analysis examines a number of fundamental issues that earlier writers have tended to skip. Why do intermediaries exist? What functions do they perform? What types of institutions are there? And why do some people and firms use the services of financial intermediaries but others do not? The literature explaining the existence and role of intermediation has isolated a number of determining factors, no single one of which can offer a complete theory of financial intermediation. *Transactions costs* have an important role to play, but so does *imperfect information* which gives rise to the costs of *verifying reported outcomes* which one party might have an incentive to misrepresent, the costs of *monitoring the performance* of a party who would reduce his or her effort level if not watched, the costs of *enforcing contracts*, and the degree of *marketability* or *non-marketability* of investments in the underlying 'real' economy.

These elements also influence the form that the intermediation might take. In the simplest case, the intermediary is a *broker* – someone whose function it is to inform and bring the prospective borrowers and lenders together. Most real-world intermediaries go beyond this, and become a party to the financing activity by holding (primary) claims issued by the borrower and issuing their own (indirect) claims to lenders. Instead of owing something to the 'ultimate' lender, the ultimate borrower thus owes something to the intermediary, and the intermediary owes something to the ultimate lenders. The advantage of this type of arrangement is that lenders do not have to monitor the borrower or verify the claims which he makes. Instead, they delegate those jobs to the intermediary, and have only to keep an eye on the intermediary itself. Among those intermediaries we can distinguish two basic types. There are *mutual funds* (unit trusts) which offer investors a proportionate share in the portfolio of assets that the intermediary acquires, and whose shares therefore fluctuate with changes in the value of the underlying collection of assets that make up the intermediary's portfolio. Many insurance companies, for example, offer unit-linked or variable life-insurance policies, especially for pension schemes, which combine to varying degrees traditional life insurance with investments in mutual funds. The other intermediaries are *deposit-taking* intermediaries which offer savers claims which are usually very liquid and whose promised values are independent of the value of the portfolio held by the intermediary. Sometimes these promises cannot be met and there is a crisis of confidence in the institutions concerned. These isues are taken up further in Chapter 6 below.

THE OPERATION OF FINANCIAL MARKETS

We then turn to the operation of financial markets. This subject has been very controversial in recent years. Much of this controversy has centred on the extent to which financial markets are *'excessively' volatile* when left to themselves, and, as a corollary, whether *government intervention* of some sort is needed to make financial markets less volatile than they appear to be. Alec Chrystal provides a perspective of this topic in Chapter 4. He looks at the 'excess volatility' arguments as they have been applied to three different markets – the *foreign exchange market*, the *stock market*, and *retail financial markets*. The arguments vary somewhat in each case, but they have in common the same underlying theme – that markets 'fail' in some important sense. In each case the starting-point is the notion of *market efficiency* – do market prices fully reflect all available information? Market efficiency implies that the market price should only respond to unpredictable events – 'news' – and that the price at any time should provide the best estimate of its value in the period – the *random-walk hypothesis*. The absence of market efficiency would imply that supernormal profits could be made by 'playing the market', and no one has convincingly established that such profits can be made without 'inside' information about special events. The market efficiency hypothesis has thus proved very difficult to reject and Professor Chrystal concludes that supporters of the excess volatility view have so far failed to establish their case. He also notes that much market volatility is a direct reaction to the volatility of government policies themselves. If one wishes to draw conclusions about the appropriate government policy response, one might therefore conclude that governments should make their own policies more steady and predictable.

Professor Chrystal notes that the foreign exchange market differs from other financial markets in that it is the creation of previous government interventions to establish different fiat currencies in each country. Even a system in which currencies are tied to a commodity such as gold would have a foreign exchange market if the currencies had different gold parities – as was the case under the classical gold standard. Exchange rates under the gold standard responded to market forces but moved, for the most part, within the gold-shipping points (those exchange rates at which it became profitable to export and import gold bullion for international payments). Professor Chrystal considers whether there may be a case for abolishing the foreign exchange market completely which would mean replacing these separate currencies by a common one. Member-countries of the European Community have this goal for European-wide transactions in terms of European Monetary Union. Conceivably that single European currency might be adopted by some other countries for international transactions, but a major role for foreign exchange markets would still remain without a concerted move to create an international money.

Some additional considerations arise when examining the operation of the stock and retail credit markets. There has been considerable concern in the stock-market literature as to whether prices accurately reflect market fundamentals – the long-run values of the income streams to which stocks are claims – and whether *programmed trading strategies* – the automatic execution of stop-loss orders using computers – are to be held responsible for the stock-market collapse in 1987. Commentators have also claimed – a view known as *short-termism* – that the stock market takes an excessively short-term view of investment activities. Professor Chrystal studies some of these arguments and concludes that they are not as persuasive as is often believed. In retail financial markets, there has also been considerable and often very public controversy over the alleged 'excessive' provision of credit by lending institutions, and this concern has led to many calls for government intervention to curb lending. These arguments tend to concentrate on the relatively visible costs of lending and ignore the many and generally less visible benefits that lending brings – successful lending does not make good newscopy. Considering the point more generally, leveraged buyouts and the much maligned 'junk bonds', for instance, opened up financial markets and provided modes of financing to enterprises which had previously been excluded from them. It is no coincidence that a free market for entrepreneurial finance is high on the agenda of those reforming Eastern European economies. Many of the criticisms also tend to confuse symptom and cause. If people have difficulty repaying loans, then the cause of the problem is (usually) the fact that they are poor, and the repayment difficulties are merely a symptom of their comparative poverty. To restrict bank lending is then to attack the symptom of a problem for which the banks are not usually responsible.

FINANCIAL INNOVATION

The introduction of a vast number of new financial products and processes, the expanding use of a new computer and communications technology, and the growth of numerous and increasingly diverse types of financial institutions have combined to produce a revolution in financial services over the past two decades. The literature on this financial revolution has pointed to three main causes – the increase in risk and uncertainty that took place in financial markets in the 1970s and 1980s; the impact of *regulatory* factors and changes in regulatory regimes on an increasingly globalised financial services industry, and, in particular, the increased competition that traditional providers of financial services have faced from unregulated competition; and, finally, the impact of various technological factors (e.g. advances in *computer technology*).

These issues are examined in Chapter 5 by Dan Thornton and Cliff Stone. They begin by reviewing the causes and consequences of the 'microeconomic' financial innovation just described, and in the process provide a concise summary of an already considerable literature. They then discuss some 'macroeconomic' aspects of innovation which are far from fully understood. Financial innovation alters the structure of rates of return on different assets, and thus influences the relative demands for financial assets. It also blurs the distinction between different types of financial intermediary – in the USA, for example, the distinction between commercial banks and 'thrifts' has virtually disappeared – in the process undermining the regulatory process which has traditionally presumed these institutions to be quite distinct. Financial innovation has also tended to erase old distinctions between financial assets, and differences between the monetary aggregates based on those distinctions. (Innovation has also given rise to many more measures of financial aggregates from which to choose). The traditional distinction between M1 assets and non-M1 assets has long since ceased to have any real substance, for example, and these developments have clouded the *monetary control problem* faced by the monetary authorities. One case in particular has attracted considerable interest because of the difficulties it has created for the monetary authorities – the 'shift' in the demand for M1 balances in the USA in the 1980s. The chapter examines this case in detail and reviews the theoretical issues it raises as well as the empirical evidence assembled to date. It concludes that the behaviour of M1 over the past decade cannot be explained without giving a leading role to the effects of financial innovation.

BANKING REFORM

Financial innovations on the scale just described would necessarily have consequences for the industry structure and regulatory framework of banking and financial services, but the banking crisis which has unfurled in the USA over the past decade has lent urgency to the need for change and has led many to conclude that a root-and-branch reform of banking is required. The crisis is especially acute in the 'thrift' side of the industry – thrifts being the US term for savings institutions and housing finance (building) societies – and it is probably fair to say that most thrifts that remain today face severe financial difficulties even if they are still solvent (and many are clearly not). The issues raised by banking reform are covered in Chapter 6 by Gerald O'Driscoll. His treatment focuses on the cause and cure of the American banking crisis. While the American banking system has many special features, the lessons drawn by Dr O'Driscoll apply in general terms to almost every financial system. Government-owned banks and private building societies and merchant banks in some states of Australia, for example, have recently undergone a crisis which bears uncanny similarities to the US situation. The US case also offers a warning for those countries that have followed the USA in introducing government-supported systems of *deposit insurance*. (Note that countries with a compulsory system include the UK, Japan, Canada and Italy, while voluntary schemes run by industry operate in France, Germany and Switzerland.)

The US systems of deposit insurance were introduced in the 1930s to protect the banking system against runs, but in doing so, deposit insurance also encourages managers to take lending risks that they might otherwise have avoided. Deposit insurance (in common with other types of insurance) thus creates moral hazard, and the integrity of the system can only be maintained if this *moral hazard problem* can be kept under control. The problem was contained well until the late 1970s, but for various reasons it got ot of control during the following decade. Many banks and especially thrifts took excessive risks that undermined their capital values and drove many into effective insolvency, and the costs of moral hazard have been exacerbated by the authorities' extreme slowness ('forebearance') in closing down those 'zombie' institutions before they could run up massive bills at the public expense. The crisis escalated in this way throughout the 1980s, and it is still far from clear that the authorities have it under proper control.

Many solutions to the crisis have been proposed. Some writers have proposed various ways of patching up the current system and hoping that it then works. Others have proposed more thoroughgoing reforms of the deposit insurance system: while most have argued for reduced coverage and 'market discipline', some have proposed its outright abolition. There have also been calls for 100 per cent *reserve banking* – the Chicago plan of the 1930s to make banks 'back' their deposits 100 per cent with assets that are sound and marketable – *mutual fund banking* – making the value of bank deposits vary in line with the value of bank assets – and *free banking* (another old idea) – the establishment of a deregulated, *laissez-faire* banking system. While the political environment in which these issues will be worked out might rule out, for the present, some of the extreme manifestations of these ideas, we note that there appears to be general acceptance that deposit insurance coverage must be unwound to some degree and that the deregulation of banking should continue.

DEREGULATION AND MONETARY POLICY

In Chapter 7 Kevin Davis and Mervyn Lewis consider some of the issues raised by deregulation and monetary policy. This chapter begins with a review of the ways in which deregulation, financial inventiveness and innovation, and technological progress interact and spur each other along. Not surprisingly, these factors interact in complex ways and it is far from easy to disentangle true cause and effect. The chapter then looks in more detail at the ways in which political forces shape financial and monetary deregulation. Various theories have been proposed to explain political behaviour. The first is the *public interest* model which supposes that the political process aims to promote the general public interest. The second is the *private interest* model which explains political behaviour (and hence, regulation) on the basis of the private interests of the key players involved. These key players are usually the politicians and regulators involved, but they can also include those who are themselves regulated. Indeed, one version of this theory – the theory of *regulatory capture* – emphasises the regulated above others, and supposes that they 'capture' the regulatory process erected over them and manipulate it in their own private interests. A third theory – the *political-support-maximising* theory – is somewhere between the public and private interest theories and maintains that politicians aim to maximise their political support to keep their hold on power. The authors examine how well these theories can account for the deregulation which took place in so many countries during the 1980s. They identify some elements common to the USA, the UK, Canada, Australia and Continental Europe.

The chapter then considers in some detail the impact of deregulation on financial markets and monetary policy. It has long been said that deregulation erodes the effectiveness of monetary policy. The argument is that it erodes the difference between 'money' and other assets, and therefore the difference between 'banks' and other financial intermediaries, and that the effectiveness of monetary policy is undermined in the process since monetary policy is (traditionally) aimed specifically at the banks. The chapter reviews this issue and suggests that the traditional analysis is incomplete; cases can easily be found where deregulation actually *increases* the effectiveness of monetary policy. This discussion is followed by a look at the evolution of monetary controls in the recent past and their likely evolution in the near future. It concludes that there is little likelihood that the authorities will lose control as some writers have suggested. Deregulation, however, does have important ramifications for the transmission mechanism, i.e. the way in which the economy can be controlled by monetary means.

CREDIBILITY AND TIME CONSISTENCY IN MONETARY POLICY

Other policy issues that have also received much attention in recent literature concern *credibility* and *time consistency*. These issues are examined by Keith Blackburn in Chapter 8. Suppose a government is considering a programme of disinflation. The ability of the programme to bring inflation down at relatively low cost depends critically on the public's perception of what the government is doing. If they think that the government is not serious in its purpose – i.e. if the programme lacks credibility – then inflationary expectations will remain high, and the government will only be able to reduce inflation at a relatively high cost in terms of foregone output and employment. If the public believe that the government is serious, on the other hand, then inflationary expectations will fall and the government can reduce actual inflation without incurring the high output and unemployment costs that would otherwise be necessary. The government's credibility thus has a critical bearing on the cost at which it can carry through its policy. Time consistency flows on from the credibility issue. Suppose that the public expects the government to act in a self-interested way. If the government says it will do X at some future time t, the public will only believe it – and, therefore, X will only be credible – if the public perceive that it will be in the government's interest to do X at t. If the public believe that it will be in the government's interest to do Y instead, then X lacks credibility. The policy X must be time-consistent if it is to be credible.

These issues mean that we have to view the monetary policy process in a very different light from the way that traditional theories have viewed it. If a government is to implement a programme at minimum cost, it must be credible. The government must make its programme time-consistent, and in order to do that it must somehow limit its own freedom to 'change its mind' and abandon the programme later on. In short, it must *pre-commit* itself in some believable way. In practice, of course, perfect pre-commitment is virtually impossible, and private-sector decision-makers will attach some positive probability to the future abandonment of a currently adopted course of action. The effectiveness of the official programme then depends on that probability, and the probability itself depends on the government's *reputation*. A good reputation is like a hostage given to the future, and helps us to believe something that we might otherwise be inclined to doubt. Paradoxically, an authority with an established reputation (e.g. for inflation control) may be able to deviate substantially to pursue other targets (e.g. exchange-rate stabilisation) without imperilling the longer-term goals: the Bundesbank and Swiss National Bank, for instance, have occasionally acted in this way. Monetary policy needs to be seen as a 'game' played over many periods of time in which authorities pursue policies which they try to make credible, but the credibility of their policies depends on their ability to pre-commit themselves and on their ability to maintain a sound reputation which itself depends on their own actions and achievements. This perspective has revolutionised our understanding of the monetary policy process, and its full implications have yet, it appears, to be fully worked out.

INTERNATIONAL MONETARY POLICY COORDINATION

We come then to the last topic in the book – the chapter on *international monetary policy coordination* by Robin Bladen-Hovell. An obvious feature of the post-War world is the increasing interdependence of the world economy, and this interdependence has important implications for government policy. It suggests that the abilities of national governments to pursue their own independent policies might have become increasingly limited, and it indicates the potentially important gains from policy coordination. Coordination necessarily embraces all facets of economic policy, for monetary policy ought not to be fashioned independently of fiscal and other policy actions internationally any more so than domestically, although in practice there may be closer links between the central banks of the major countries than is the case with their fiscal counterparts – certainly this has been so historically.

The absence of policy coordination has been a subject of concern since at least the early 1970s. In 1972, for example, the coincidence of tight monetary policies in Germany and expansionary economic policies in the USA saw a flood of dollars flow from the USA to Germany and other European countries, expanding international reserves and money supplies. Commodity price rises at a world level, and thus indirectly the rise in oil prices in 1973, have been attributed to this monetary expansion.[2] A decade later in the early 1980s, the combination of tight monetary policy and expansionary fiscal policy in the USA saw upward pressures upon world interest rates reinforced as European countries moved to counter the inflationary pressures from the strengthening dollar by restrictive monetary policies. Dealing with the aftermath of this episode was a major issue in international policy discussions throughout most of the 1980s. It led to the Plaza Accord of 1985, for example, which was an attempt by finance ministers to coordinate the macroeconomic policies of the G-7 nations – the seven biggest Western economies – in order to avoid a 'hard landing' for the US dollar. The commitment to coordinate macroeconomic policies was subsequently reaffirmed at each annual economic summit, and though there is sometimes controversy over the way that policies should be coordinated, no major government is opposed to the principle of coordination *per se*.

As Dr Bladen-Hovell observes, these practical considerations have stimulated a large theoretical and applied literature that tries to explain the nature and possible size of the gains from policy coordination. The theoretical work takes a *game-theoretic* approach – it sees each country trying to achieve certain policy objectives in an interdependent world economy where the ability to achieve an objective successfully depends in part on what policies are pursued by other governments. The gains from coordination then arise from successful attempts to avoid damaging *spill-overs* which occur when one country's policies have a harmful impact on another. An example would be a sudden shift in monetary policy by one country. The exchange rate might then 'overshoot' its long-run path and have a disruptive effect on he current and capital account positions of other countries. The theoretical literature also raises credibility and time-consistency issues – as noted in the previous chapter, the effectiveness of policy actions depends much on the credibility of the government that implements them. Time consistency is a major problem in this area because governments have no easy way of pre-committing themselves, and the absence of pre-commitment can itself undermine the efficacy of the coordinated policy. If the theoretical work indicates that there are gains from coordination, the empirical work nonetheless suggests that these gains might actually be quite small in practice. This evidence comes almost entirely from simulation experiments performed on large-scale econometric models of the world economy, and most of these exercises suggest potential gains of around 1 per cent of GNP, if not less. These results are necessarily tentative, and it is possible that future studies might give different answers.

What is interesting (and here the final chapter links back to Professor Goodhart's study of monetary standards) are the parallels which can be drawn between the Plaza Agreement and the Louvre Accord of the 1980s and similar arrangements during the last period of floating exchange rates in the form of the Tripartite Monetary Agreement of 1936. Then the coordination of policies and interventions in currency markets to stabilise exchange rates served as a precursor of a world-wide return to fixed exchange rates. But it is too early to judge whether there will be a repetition.

2 Alternative Monetary Standards

CHARLES A. E. GOODHART

INTRODUCTION

During the course of the past two decades the interplay of the pressure of events, together with the development of academic and informed thinking, led the major Central Banks of the industrialised world to experiment with various alternative methods of monetary management and control – different *monetary standards or regimes* as they are usually termed. In particular, Central Banks responded to the worsening inflation of the 1970s by adopting quantitative monetary targets as their main intermediate monetary objective. Such targets were 'intermediate' in the sense that they lay between the operational instruments of Central Banks (e.g. open market operations to vary either prices, i.e. interest rates, or quantities, the monetary base, in money markets) on the one hand, and the ultimate objectives of policy, especially the control of inflation, on the other.

As described further below, such targetry led to tight monetary policies in the early 1980s, which *did* result in a significant reduction in inflation, albeit at the expense of a severe, but temporary, recession (1980–82) and a longer-lasting problem of debt overhang among less developed countries. In the event, however, the relationship between monetary expansion and the growth of nominal incomes, i.e. the velocity of money, proved much less stable than had been expected, at least for the initially chosen key monetary aggregates (£M3 in UK, M1 in USA).

Whereas the instability in the demand for money functions of certain other monetary aggregates (e.g. M0 in UK, M2 in USA) was somewhat less marked, there was diminished faith in the applicability of monetary targetry for the succesful conduct of policy, just at a time, in the mid-1980s, when attention had been turning away from overriding concern with controlling inflation to other objectives, such as exchange-rate stability and the resumption of full employment.

This latter historical story is told in much greater detail in my survey paper on 'The Conduct of Monetary Policy', *Economic Journal*, June 1989. The distinction between that paper, and this chapter, is that the former paper is much more concerned with short-term macroeconomic policy matters, concentrating on issues of monetary policy and theory that were of particular importance in the context of the past two decades. By contrast the purpose of this chapter, is to examine briefly major structural changes in monetary systems and methods of management and control stretching over several decades, even centuries.

THE MAINTENANCE OF CONVERTIBILITY

The *convertibility* of deposits into some generally accepted external source of value represents a fundamental cornerstone of bank intermediation. While the crucial development in early banking lay in the appreciation that a *proportion* of the specie (gold, silver) left with bankers for safe-keeping and convenience could be loaned out (with a prudently acceptable balance between greater profit and increased risk), the banker *had* to ensure that his clients would be confident of converting the bankers' notes and deposits back into specie on sight or at notice; otherwise they would withdraw their existing balances with the bank, and the contagious effect of such withdrawals could then precipitate a 'run'. A rigorous theoretical analysis of the conditions that lead to bank runs, in a modern rather than an historical context, is to be found in Diamond and Dybvig (1983).

Banks can provide money to needy borrowers either by using their own capital, or by making loans of the funds deposited with them. Governments have often found themselves in the position of a needy borrower, especially when wanting to finance an expensive war. In turn, governments have had the power to provide valuable favours to a bank, in exchange for funds, in the form of a (local) monopoly over note issue, a monopoly over the handling of tax revenues, a privileged ownership structure (e.g. being specially Chartered as contrasted with a private partnership). Thus the Bank of England and the Banque de France were originally established (1694 and 1800 respectively) by their governments to provide funds for them in exchange for such monopolistic favours.

Indeed, as has been shown by Cameron (1967), these early (pre-1850) government banks on occasions used their privileged, monopolistic position to hinder the establishment of other strong, competitive banks; this is one reason why the Scottish banking system, which had a separate, independent structure, proved more robust in the eighteenth and early nineteenth century than the English banking system. Moreover, at times of particular stress and need for funds under pressure of war, governments frequently called on these banks, which they had specially chartered, for such massive extra loans that the ratio of loans outstanding to specie reserves became unduly stretched. In the face of external drains of specie, as domestic monetary expansion turned the balance of payments adverse, and internal drains, as rising nominal incomes led to increasing requirements for coin, there would be an increasing danger of 'runs' even on the governments' own chartered bank, and subsequent financial panic and crisis.

In order to avert such a potential catastrophe the government would then decree that their own main chartered bank's notes were 'legal tender' for the payment of taxes, and release the bank from its obligation to maintain convertibility. The Bank of England went through just such a period of inconvertibility, and restriction of specie payments, during the years 1797 to 1821, and many other European government banks, e.g. in Belgium, France, Austria, Denmark, etc., were forced into temporary periods of inconvertibility by the urgent needs of war finance at one time or another during the nineteenth century.

Nevertheless, even when the pressures preventing the resumption of convertibility seemed endemic, it was always recognised that such convertibility into specie was the appropriate, proper regime for a bank. The episodes of war-time monetary expansion and inconvertibility were, almost invariably, accompanied by worsening inflation; while there was some controversy, e.g. the

Bullionist controversy in England, about the extent of responsibility of monetary expansion, as contrasted with specific demand and supply side factors, for such inflation, the consensus was that the forced adoption of fiat, legal tender (the *cours forcé*) was a sign of political weakness and the harbinger of inflation.

Meanwhile, the strong, central position of the government's bank led (many of) the smaller banks and discount houses to keep their reserves largely in the form of notes issued by, and deposits with, this central bank. This had a number of advantages for the smaller banks who might obtain some benefits in the form of interest on deposits, or access to borrowing facilities, or clearing facilities, or other correspondent services, so that such reserve holdings with the central bank came, in their view, to be preferable to holding large quantities of (sterile) specie in their own vaults. In turn, the balances held by such correspondent banks with the central bank increased the latter's balance sheet position.

This led, without any official prompting, to a pyramiding of the reserves of the banking system, with the generality of banks keeping the majority of their reserves with the central, government-chartered, bank, and with the bulk of the whole system's reserves of specie (gold and/or silver) concentrated in this central bank. This naturally led to considerable discussion about what was the responsibility of the central bank for managing the system that had evolved in this way. These discussions gave rise to the debate between the 'currency' and the 'banking' schools of thought in the UK in the first half of the nineteenth century, leading up to the 1844 Bank Charter Act (see Fetter, 1965); in addition there was a third group which deplored both the privileged position of the central bank and the pyramiding and centralisation of reserves that had occurred, (as recorded by White, 1984); while this latter group included several notable figures, a major problem (as Walter Bagehot, a convinced sympathiser, recognised in *Lombard Street*, 1873) was that the removal/abolition of the Bank of England was just not practical politics.

The currency school argued that monetary problems arose when the money supply, which this school defined as consisting of coins and bank notes, *but not bank deposits*, rose too fast relatively to the available specie reserve base. They argued that so long as the issue of bank notes was constrained to adjust automatically in line with the specie base, all would be well and that the central bank, in this case the Bank of England, need have no further responsibility for the working of the system as a whole – no systemic responsibility – and could revert to operating as any other profit-maximising commercial bank.

The banking school contested the concentration of the currency school on one narrow monetary aggregate, and argued that the central bank did have a responsibility to maintain both convertibility and the soundness of the banking system as a whole by the appropriate discretionary management of its portfolio. Thus it should ensure convertibility by maintaining a prudent balance between its earning assets and its gold reserves (a ratio that became known as 'the proportion'), and seek to ensure the prudential *quality* of bank loans by refusing to discount low-quality paper.

In the event the currency school won the immediate battle, since the 1844 Bank Charter Act was designed according to its precepts, including the division of the Bank of England into two separate Departments (Issue and Banking) – a division which had become an anachronism by the 1870s and continues to be a source of statistical confusion to this day, with the Issue Department treated as part of the public sector, and the Banking Department as part of the banking sector. But the banking school won the war. A series of financial crises in the mid-nineteenth century required the suspension of the 1844 Act, to allow an emergency increased issue of Bank of England notes, if they were to be allayed. The experiences seemed to demonstrate that the monetary and banking system needed to be managed in order to avoid crises. The monetary rule of the currency school was not satisfactory in practice.

The ultimate objective of the central bank, however, remained convertibility into specie. The main indicator which it watched was the proportion of gold reserves to earning assets. The main instrument which it developed, about which more in the next section, was to use its position as the main source of cash reserves for the commercial banking system to inject or withdraw further reserves (originally through a variety of devices, now primarily by open market operations) to control interest rates. When the central bank raised interest rates, it would make the deposit of specie and coin with commercial banks more attractive (higher interest rates being paid on deposits) and by the same token would make borrowing from banks more expensive, and hence less attractive: so an increase in interest rates would help to stem both internal, and external, drains of specie from the banking system. When the central bank's gold reserves declined, it would withdraw cash reserves and raise interest rates, and vice versa.

Ideally such variation in interest rates would not only maintain convertibility, but also stability in the banking system. In practice unforeseen shocks (or bad management) could still lead to financial crises developing. In such cases commercial banks facing runs to withdraw deposits into gold coin, or into central bank notes, would turn to the central bank for assistance. In such cases Bagehot emphasised that the central bank should lend freely to reputable and prudently managed banks, but at high interest rates.

Thus by the latter half of the nineteenth century, the gold standard regime was in place. Although its decisions remained discretionary, the central banks mostly followed the rules of the game, raising interest rates in the face of declining gold reserves, and vice versa. In addition it increasingly accepted a further responsibility for sustaining the health of the banking sector as a whole, and staving off financial panics by appropriate last-resort lending (see Goodhart, 1988 and several of the papers in Capie and Wood (eds) 1990).

Even in those countries without a formal central bank, the natural evolution of the pyramiding of (smaller) bank reserves with, and the concentration and centralisation of specie reserves in some set of major, central commercial banks, or bank, occurred, as in the USA or in most countries, such as India or Brazil, prior to the formal establishment of central banks there. In those countries where a single commercial bank dominated, it tended to assume quasi-central-bank functions. In those countries, such as the USA, where the pyramiding/centralisation went to a *group* of powerful New York banks, the Clearing House which they had established and run assumed certain quasi-central-banking functions, see Timberlake (1978 and 1984).

The rules of the gold-standard regime required the central bank to tighten interest rates just at the time when increasing optimism was leading to faster monetary expansion, and hence a declining proportion. It was generally easier for central banks, which were this time no longer seeking to maximise profits, to do this than for large commercial banks. The consensus was that, without a central bank to manage the monetary system, crises were more likely and more severe. So, by the start of the twentieth century central banks were in vogue, and by the middle of the century virtually every country had one.

The basis, the rules of the game, on which central banks had been operating, however, changed dramatically with the onset of war in 1914. As had happened in previous war-time periods, the exigencies of government finance rapidly led to such monetary expansion among the European combatants that they were forced off into inconvertible, fiat currency. Inflation, and in some cases hyperinflation, followed.

There was naturally a desire in the 1920s, to return to the pre-1914 gold age, but the disruption of the 1914–18 war had been so great that the return to the gold standard proved hard to arrange smoothly. Much of the world's gold reserves had been accumulated by the world's emerging leading creditor nation, the USA, during the war. Rectification of this imbalance required either inflation in the USA or deflation elsewhere. The structural upheavals caused by the war meant that the parities of 1914 would no longer be appropriate, but nevertheless attempts to go back to those in some countries – e.g. the UK – caused stagnation there while the adoption of more competitive parities elsewhere, e.g. France, meant that real exchange rates, and competitiveness, were not in line with their underlying equilibrium values. Beyond this, the dissension over German reparations and war debts continued to hinder international cooperation.

In this context the Federal Reserve Board (the 'Fed') in the USA did not have the previously relatively clear guidelines of the pre-1914 gold standard by which to steer. It hardly wanted to inflate consciously, simply because it had so much gold, yet it may have somewhat muted and delayed its contra-cyclical response to the stock-market boom of the late 1920s because of its concern with its international responsibilities. Thus Friedman and Schwartz wrote that:

> Inevitably in the absence of any single well-defined statutory objective, conflicts developed between discretionary objectives of monetary policy. The two most important arose out of the re-establishment of the gold standard abroad and the emergence of the bull market in stocks, *A Monetary History of the United States*, p. 297 (and ch. 6 as a whole).

Even worse was to follow. One of the reasons why the Fed failed to adopt a more expansionary, contra-cyclical policy when the initial downturn in 1929 moved into extremely severe recession, with large-scale bank failures and severe monetary contraction in 1931–3, was the outflow of gold, especially after the UK left the gold standard in September 1931 (see Friedman and Schwartz, 1963, ch. 7).

A conclusion which Friedman and Schwartz drew from this débâcle was that a central bank's discretionary management is more likely to be inept when it seeks to achieve several, potentially incompatible objectives at the same time. In this case in the inter-war period there were certain conflicts between external and internal objectives. Yet it is by no means clear that the appropriate objective *should* necessarily be an internal one, e.g. domestic price stability, rather than an external one, e.g. holding the exchange rate pegged, or fixed, against some external source of value. If the latter external source of value can at the same time provide a reasonable guarantee of price stability, then the external objective would also provide the additional benefit of stable exchange rates.

Indeed, the breakdown of the gold standard in the early 1930s, and the increasing concentration of national central banks on inward-looking autarchic monetary policies, led to such chaotic exchange-rate movements and such restrictions on trade, as well as on capital movements, that the architects of the international monetary system at Bretton Woods in 1944 determined that a more structured system of exchange rates was necessary, in which these would normally be held pegged against gold, or the US$, but could be adjusted (revalued) in those cases in which a 'fundamental disequilibrium' was held to exist.

THE BREAKDOWN OF THE BRETTON WOODS SYSTEM

Indeed, at the end of the 1960s, the major countries of the world still adhered to the Bretton Woods system of pegged but adjustable exchange rates. Under such a system, the main requirement and objective of the central bank is to maintain the value of the domestic money stock in some nearly-fixed relationship to some other external standard of value; under the Bretton Woods system the external standard of value was initially gold, whose value in terms of US$ was in turn held fixed. After a steady process of mild inflation in the 1950s and 1960s had led to the fixed $ value of gold becoming unrealistically low in real terms, a run on (US) gold reserves developed. In 1968 the USA was forced to abandon pegging the gold price, and the Bretton Woods system became one of linking currency parities to the $, *de jure* as well as *de facto*: the interest rates available on $ reserves had made them more attractive than gold for other central banks to hold, until there was a serious prospect of forthcoming gold revaluation, as Triffin (1960) had foreseen would happen.

As already noted, the maintenance of the convertibility of the domestic money stock into an external standard of value has been the normal procedure for *all* central banks (with the important exception of the US Federal Reserve System) for the greater part of their history.

As described in the preceding section, the primary instrument that they had developed for achieving this objective was their ability to control interest rates. When a tendency for the value of domestic money to depreciate relative to the external standard of value occurs, an increase in interest rates will not only have a deflationary effect on domestic credit expansion, output and inflation, but will also attract capital inflows from abroad. Both historical experience and economic theorists of all schools agree that the medicine will work.

Nevertheless the medicine is often unpalatable. Besides having the generally *desired* effect of maintaining the internal value of the currency, and restraining inflation, an increase in interest rates not only adversely affects the level of output but also, and perhaps more important, its composition, with a particularly severe effect on activity financed by borrowing, such as housing. This is politically unpopular.

In order to alleviate the adverse domestic consequences of such distributional effects on expenditures, while at the same time maintaining external convertibility, central banks have repeatedly been forced, often by outside pressure, to bring other more direct methods of control in support of, or even instead of, their traditional interest-rate adjustments. Exchange controls provide, perhaps, the most common example. They operate, however, by impairing the ability of the ordinary private citizen to take full advantage of the external convertibility that is otherwise formally preserved. In addition, direct-lending ceilings to limit and to redistribute domestic credit, and tariffs and export subsidies, are further mechanisms which can be used to try to maintain the convertibility objective at a generally lower level of interest rates than would otherwise be required. While in the short turn the advantages of such direct controls may seem considerable, even self-evident, the inefficiencies and distortions that increasingly ensue, the longer such direct controls are kept in place, make their adoption questionable at all times.

Historical experience has abundantly demonstrated that the main threat to the maintenance of external convertibility and to price stability has come from governments being forced, usually as a result of war, defence expenditures, or the political unpopularity of explicit taxation, to resort to the printing press – that is to an inflation tax – to finance their actions. Monetarists would add to the list of inflation-causing factors the siren-song of Keynesian support for deficit budgeting whenever output fell below some, often over-optimistically estimated, full employment level.

The examples of countries being forced into inflation by the pressures of war, or by the attempt to maintain public-sector expenditures well in excess of governments' political ability to finance through taxation, have been historically obvious, even dramatic. What then became a more nagging worry in the post-war world has been the attempts of governments to encourage faster growth, or even just recovery in output, by means of fiscal and monetary expansion to an extent that endangers the pegged exchange rate, unless a fairly savage dose of deflation is applied. The problem then is that the relative inflexibility of labour and goods markets – that is of wages and prices – makes so much of the initial adjustment fall on employment and output, rather than on wages and prices. Faced with an exchange rate out of line with equilibrium, which may have resulted in the first place from excessive political pressures, how strongly can, or should, a central banker argue for the defence of its current level, if that would require domestic adjustment of a severity which might possibly threaten political consensus and even social stability? But, if financial stability is not maintained at an early stage, will not an even more difficult spiral of exchange-rate depreciation and worsening domestic inflation set it?

So, the maintenance of a regime of convertibility into an external standard of value, the historical commonplace for central banks, may sound easy. All it involves is varying interest rates inversely to the strength of the balance of payments. In practice, however, its conduct in the post-war world involved continuing arguments both on the weights to be placed on interest rates or direct controls as instruments, and on whether it was better to defend the existing exchange rate or to adjust its value to another level.

Despite these various difficulties the periods when the main industrialised countries of the world jointly adhered to a generally fixed exchange-rate system, that is, the gold-standard period, roughly from 1870 to 1913, and the Bretton Woods period, from 1945 to 1971, were the outstanding occasions of world economic success, combining generally low inflation, with little inter-country dispersion around the mean (thus it is often now forgotten that in the 1950s and 1960s the UK was a relatively low-inflation country), with relatively rapid growth, though the latter was not steady over time and varied quite sharply between countries.

Why, then, did the major countries of the world abandon a system of proven success in 1971–3, without the excuse of a major war as in 1914? Of course, the success of the Bretton Woods period is clearer in hindsight: at the time the discipline entailed in the pegged-exchange-rate system was felt to be irksome. The British disliked it, because the stop-periods in the stop–go cycle, enforced in order to maintain the sterling exchange rate, were held to prevent the achievement of a satisfactorily faster rate of growth: the Germans disliked it because the maintenance of a fixed exchange rate forced them to accept the faster rate of inflation being generated in the USA by the Vietnam War: the USA disliked it because the pegged-exchange-rate system allowed other individual countries to shift their peg on competitive grounds against them, but hardly allowed them, despite the high-level labours of the Smithsonian round, to adjust the dollar *vis-à-vis* everyone else: the French disliked it because it allowed the USA too much leeway to finance the Vietnam War by running a current account deficit, since other central academic economic opinion had become opposed to pegged exchange rates, with a strong theoretical attachment to free floating.

There was, in addition, a second reason. The development of an international capital market, with improved communications, etc, was vastly increasing the volume and rapidity of cross-country capital flows, especially when the market smelled the chance of chasing a central bank facing a one-way option. In 1972 a second-rate sterling crisis that hardly hit the headlines was nonetheless sufficient to denude much of our own usable reserves in the UK within a fortnight. In earlier years the size of central bank reserves, relative to potential market flows, allowed the authorities to use intervention as the short-time adjustment, allowing them more time to review whether, and by how much, a change in interest rates was required. The failure of central bank reserves to grow in line with the expanding international capital market was, however, in some part the result of conscious decision by policy-makers to restrain such international reserves out of fear of their possible world inflationary consequences.

Anyhow, as the size of the international capital market grew, relative to central bank reserves, even to the extent that these could be augmented by cooperation among central banks with exchange, etc., the extent of reliance that could be placed on (sterilised) intervention declined, until it is now widely seen as an instrument of strictly limited usefulness. Under such circumstances the maintenance of exchange-rate stability seems to imply a willingness to allow domestic interest rates to adjust rapidly to all shocks affecting the exchange rate, whether those shocks originate at home or abroad (except to the extent that exchange controls on capital flows can dampen the impact of such shocks on domestic interest rates). The virulence of external shocks in the 1970s, notably the oil shocks, however, was so great that it is debatable whether the fixed-exchange-rate system could have endured, even had there been a greater will to defend it. I shall review in the final section present prospects for restoring such a system.

MONETARY TARGETS

For several countries, including the UK, the collapse of the Bretton Woods system was a semi-conscious rejection of financial discipline in pursuit of faster-growth objectives. The experience of the years, 1972–5, thereafter, however, confirmed the worst fears of those who claimed that the supposed trade-off between inflation and higher output was illusory, even possibly perverse, in all but the short-run (see Friedman, 1968 and various subsequent papers, and Phelps, 1972). While there remains debate about the wider question of how far the oil shock of 1973 was *sui generis*, or itself an inevitable response to more expansionary Western economic policies in 1971–3, and whether inflation which followed the oil shocks in 1973 could be attributed more to the oil shock or to those expansionary policies, there was a general consensus that those countries which maintained a relatively more expansionary policy through that period, such as the UK and Italy, did worse generally, on inflation and ultimately also on output, than those countries such as Germany that battened down the monetary hatches early on. The former group of countries subsequently had to reverse their relatively expansionary policies.

This experience pointed to an urgent need to establish an alternative bastion of financial discipline, to replace the exchange rate, as a constraint against over-expansionary policies, and as a guarantee against ever-worsening inflation and financial chaos. The case for the adoption of such an alternative domestic financial target, in the form of an intermediate monetary target, had long been pressed by monetarists. They argued that the medium-term stability of velocity, the close relationship apparent throughout history between inflation and monetary growth, made a monetary target not only a necessary and sufficient guard against worsening inflation, but also a more efficient form of constraint than a pegged exchange rate, since it freed domestic monetary policy to control domestic inflation. Moreover, it was recognised that volatile expectations about future inflation made it increasingly difficult to use interest rates as a yardstick to judge the stance of monetary policy: the case for shifting the focus of attention for domestic monetary policy purposes from prices, in the form of interest rates, to quantities, in the form of growth rates of the monetary aggregates, seemed demonstrably established. Concerns over which monetary aggregate to choose and possible instabilities in short-run relationships between monetary aggregates, activity, inflation and interest rates were dismissed as second-order problems.

The general case for intermediate monetary targets was also accepted by many moderate Keynesians, at least outside the UK, partly on the grounds that velocity was sufficiently stable for monetary movements to represent a reasonable leading indicator of future movements in nominal incomes. In consequence, an interest-rate adjustment that would restore monetary growth to its target path should also help to restore nominal incomes to its target path. In addition, the adoption of a monetary target not only allowed central banks to argue the case for adjusting interest rates on apparently objective grounds, but even in some cases allowed them to operate in such a way – for example, through some version of monetary base control – as to be able to claim that the resulting interest-rate changes were nothing to do with them, but only the result of free-market actions, in a system where the central bank set the *quantity* of money and its *price* – i.e. the level of interest rates in the short run – was freely determined to equilibrate demand and supply. This latter had obvious 'political' advantages. Thus there was a sizeable constituency in favour of monetary targets, opposed really only by those who thought that financial discipline and the control of inflation was an undesirable constraint, or a strictly subsidiary objective, or could be achieved at less cost by prices and incomes policies.

Indeed, in some quarters the main subject of discussion was whether the public announcement of a commitment to a medium-term strategy for rapid monetary deceleration, supported by credible policies, would not allow for a faster deceleration of both monetary growth and inflation, without much, or any, accompanying depression of output and employment, because of expectational effects. Analogies were drawn with the monetary reforms which had terminated certain European hyperinflations without significantly worse unemployment then resulting (see Sargent, 1986, expecially ch. 3 on 'The Ends of Four Big Inflations' and ch. 4 on 'Stopping Moderate Inflation: The Methods of Poincaré and Thatcher').

In the event, a more cautious gradualism was generally adopted. Even so, the effects on output and employment were as severe as the most old-fangled Keynesian economists warned. Some economists and commentators blamed this on a lack of commitment, and/or on inappropriate supporting policies, by the central bank and/or government, so that the promise of lower future monetary growth (and inflation) was not treated as credible. Other economists, including myself, argued that the normal market mechanisms through which wages and prices were set were not such as to allow government promises of future lower monetary growth to have much current impact on wage or price-setting decisions today. (The difference in hyper-inflationary conditions is that normal market mechanisms for wage- and price-setting will already have largely broken down in chaos.) So monetary targets did not prove a painless panacea, but few had thought they would.

However, it was not so much the pain and stress of the severe (in the UK at least) recession in 1980/82 that led to a withdrawal from monetary targetry, but rather the comparative *success* of such tight monetary policies in bringing inflation down to levels (e.g. below 5 per cent) by the mid-1980s, at which its further containment no longer seemed of overriding priority. In these circumstances many pragmatic politicians, and even some central bankers, gave more weight to other issues, considerations and priorities, e.g. exchange-rate stability, the growth of employment, etc. Even so, had the link between monetary growth and nominal incomes remained predictable, it is extremely doubtful whether any major country would have abandoned targetry simply because inflation seemed less immediately threatening.

A more serious problem was that the vaunted stability of velocity was found wanting, at least in a number of countries for periods long enough to cause serious policy problems. The relationships bewteen £M3 and subsequent movements in nominal incomes in the UK and between M1 and nominal incomes in the USA and Canada, have all been subject to such sizeable and unpredictable (at least unpredicted at the time) shifts, that the emphasis on the achievement of such single targets had to be relaxed. What has been increasingly appreciated is that the stability of the time-series relationships between any particular definition of money and nominal incomes depends on the institutional structure of the system. The very pressures, of worsening and more volatile inflation, that led to the adoption of monetary targets also encouraged innovation and competitive pressures that resulted in changes to the structure. Moreover, as some of us have noted, the adoption of a new target, to take advantage of an apparent statistical regularity, is liable of itself to result in changes to the structure of the system that will cause the prior regularity to collapse.

In particular, the onset of high and fluctuating inflation brought with it, as both lenders and borrowers tried to adjust, high and fluctuating market interest rates. Up until the 1970s banks had generally been prepared to set interest rates on their deposit liabilities in a passive, administered context. Demand/sight deposits were generally offered at no interest, while the rates provided on time-deposits were subject to various constraints through cartel agreements, legal certificates under Regulation Q, etc. This meant that the authorities, by shifting market rates relative to such passively-determined bank rates, were able to affect the flow of deposits into the banking system, and hence the volume of funds that the banks could lend themselves. Since the beginning of the 1970s, however, banks have reacted to external market pressures by offering a larger and larger proportion of their liabilities at market-related interest rates. Whenever a profitable outlet for additional lending could be identified and established, bank and other financial intermediaries would bid for funds, largely in wholesale markets, to finance such lending. Moreover, the demand by borrowers for loans from banks has itself turned out to be relatively insensitive to interest-rate movements, perhaps in part because of tax offsets generally allowed. In consequence, both the elasticity of the response of monetary aggregates, and the possibility of imposing a credit squeeze, following interest-rate adjustments, have diminished. Particularly in those countries allowing tax advantages and offsets for borrowers, the resulting volatility and average level of interest rates increased.

Another partial consequence of this was that much of the effect of domestic monetary targetry was transmitted through exchange-rate adjustments. There have been several examples in recent years of countries in which the confrontation between a tight monetary policy and expansionary pressures elsewhere in the same economy (e.g. UK, 1980–1; USA, 1982–5) was reflected in an appreciation in the real effective exchange-rate to levels that appeared grossly out of alignment with existing fundamentals.

As stated at the outset, a more detailed account of these recent events is available in my survey paper on 'The Conduct of Monetary Policy', *Economic Journal*, June 1989. The aim of this chapter, instead, is to review a rather longer horizon, and to consider next the range of monetary regimes that we might possibly adopt in future.

WHITHER NOW

There are, perhaps, some five possible alternatives now. In view of current steps towards economic and monetary union (EMU) in Europe, the first, most immediate, option for the UK is simply to stay in the Exchange Rate Mechanism (ERM) of the European Monetary System (EMS), currently a pegged but adjustable exchange rate system, but one which is now intended to move on to the adoption of irrevocably fixed parities, and then ultimately to a single European currency. (The UK joined the ERM in October 1990.) Whereas such a progression towards monetary union is underway in Western Europe, it remains hard to observe any significant progress towards the readoption of external, exchange rate, constraints on domestic monetary policy between the three main (G3) bloc centres, i.e. Europe/DM, America/$, and Asia/Yen. Consequently the regime shift which is currently most relevant for the UK is not at present politically (or economically?) feasible at the world level.

The adoption of an irrevocably fixed parity against some external source of value, e.g. gold or the DM, does limit, though it does not completely remove, a central bank's powers of independent action, e.g. in prudential supervision, or lender-of-last-resort functions. Of course, a single European currency would require a single focus of monetary decision-making, a European System of Central Banks, as set out in the Delors Report of 1989. An even more radical option now canvassed by some theoreticians is not only to fix the money stock to some external source of value, perhaps a basket of goods or a labour standard as an 'ideal' index of value, but also to abolish central banks as such, and to rely on competitive forces, and/or on structural changes in the banking system, to maintain financial stability.

A third option would be to move on from monetary targets to nominal income targets. A fourth possibility would be to hope for a return to stable predictability in monetary velocity, so that monetary targetry, after the present hiatus, could be resumed. A fifth option would be simply to go back to the previous regime of purely discretionary monetary management. In practice, however, such discretion is conditioned by continuing observation and assessment of developments amongst both nominal income and monetary indicators, so the final three alternatives are not really distinct from each other, being more a matter of the balance of emphasis in the continuing conduct of domestic monetary policy, whereas the first two involve a clear shift in the locus of decision-making, sharing it with other countries in the first option and abandoning it altogether in the second.

(i) Readoption of fixed exchange rates

Although this alternative would undoubtedly severely limit national autonomy in conducting monetary policy (except for the central, hegemonic, country in such a system, e.g. for Germany in the EMS, or the USA in the Bretton Woods system), and would strictly limit the ability of national policy-makers to address purely domestic objectives, there is growing doubt about how valuable that freedom really is. Recent history now makes the 1950s and 1960s, when Bretton Woods still held, look like a golden age compared with the disturbances of the 1970s and 1980s, two decades of general floating. The causal connections, such as they may be, however are mixed; thus the disturbances of the 1970s and early 1980s may have forced floating on us willy-nilly; but the desire to return to an apparently more stable system is strong, particularly within Europe.

Moreover, practical experience has demonstrated that flexible exchange rates do not adjust smoothly. Not only is there much short-term volatility, though the real costs of that are probably limited and often avoidable by hedging, e.g. in forward and futures markets, but it is also the case that major exchange-rate relativities have moved in certain cases far from their apparent comparative price-competitive equilibrium. There is less doubt that such misalignments have involved serious costs, in terms of inefficient allocations of resources and increased risk and uncertainties, in the countries involved.

Moreover, analytical argument suggests that the supposed benefits of having domestic freedom for monetary control are not all that great. With the continuing development of a single world capital market, the elasticity of cross-currency capital flows has almost certainly increased and is almost bound to increase further. This will tend to force *ex ante* real interest rates into equality in all countries. All that the local central banker will be able to influence will be *nominal* magnitudes, e.g. the rate of inflation, the movements in nominal exchange rates and interest rates. The question then arises as to what great value it is to have one's own local man doing that rather than relying on Mr Greenspan or Mr Poehl.

In general, countries with a dominant currency (and economic position), such as Germany within the EMS, have not objected if other countries have sought to link their currencies in some pegged (but adjustable) relationship to their own, so long as they themselves continued to be allowed absolute sovereignty and command to pursue their own national policy as they thought fit. Many smaller countries, for the reasons already considered, have thought that the benefits in greater external stability (and counter-inflation credibility) arising from such a link outweighed the loss of domestic autonomy. Greater problems arise when the countries considering an exchange-rate link are more equivalent in financial strength. In virtually no case, prior to the 1990s, had the country whose currency would seem to be the most obvious central anchor of the system, been prepared to cede any significant part in the decision-making process concerning its own national (sovereign) monetary policy to other countries making up that system. Now, however, the Delors Committee Report (1989) does envisage a significant transfer of power from national Central Banks, including the Deutsche Bundesbank, to a federal European System of Central Banks (ESCB), though an ESCB whose proposed independence from political oversight, constitutional prime objective (price stability), and structure would seem to be largely modelled on the Bundesbank itself. More controversially, the Delors Committee Report claims that an accompanying transfer of powers over other economic policies, e.g. constraints over budget deficits and incomes policies, to a federal European centre in Brussels would also be necessary if the further steps – Stages 2 and 3 – towards monetary union were to be successfully implemented.

Moreover, there remains some concern about the technical problems of running a pegged, but adjustable, system of exchange rates, e.g. the ERM and Stage 1 of the Delors Committee Report, without the support of exchange controls in those cases where the economies of the countries involved have not succeeded in achieving underlying economic convergence, e.g. with similar trends in unit labour costs. Underlying divergences in inflation trends would, at times, lead to the development of one-way options, or unless the realignments are made promptly and in quite small, frequent steps – which latter course undermines the objectives of stability and monetary discipline that the system is intended to provide. It is no accident that Mrs Thatcher insisted at the Madrid summit in June 1989 that the UK would only join the ERM when the UK's inflation had fallen into line with that in Europe, and it was demonstrated that the ERM could continue to function well even after the abandonment of exchange controls. (The fact that the UK then joined anyway is another matter.)

It will be hard enough to overcome the technical and political obstacles confronting the achievement, in stages, of monetary union within Western Europe. It would be even harder to achieve either economic convergence, or political consensus on appropriate policies, or on the distribution of adjustments necessary to achieve such policies, between the major block currencies, DM, $ and Yen. With each bloc having relatively a free flow of labour and goods within themselves, with a comparatively small flow between the blocs, adjustment to imbalances in the balance of payments between these blocs would be difficult to achieve smoothly without the support of changing (real) exchange rates. Consequently there may be no real alternative to a relatively free float between major bloc currencies, (though the path of that float should be capable of some influences from inter-governmental cooperation). The world is not yet ready, economically or politically, for a single world currency. Indeed it remains to be seen whether Western Europe does manage to move to a single European Currency.

(ii) Free banking

As was noted earlier, there were many commentators and economists, e.g. Bagehot, who argued that both the natural and proper condition for banking was one of free competition between many private banks, the number of which would depend on economies of scale in the business. Central banks, they claimed, had been imposed on the banking system by the intervention of governments. Both the resulting monopoly position of such central banks, and their close involvement with government, were seen as deplorable in theory, and liable to lead to endemic inflation in practice. So proponents of this view (e.g. Hayek, 1976) advocate a new regime, or constitution, in which central banks would be abolished, and banks would be left free, hence the term 'free-banking', to operate according to the dictates of their own commercial objectives, subject only to the same kind of legal constraint, e.g. on mergers and the misuse of monopoly power, as apply to any other industry.

The dominant impulse of the advocates of a new monetary constitution is the conviction that virtually all, perhaps all, inflation arises from political mismanagement, a view which a study of history demonstrates has to be taken seriously. Furthermore central banks are held to be compromised, either through being themselves subject to political pressures, or because their nature as a large public-sector bureaucracy makes their pursuit of the goal of price stability less than whole-hearted. I do not myself accept the latter argument; though I do recognise the strength of the view that the issue of how to ensure the stability of the currency in a democracy is largely a constitutional question. Be that as it may, the advocates of a new monetary constitution seek to remove the conduct of macro-monetary policy from the hands of the authorities, by in effect making it into an automatic system.

There are various forms of automatic system proposed – for example, a return to the gold standard, the adoption of a fancier kind of commodity-based scheme in which all monetary units would represent a basket of standard raw materials, or alternatively Friedman's suggestion of a monetary bureau that would expand the base, every working day, at a fixed rate. The idea of removing any political influence, or discretionary management, from monetary affairs may sound academic and impractical. Nevertheless one must always remember Keynes's dictum about those in authority distilling the lessons of previous academic economists. Moreover, the earlier establishment of the Gold Standard Commission in the USA by President Reagan suggested that, were it not for bitter divisions in the ranks of the more right-wing thinkers about *which* monetary constitution to adopt, there might well be a strong constituency, at least in the USA, for such a change to be attempted.

One of the common features of such proposals is that the government/central bank should cease to issue and provide money, e.g. Bank of England notes. Some economists of this view have argued that the resulting external sources of value into which banks should be free to make their deposits, and bank notes (under these proposals, commercial banks would regain the right to issue notes) could also be chosen freely, and competitively. In practice the confusion that would result if some banks pegged to gold, others to wheat, others to coal, others to a basket of goods, would disrupt the efficient operation of the payments system. Since this latter is a public good, there is a case for the government defining what the common external source of value should be, but not getting involved in issuing money against it. Just as the authorities define a yard, or metre, as a certain distance, so they could play a metric role, defining a $ or £ as equal to a certain amount of a good (ounces of gold) or goods, e.g. a basket of goods.

The latter is preferable in principle since it reflects more closely what people actually buy, hence ensuring price stability, and reduces the impact of relative demand/supply shocks on a single monetary good, (e.g. the discovery of gold in California in 1849). But one could hardly exercise convertibility directly into a statistically appropriate basket of goods. Instead the community would perhaps revert to full-value gold or silver coins, but the market value of such coins in terms of both the $/£ *numéraire*, and also of bank deposits, would change continuously over time, as the value of gold shifted relative to the basket. This has sometimes been described as 'indirect convertibility', e.g. by Greenfield and Yeager (1983) and Yeager (1985). That would make it harder to use such full-value coins for transactions purposes, but a combination of (commercial) bank notes, credit/debt cards, and subsidiary (base metal) low-value coins would be used for such purposes instead.

Besides doubts whether governments would ever be willing to relinquish their monetary powers in this way (for three main reasons, (a) power is enjoyed by those who have it, (b) the issue of bank notes provides a small, but useful, command over extra real resources (*seigniorage*) in normal times, (c) the use of the printing press as the final available source of finance may be vital to a government *in extremis*), such a return to free banking raises two questions: first, how would interest rates be determined in such a system, and second, would the banking system be prone to 'runs', panic, etc., without a central bank?

First, assume that banks could/would pay interest on *all* their liabilities, notes and deposits. There *are* some possible technical ways of paying interest on notes, either by issuing notes in smart card form which incorporate a continuous compound rate of interest, or by holding a lottery based on the identifying serial numbers of the notes outstanding, so the expected mean return equals the market rate. In such cases with all liabilities bearing interest, competition would force such rates into equality, after taking account of normal business costs, etc., with the underlying market rate of interest determined by the forces of productivity (and investment demand) and thrift (the propensity to save). It is its monopolistic ability to issue legal tender, zero-interest money that gives a central bank its monetary command over nominal interest rates; and with sticky, sluggishly adjusting prices, also over real interest.

It has been argued (e.g. Wallace 1983) that if commercial banks were left free to issue bank notes, but that they found themselves unable to, or prevented from, paying any interest on these, then they would go on issuing these until interest rates were driven so close to zero, that no profit could be made from printing more notes to buy up (riskless) government debt, thereby presumably causing hyperinflation. This argument would hold if the commercial banks' notes were legal tender.

Otherwise, as history shows, since there have been many earlier periods of free commercial note issue, an increased issue of notes will raise the probability of notes being presented for redemption. The need to sell assets (e.g. government debt) to meet the drain of specie reserve would lower the price of such assets and raise the possibility of runs on the banks and their insolvency. Accordingly there would be an equilibrium trade-off between return and risk. Since risk cannot be fully eliminated, the equilibrium return would not be driven to zero.

This then raises the second question of whether a free banking system would be inherently stable, or whether, without a central bank to provide prudential supervision and lender-of-last-resort services, it would be more prone to runs, panics and financial crises than in the past. Some economists (e.g. Dowd, 1989; Selgin, 1988) have argued that the normal working forces of competitive markets would make the system stable. Others have argued that the appropriate structural reforms (e.g. limiting the assets that banks could buy, *or* requiring banks to revalue all their assets continuously to their current market values, i.e. 'mark to market', and increasingly constraining the banks' freedom to operate as their free capital became further eroded, *or* basing the payments mechanism on deposits, units, whose capital value varied instanteously in line with their asset portfolio) could easily make banks proof against runs in a free banking milieu, without a central bank (see Goodhart, 1990, and Shadow Financial Regulatory Committee, 1989).

These latter structural reforms would, however, generally prevent banks from undertaking the fixed interest loans of a non-marketed, and perhaps inherently non-marketable, form, i.e. advance to small businesses and persons, which has been a staple of their activities. Given the problems such small agents would have in borrowing directly from capital markets (e.g. high transactions costs, information asymmetries) some financial institutions will still have to specialise in making such loans, will need to issue fixed interest liabilities against their fixed interest assets, and will maintain the risk characteristics of existing banks. So, even if 'safe' intermediaries can be developed to run the payments system, we may still need banks' credit-creating operations and a central bank to support these.

Some features of this alternative are visionary, and currently mostly of academic interest. If we then exclude either of these first two alternatives, we then turn to variants of presently available methods for existing central banks to conduct monetary policy for the achievement of domestic objectives.

(iii) A nominal income target

If velocity was exactly predictable, then a monetary target would be identical to a nominal income target, since velocity is *defined* in terms of the relationship between the money stock on the one hand and of prices and output on the other. Anyhow, the ultimate objectives with which the authorities are concerned, output, employment, and price stability, relate to nominal incomes, not so much to the intermediate monetary variable, since the monetary aggregate itself is a statistical abstraction of no direct or immediate concern to anyone. Particularly therefore in the aftermath of velocity having proved to be more unpredictable than expected, many moderate Keynesians (in the USA) and moderate monetarists (in the UK) are suggesting a shift to targeting the path of nominal incomes itself.

This, however, implicitly involves giving exactly equal weight to a percentage deviation of real output from its desired level as to a divergence of prices from the objective for the price level, since nominal incomes equals prices time output, $Y = P \times Q$. Hall (1986) has suggested an improved method of targeting in which the weights on output and price level deviations could be chosen in such a manner as to reflect more closely some social welfare function weighting of output losses (unemployment) and price level instability and uncertainty.

While this latter suggestion could represent a considerable improvement over a simple nominal income target, there remain several serious objections to the adoption of nominal income targets. For those central banks which are constitutionally independent of the executive government, such as the Federal Reserve Board and the Deutsche Bundesbank, such a move could lead them into an awkward relationship with government. What if the central bank and the government might want to set different nominal incomes objectives? Moreover, nominal incomes are influenced by fiscal and other policies, as well as by monetary policy. How could a central bank unilaterally commit itself to achieve a nominal income target, when many of the relevant policy instruments were controlled elsewhere? These problems, essentially relating to policy coordination, are less pressing in countries where all policy is already coordinated under central political direction

But many problems remain. For example, a rise in nominal income is composed of an increase in output, which is a good thing, and an increase in prices, which is a bad thing. How can you combine a good and a bad into a single target? To put the same point better, one may well want to react to a shock to prices by encouraging though policy measures a (partial) offset to output, in pursuit of stability. But if there was a shock to output, say it fell suddenly on account of a bad harvest, would one consciously seek *higher* prices in order to attain a nominal incomes target? The problem above could be reduced by the sensible adoption of an improved, Hall-type, system of targets.

Indeed, the above is something of a debating point. Much more serious is the fact that the national income data are generally quite long delayed, of uncertain accuracy and subject to major revisions, and, above all, represent the *lagged* consequences in the economy to *previous* policy initiatives. What one needs for policy purposes is not an accurate measure of where the economy *was*, but a reasonable indication of where it may *go* in future if no policy action should be taken now. By their nature past and still unreliable indications of GDP cannot give you that: you need, instead, some information, some leading indicators about future developments; and here current financial developments, if carefully and sensibly assessed, may help. By their nature there is really no way in which quarterly observations of past GDP can help to guide and direct a central bank's *day-to-day* decisions on market operations in money and exchange markets.

Where it may, however, be sensible to place more emphasis on a nominal income path is, rather, in establishing and publicly explaining the longer-term strategy and framework of policy over a run of years, within which intermediate targets, and shorter-term operating rules, will still be needed for the conduct of policy through each year.

(iv) Monetary targets

It was, indeed, one of the intended purposes of monetary targetry, that the course of the chosen aggregate should provide a reasonably clear leading indication of where the economy was currently heading. The problem is that they no longer appear able to do so in a sufficiently clear and reliable manner. In the case of those aggregates which seemed to have a leading, predictive relationship with subsequent nominal income movements, e.g. £M3 in the UK, the (velocity) relationship between them has become quite unstable. In those cases where the demand for money function still fits quite well, e.g. M0 in the UK, the relationship is concurrent, so that the M0 statistic does little more than provide a noisy signal of what is currently happening to consumers expenditures in current prices, which one knows anyway from retail sales and RPI data.

It is certainly possible that the current disturbances to monetary relationships just reflect a temporary flood of innovations, and that stability and predictability will be restored. We will see. But for the time being monetary targetry has been largely abandoned.

(v) Discretion

There appear, therefore, to be serious objections to all these alternative approaches *except* for Alternative (i), the adoption of an exchange-rate commitment, for the UK and other European countries. For the rest, in the absence of any clear and practicable alternative, central banks have reacted to structural change and to breakdowns of previously stable relations between money and nominal incomes by adopting a more pragmatic and discretionary approach. They take into consideration a wider range of variables in coming to a view on the stance of policy and its appropriate adjustments. In many ways this is congenial to central bankers, since they are at heart pragmatic people and their discretion is legendary. Nevertheless it is not an entirely comfortable position for them.

3 The New Theory of Financial Intermediation*

JOHN CHANT

Financial institutions that borrow from ultimate lenders and lend to ultimate borrowers are prominent features of any modern economy, yet present an apparent paradox. The lenders could lend directly to the borrowers without the use of the intermediary, and indeed many do. The purpose of this chapter is to contribute to the understanding of the workings of financial institutions and the benefits that they provide to lenders and borrowers. A number of issues relating to financial institutions and their functioning are examined. Why do financial institutions exist? What functions do they perform? Why do some borrowers and lenders use the services of financial institutions while others do not? Do different types of financial institutions serve different functions?

The literature explaining the existence and functions of financial institutions is extremely diverse. No single explanation of the phenomenon of financial intermediation has emerged. One source of diversity arises from the various types of activity that take place through financial institutions. While explanations for several different types of financial institutions are reviewed in this chapter, the primary objective is to explain deposit-taking institutions, which offer fixed-value claims to their customers and are such a predominant feature of modern financial systems. Much concern is currently being expressed in public discussions about the deregulation or regulation of their operations. Any approach to the regulation of financial institutions should be based on a sound understanding of their function.

This chapter examines financial institutions from the perspective of the 'new' theory of financial institutions that has emerged in recent years, mainly in response to parallel developments in the economics of information and transactions costs. Prior to recent developments, the 'old' theory identified the services offered by financial institutions as the transformation of the assets: financial institutions issue claims to their customers that have characteristics different from those of the assets held by the institutions themselves.[2] Moreover, it viewed financial institutions as passive portfolio managers choosing their portfolio on the basis of returns and risks that they face in the market. The 'new' theory of financial institutions goes beyond the 'old' theory in two dimensions. First, it identifies and analyses more carefully the different types of transformation services supplied by financial institutions. Second, it explores in greater depth the way that financial institutions can carry out these transformations by altering risks and returns through applying resources to acquire better information and overcome transactions costs.

TYPES OF INTERMEDIARIES

The essence of financial intermediation is the interposition of a third party between the ultimate borrower and ultimate lender in the saving–investment process. The simplest form of intermediary is the *broker* who facilitates transactions between lenders and borrowers without acquiring the debt of the borrowers or issuing claims to the lenders. In contrast, the 'true' financial intermediary becomes a party to the financing activity by simultaneously holding claims on the borrower and issuing claims to the lender. Among true intermediaries, a distinction can be made between mutual funds and deposit-taking institutions. A *mutual fund* offers investors a proportionate claim on a portfolio of assets that fluctuates in value with the value of the underlying collection of assets that make up the intermediary's portfolio. The *deposit-taking intermediary*, the focus of this study, offers investors a claim, the value of which is stated by contract to be independent of the value of the portfolio held by the intermediary.

In a simple economy with perfect certainty and the absence of any transactions costs, there would be no need for financial institutions. The analysis proceeds by asking what departures from this idealised economy create a role for financial institutions. Several theories are identified, each of which stresses a different set of causes for the emergence of financial institutions. A number of questions are asked about each theory. What economic problems exist for lenders and borrowers that cannot be resolved in a mutually beneficial way through a direct contract between them? Under what assumptions can this problem be resolved more efficiently through financial intermediation? What type of financial intermediary is required to resolve the problem?

Emphasis, as already mentioned, is placed on the ability of each theory to explain the need for deposit-taking institutions. Any explanation must take into account four prominent features that characterise these institutions. First, they issue liabilities that promise to pay a predetermined money value regardless of the performance of the intermediary's portfolio. Second, the majority of their deposit liabilities have a short-term maturity. Third, while some of their liabilities are in the form of chequable deposits, the majority are not.[3] Finally, deposit-taking institutions differ from other intermediaries, not only in terms of their liabilities, but also with respect to the markets in which they operate. Brokers and mutual funds deal most commonly in so-called marketable securities, whereas deposit-taking institutions hold a large proportion of non-marketable securities (including loans or advances) in their portfolios.[4]

THE APPROACH TO EXPLANATION

The cost of performing transactions is a central element of the existing theory of financial institutions. Indeed Benston and Smith (1976) argue that 'the *raison d'être* for this industry is the existence of transactions costs'. Following this approach, a simple theory of financial institutions could be derived, based on the argument that these institutions simply have access to superior technology for overcoming transactions costs. However, such an explanation carries the danger of being tautological to the extent that it fails to explain the sources from which the cost-advantage of financial institutions arise.

In the discussion that follows, intermediaries are assumed to have access to the same technology in all activities as other members of the general public. This assumption does not deny that the use of intermediation can have a cost-advantage over direct finance. As Gurley and Shaw, pioneers in the modern theory of financial institutions, state:

> Financial intermediaries exploit economies of scale in lending and borrowing. On the lending side the intermediary can invest and manage investments in primary securities at unit costs far below the experience of most individual lenders (Gurley and Shaw, 1960 p.194).

Any cost-advantage is assumed for the present to arise from the organisation of the activity through an intermediary using existing technology and not from the assumption of any inherent advantage of those who choose to be intermediaries.

A SIMPLE ECONOMY

The simplest economy to consider is one characterised by complete certainty. Households are assumed to know their incomes and consumption demands for all times in the future. In addition, production technologies and supplies of productive inputs are also known with certainty. In this simple economy, all transactions can be carried out without cost. Moreover, transactions over time can be enforced without cost.

Households in this economy receive income from supplying productive services over a number of periods. Any lack of correspondence between the household's pattern of income and its pattern of consumption over time means the household must sell or purchase assets.[5] In a pure exchange economy, the household can either exchange claims for consumption at different times with other households or hold durable consumption goods. In a production economy, households can acquire capital goods and sell them at a later date to finance their consumption.

The production technology may require people to use productive capital in amounts different from the amount that they own. In the absence of transactions costs, the ownership and use of productive assets can be separated without consequence. The terms of the arrangements by which one household permits another to use its productive assets are negotiated, monitored and enforced without cost. As Benston and Smith observe:

> it should be obvious that in a market without any frictions such as transactions costs, information costs, or indivisibilities, financial intermediaries would not exist (Benston and Smith, 1976, p.217).

The assumption of perfect certainty rules out many types of transactions costs used to explain the existence of financial institutions. Under this assumption, neither the lender nor the borrower needs to incur any search costs in finding others with whom to trade financial claims. Also the outcomes of investments over time are known so that investors are obliged neither to screen investments in advance nor to determine their subsequent outcomes.

The following analysis of the theory of financial institutions proceeds by adding more realistic elements to the simple economy discussed above. First, individuals are assumed to be subject to risks that cancel for the economy as a whole. Next, the uncertainties facing individuals do not offset each other so that some uncertainty remains at an economy-wide level. Finally, information costs are introduced so that individuals can to some extent, control the uncertainties they face by directing resources to activities such as search, monitoring and enforcement.

UNCERTAINTY AND INTERMEDIATION

Uncertainty about the outcomes of transactions made over time can enter the economy in different ways. *Social uncertainty* exists when the uncertainties facing individuals are combined in a way that results in uncertainty for the economy overall. Individuals can still face *private uncertainty* even when the underlying certainties offset each other for the economy as a whole. Both social and private uncertainty are assumed, for the present, to be inherent in the economy in the sense that individuals cannot reduce these costs through the application of additional resources.

Private risk

(a) Investment uncertainty

The simplest case of uncertainty arises when the outcomes of individual investments are uncertain, but the outcome of the investments in aggregate is known in advance. Suppose there are n identical individuals with X to invest and that each of the possible investment projects in the simplest case costs X. Each investment project gives a payment in the second period of either $X(1 + r + e)$ or $X(1 + r - e)$ with equal probability. An investor holding only one investment has an expected gross return of r from the investment with equal probability of e greater or less than r. If a fixed cost c is incurred in acquiring each asset, the net return expected by this investor from acquiring one asset equals $r - c$.

Investors are often assumed to be *risk-averse* in that they value an uncertain income stream less than a known income stream with the same expected value. These investors can reduce uncertainty by holding more than one investment because some of the independent risks will offset each other.[6] In so doing, the investors would incur additional costs. Risk-averse investors would continue to divide their resources among more investments until the additional costs of holding further investments offset the added benefits at the margin. Each investor could achieve this degree of diversification at a cost of qc, where q is the number of securities at which the benefits from this diversification are maximised and c, as before, is the fixed cost of acquiring each asset. The n individuals in the economy would carry out diversification at an aggregate cost of nqc.

An intermediary could reduce the costs to individuals of holding diversified portfolios. Consider the case where the intermediary holds the number of securities that would have maximised the benefits to individuals from diversification. In assembling this portfolio the intermediary incurs a cost of qc, the fixed cost c for each of q assets. In addition, the intermediary must negotiate with each of its customers at a cost of v for each of the n investors. The total cost for the intermediary equals $nv + qc$ and the cost of this degree of diversification to each of its n customers is $v + qc/n$. Investors would find indirect finance a more efficient means of diversification whenever $v + qc/n$ is less than qc. This condition shows that intermediation is more likely the larger the number of investors over whom the intermediary can spread its costs.

This theory of intermediation is limited in that it can explain at most brokers and mutual-fund intermediaries. A broker would emerge only if the costs involved in achieving diversification were search costs and did not arise from the direct holding of securities. With the presence of only search costs, the broker could direct his customers towards acquiring appropriate securities so that they could gain their desired level of diversification. A mutual-fund intermediary would be more likely to emerge if the costs involved were directly related in some degree to the holding or acquisition of securities. Such costs could not be avoided by using a broker and would require the intermediary to hold securities.[7]

(b) Individual consumption risk

The model of diversification developed above limits uncertainties to the outcomes of investments. Diamond and Dybvig (1983) (hereafter referred to as DD) develop an alternative model in which the uncertainty arises from consumers' demands. In the DD model investors can be of two types. Some must consume in the next period, whereas others can delay their consumption to a latter date. In the simplest model, the proportion of each of these types of investors is known over the economy, but at the time they make their investment decisions individuals do not know which type they will subsequently be.

DD assume a technology that requires investments to be committed for two periods in order to be productive. If production is interrupted after only the first period of an investment, its return will be lower than if it is allowed to continue through the second period. The possibility of intermediation arises in the DD model because the individuals are risk-averse and the technology of production makes their future consumption uncertain. Individuals can consume more if they can delay their consumption for two periods than if they are forced to consume after only one.

According to DD, financial institutions emerge as a device through which investors can alter the pattern of their consumption across different outcomes relative to that possible for the investor in isolation. Financial institutions perform this role by first pooling the resources of many investors and then making larger payments to those who consume 'early' and smaller payments to those who consume 'late' compared with what they would get without financial intermediation, but payments are such that everyone prefers to deal with the intermediary because they do not know in advance when they will want to consume. In effect, DD's financial institutions insure individuals against the risk that they will be forced to consume after only one period and forego the returns for longer periods of investment.[8]

It might appear that DD have created an example in which intermediation arises in the absence of transactions costs. Such an impression is potentially misleading. In the absence of any transactions costs each individual could make a contract with every other individual that would achieve exactly the same outcome as using the DD intermediary. This contract would take the form of a mutual insurance contract that indemnifies the holder for the costs of some stated event. In particular, it would specify a payment to be made between individuals in the circumstance that one was forced to interrupt his investments to fulfill his consumption needs. Like a contract with an intermediary, this payment would permit the investors who are forced to consume in the next period to obtain consumption greater than that possible from their investments alone.

A problem arises with these private contracts because of moral hazard. After the event, investors who can delay their consumption to the later date have an incentive to misrepresent themselves. By declaring himself as having to consume in the first period, such an investor can claim indemnity from other individuals and also protect his own resources from claim. Private contracts would break down because unscrupulous investors could gain an unwarranted payment from others and avoid legitimate claims from others on their resources.

The pooling of assets with an intermediary turns the investor's decision into an either/or choice. Making a claim in the first period leads to a payment from the intermediary together with the forefeit of any claim to payment at a later date. As long as the present value of the payment at the later date exceeds that of the payment in the next period, investors who are able to delay their consumption have an incentive to be truthful.

The either/or choice is strictly a result of the assumption in the DD model that two types of investors consume in different periods. It fails to overcome the problem of designing an intermediary to diversify consumption risks in the standard two-period model. In that model any consumption risk must reflect different consumption needs in the same period so that the either/or choice is between a large or a small payment at the same time and thus an incentive always exists to choose the larger payment. When the payments are separated over time as in the DD model, the intermediary can arrange the size of the payments to create self-policing of investors' declarations.

The DD model succeeds in explaining the emergence of a deposit-taking institution when individual consumption risks – the risks of needing to consume early – cancel over the population of investors. The payments that the intermediary must make in each period are known, as are the number of claimants. Still, the significance of this result should not be overestimated. When DD extend their model to the case where the proportion of different types of investors is uncertain, the analysis breaks down. Any fixed payment promised to investors who must consume in the first period makes the payment to the remaining investors depend on the actual number of each type. In the DD analysis, the existence of an intermediary is explained by its ability to reshape the pattern of consumption across the prospect of being one or the other type of investor. Consistency with this objective requires a payment to investors who must consume in the next period that depends on the realised proportions of these investors relative to the others. Thus, when the DD model is extended to incorporate uncertainty about the proportions of investors, it explains an institution that offers obligations that depend on outcomes rather than a deposit-taking institution that offers fixed-money claims.

Social risk

Up to this point the only uncertainty analysed has been uncertainty with respect to individual investments (i.e. over the economy as a whole the proportion of poor investment is known with certainty). This analysis can now be extended to consider uncertainty with respect to outcomes for the economy as a whole. As a simplification all investments are assumed to have equal returns given the outcome for the economy so that the only source of uncertainty is aggregate uncertainty.

If investors differed in their attitudes toward risk, it would be possible to shift risk among them according to their willingness to accept risk.[9] Investors would want to exchange securities if, with their existing holdings, some investors had different valuations for risk at the margin than others. An opportunity exists for the individual more willing to take risk to issue risk-free securities to the other at an interest rate lower than the return of risky assets. Whether he could issue risk-free securities would depend on the size of his wealth relative to the worst possible outcome for the risky asset. If his wealth is inadequate to cover all contingencies he could issue only low-risk securities. As the volume of this lending grows, one indivdiual's exposure to risk decreases whereas the other's increases. At the margin, the investor taking on risk would require more compensation than before to take on risk; the other would be less willing to pay to escape risk. An equilibrium is established where the more risk-averse investor holds a portfolio that consists of both risky assets and the risk-free securities issued by the other, whereas the other investor holds risky securities in an amount that exceeds his net wealth and finances them by borrowing from the other.

This exchange of claims among investors need not lead to intermediation. Investors could achieve the desired risk-sharing in the absence of intermediaries. In the simplest case where the desired lending of one investor corresponds to the desired borrowing of another investor, each would need to transact with only one of the other type. When amounts differ among types, each investor need trade with only the minimum number of the other type required to achieve his desired volume of transactions.[10]

The effect of transactions costs on the analysis depends on the exact nature of the cost. If the cost per transaction were the same for the investor as for the intermediary, the intermediary would not be able to perform the risk-sharing more cheaply because it would have to engage in at least the same number of transactions as would the investors themselves. An intermediary would have an advantage only if some costs rose less than in proportion to portfolio size.

Social and private risk

The combination of private and social risks can explain certain additional characteristics of financial institutions that are absent when each type of risk is analysed separately. Private, or diversifiable risk, leads to the pooling of assets in a collective portfolio in the presence of any transactions costs. By itself, diversifiable risk justifies the emergence of only mutual fund intermediaries. But some risks remain even with a completely diversified portfolio. The prospect of mutually beneficial exchange arises if investors differ with respect to their attitudes towards risk. In contrast to the case where social risk exists in the absence of other sources of private risk, the need for diversification makes it more costly for individuals to transfer risk directly because investors would want to transact with more than the minimum number of investors in order to gain the benefits from diversification.

The intermediary explained by the combination of both pure private risk and social risk goes beyond a simple mutual fund, but still does not possess all the prominent characteristics of deposit-taking intermediaries discussed earlier in the chapter. In particular, this theory developed to this point does not suggest that deposit-taking intermediaries would specialise in the holding of non-marketable securities.

INFORMATION COSTS

The models considered so far have the common assumptions that the possible outcomes of investments can be ascertained in advance and that all contracts can be enforced in each case without any resource costs. Moreover, none of these models can explain the phenomenon of deposit-taking institutions that issue liabilities with a fixed-money value and specialise in the holding of non-marketable securities. This failure is a definite shortcoming because such institutions are a very significant part of a developed financial system. In this section, the theory is extended to include information costs to determine if they contribute to a theory of intermediation that better explains deposit-taking institutions and their activities.

Identification costs

The model can be extended by adding search and verification costs. Search costs are incurred in seeking out investment opportunities. Verification costs are the costs of assessing the eventual productivity of an investment once that investment has been identified.[11]

Chan (1983), following Leland and Pyle (1977), builds a model of financial intermediation in which the advantage of indirect finance arises from spreading the search costs among many investors. In isolation each investor would incur the cost of the search for investment opportunities until he finds a productive investment. The intermediary can search among investments and once a productive investment is found offer a share of it to other investors. A crucial assumption in this analysis is that investment projects can absorb more resources than are available from the typical investor.

Two difficulties arise from Chan's model. First, the model explains only a limited form of intermediary – the broker – because it lacks any reason for the intermediary to take the investment into his own portfolio or to offer claims to ultimate investors. The intermediary performs only an identification function and once this function has been fulfilled its role is complete. Second, consideration of the difficulties inherent in keeping information private creates problems for Chan's explanation for the persistence of intermediation. The broker's client is in exactly the same position as the broker after he gains the information through search. Under such perfect information the broker would be unable to realise any return from his information.

Leland and Pyle (1977) suggest that the creation of a true intermediary provides a solution to overcome this problem. By holding the investment in its own portfolio, the true intermediary need not disclose the nature of the investment and can protect its returns from search. As Leland and Pyle recognise, by itself this extension fails to explain completely the emergence of a true intermediary. The customer must be satisfied that the intermediary holds productive investments. Thus, although solving the appropriability problem – the problem of ensuring that there is some return to collecting information – the creation of an intermediary generates in its place a credibility problem. Unless investors can be assured that the intermediary holds productive investments, they will not hold the intermediary's liabilities. Simple disclosure of the assets in the intermediary's portfolio to satisfy investors does not solve the problem; it just reintroduces the appropriability problem that the intermediary is designed to overcome.

The presence of verification costs as distinct from search costs alters the analysis considerably. Verification costs could take either of two forms:

(i) a lump sum charge that is independent of the accuracy of the measurement, *or*
(ii) a charge that depends to some degree on the precision of the measurement.

Unlike the benefits of search, benefits of verification cannot easily be shared among investors.

Verification costs explain the existence of financial intermediation to the extent that the intermediary is capable of spreading some of its verification costs among its customers. If the verification costs are independent of the accuracy of measurement, the intermediary cannot offer any advantage over direct finance. To establish the value of the assets he is acquiring by investing in the intermediary, the client would have to duplicate on his own the intermediary's verification process. Indirect finance would just add another level to the verification costs.

Indirect finance may, however, benefit investors when verification costs depend on accuracy. If investment through the intermediary permits investors to verify at a lower degree of confidence then they would need if they invested directly, then it would be possible for the total cost of investing through intermediaries to be less than the costs of direct finance.

How can the presence of an intermediary reduce the need for investors to verify the quality of the investment? The intermediary could establish some device to permit the investors to reduce their effort. One such device would be the commitment by the owner of the intermediary of some of his wealth to the intermediary's portfolio together with the obligation that the investors have a prior claim on the assets. As a consequence investors would be able to reduce the accuracy of their verification because the value of the assets held by the intermediary would exceed the amount necessary to cover their claim. For example, if the owner's wealth subscribed to the intermediary equalled the sum of claims to investors any investor would need to verify only that the value of the assets is not less than 50 per cent of the value reported by the intermediary. The existence of an intermediary would depend on the costs saved through less-intensive verification relative to the opportunity cost to the owner of using wealth as a substitute for verification.[12]

The economies arising from savings in verification costs would appear to explain either a mutual-fund or a deposit-taking intermediary, but not a broker. Use of a broker would not eliminate the need for an investor to verify the investment. On the other hand, a subscription of part of the intermediary owner's wealth into a mutual fund could reduce an investor's need for verification. This subscription would not offer the investor greater protection, but, according to Leland and Pyle (1977), it would be an indication to the investor that the owner believed that the investment was productive. Alternatively, the owner could subscribe his own capital to an intermediary and provide investors with a guaranteed claim to overcome the credibility problem.

The introduction of search and verification costs both contribute to explaining different types of intermediaries, though not without some problems. An intermediary that performs search services would still need to establish some device in order to derive the full benefit for itself from the greater efficiency of collective search. Verification, in contrast, is an activity that yields purely private benefits. A need for intermediation arises because some forms of guarantee can serve as a substitute for verification and, as a consequence, lead to real resource savings.

Monitoring and enforcement[13]

The analysis of search and verification deals with only one dimension of the problems that arise when information has a cost. In this first stage, projects are sought out and examined with respect to their expected productivity. But once an investment is verified other problems arise. Can the investor be assured the funds will be directed towards the agreed-upon purpose? Moreover, once the funds are commited, will the obligations of the borrower be fulfilled?

In the real world, the outcome of an investment is not independent of the amount of resources used by the suppliers of funds to supervise the investment. *Monitoring costs* are incurred throughout the life of the investment to ensure that the funds are used for their intended purpose and that any commitment with respect to the use of the complementary inputs is honoured. *Enforcement costs* are necessary to make borrowers fulfil replayment obligations once the outcome of the investment is known and repayment becomes due. For present purposes, the distinction between these costs does not matter: the important difference is between these costs that are necessary after the funds are committed and the search and verification costs that are incurred prior to commitment.

Individual lenders are quite able on their own to monitor and enforce the contracts they make with borrowers. Two conditions must be present before a role is created for intermediation. First, the costs of monitoring and enforcing the behaviour of any borrowers must rise less than in proportion to the scale of funds. Second, the funds needed by any one borrower must exceed the resources committed by any one lender. The fulfilment of the first condition establishes the presence of economies of scale, whereas the second condition allows the realisation of the scale economies. The second condition can be achieved either by:

(i) the assumption that the scale of investment projects exceeds the resources held by potential lenders, or
(ii) the assumption that lenders are risk-averse and avoid risk by holding a diversified portfolio.

Consider the alternative ways in which a lender can overcome the problems of monitoring and enforcement. Under some circumstances direct finance may be more expensive than some form of delegated monitoring and enforcement that consolidates this function for a number of lenders under one agent. Still, the consolidation of these functions does not eliminate the problems. Rather, the ultimate lenders must be concerned instead with the behaviour of the agent delegated to monitor and enforce. The delegation of these tasks either to a broker or to a mutual-fund intermediary is not a satisfactory solution because the outcome of the investment is borne solely by the lender, despite the actions of the agent. Incentive systems could be devised to overcome these problems, but in any system the payment to the agent must depend in some way upon performance.

The deposit-taking institution appears to provide an efficient solution to monitoring and enforcement problems. The agent who is delegated with the responsibility for monitoring and enforcement guarantees a fixed payment to his depositors and becomes the residual claimant to the remainder of the income. Thus, his returns are directly dependent upon his performance. By this interpretation, the deposit-taking institution serves as a device to overcome the problems inherent in any delegation of monitoring and enforcement to agents.

The question still remains of the credibility of the fixed-value commitment incorporated in the deposit claim. If the agent performs his monitoring and enforcement duties, he gains all the benefits from greater effort and could be expected to maintain a level of activity at which the additional gains from further effort match the additional costs. The establishment of a deposit-taking institution just shifts the monitoring and enforcement problem away from the ultimate borrowers to the level of the agent himself. How do lenders assure themselves that their agent fulfils his commitment to a degree sufficient to ensure the fixed value of their claims?

The solution is identical to that described earlier to enforce appropriate behaviour from the agent who verifies. The agent must subscribe sufficient wealth to the institution so that either:

(i) the added wealth is adequate to protect depositors whatever the degree of supervision that the agent chooses to perform, *or*
(ii) that the losses to him from failure to perform his function exceed the benefits from doing so.

In effect, the intermediary must post a performance bond in the form of shareholders' capital.

This explanation of intermediation in terms of monitoring and supervision now appears to explain too much. Indeed, all the devices available to intermediaries for reassuring their creditors can also be used by ultimate debtors in borrowing directly from ultimate lenders. Thus, monitoring and enforcement costs alone serve to explain only appropriate behaviour of lenders, but not the presence of deposit-taking intermediaries. As will be seen in the subsequent analysis, monitoring and enforcement costs do play an important role in the composite theories that serve to explain deposit intermediaries.

Intermediation and the marketability of securities

The discussion of theories presented above distinguishes among brokers, mutual-funds and deposit-taking intermediaries according to their form of organisation. As discussed earlier, observation sugests that these institutions differ not only in form, but also in terms of the types of business they perform. Brokers and mutual-funds intermediaries appear to concentrate on transactions in marketable securities, whereas deposit-taking intermediaries concentrate a large part of their holdings in non-marketable securities.

Any explanation of the various forms of intermediaries should be able to explain the apparent specialisation of the various intermediaries into different types of activity. So far, no use has been made of the distinction among the types of business associated with each kind of intermediary. These differences suggest that a single theory of intermediation would not be suitable to explain all forms of intermediation and that the distinction among types of intermediaries are differences of substance. In particular, brokers and mutual-funds intermediaries may be found to perform functions different from those performed by deposit-taking intermediaries.

Marketable and non-marketable securities

The distinction between marketable and non-marketable securities may provide some useful clues for evaluating various explanations for the existence of financial institutions. It is useful at this point to discuss this distinction, at least in a preliminary way. In a literal sense, the term 'marketable' is applied to securities that have gained the approval of regulators for distribution to the general public. In that sense, they can be transferred without any legal restrictions with respect to holders.

In economic terms, the distinction between marketable and non-marketable securities is a question of degree. In a trivial sense any security can always be marketed at some price. The legal sense of the word captures some of the essence of the economic usage. Securities legislation requires borrowers to make detailed information available with respect to the identity of principals, their financial condition and commitments and many other factors. The accuracy of this information may be attested so that it is not necessary for every lender to repeat the entire exercise of determining this information. Still, this public provision of information need not eliminate the need for individual lenders to seek out information. Despite the public release of information, potential holders of marketable securities may investigate many dimensions of the security and its issuer. In contrast, the lender takes on the responsibility of collecting information for non-marketable securities. Some of this information may be the same as required under securities legislation. In some cases, this information may be gained through a continuing business relation with the borrower built up over a longtime. The intangible quality of this subjective information may restrict the ability of lenders to transfer it to other parties in any convincing way.

While the idea of the legal responsibility for supplying information is an element of marketability, more than this appears to be involved in the concept. Differentiation among securities would exist even in the absence of securities legislation. The distinction between marketable and non-marketable securities apears to correspond with the degree to which information required to verify and monitor the value of the investment is publicly supplied by the borrower. While the matter is one of relative emphasis, marketable securities are identified with those for which the borrower supplies the bulk of information required by investors. In the case of non-marketable securities, the lender gathers more of the information.

What types of borrowers are likely to convey information to the general public themselves? The size of the borrowing and the credibility of the information appear to be important. If the size of a borrower's demand for funds is such that it requires access to the funds of many lenders, the borrower would be more likely to supply much of the information on his own and thus alleviate some of the need for each of the prospective lenders to acquire the information themselves. Similarly, only those firms that have a 'track record' that permits them to supply credible information would be able to issue marketable securities.

The issuers of marketable and non-marketable securities may also differ with respect to their need for monitoring. With marketable issues, the distribution among many lenders diffuses the incentive for any one lender to monitor and enforce the performance of the borrower with respect to the terms of the contract. Any lender who chooses to supervise the investment would be able to gain only a share of the benefits for himself. The remainder would flow to all investors at large. In this circumstance, lenders must be assured that an effective mechanism exists to enforce performance by the borrowers.[14]

Doubts in the minds of investors with respect to the monitoring and enforcement mechanism may limit the ability of a borrower to issue marketable securities. Instead, the borrower may be constrained to issue securities only to lenders who intend to monitor and enforce the terms of the contract on their own. In some cases the monitoring and enforcement role required of the lender may be quite minimal. For example, the borrower may have established his reliability with one lender, but may be unable to convey this reliability to a wider group of lenders at reasonable cost.

Finally, some borrowers may prefer to issue non-marketable issues for reasons of confidentiality.[15] Even though borrowers may be of an adequate size and may have credible monitoring and enforcement mechanisms in place, they may still prefer the use of non-marketable securities because of a desire to restrict the distribution of information about their activities for competitive reasons. The issue of marketable securities requires the firm to make broad disclosure of its activities and plans. This information is generally presented in such a way that it becomes accessible to a broad audience which includes competitors. Raising funds through non-marketable securities, on the other hand, allows the information to be confined to a smaller range of actual lenders.

THE ROLE OF DEPOSIT-TAKING INTERMEDIARIES

Deposit-taking intermediaries, as we have seen, are identified with both the holding of non-marketable securities and the issue of fixed-value deposits. The holding of non-marketable securities suggests that these intermediaries must either participate in the monitoring and enforcement function to a greater degree than other intermediaries or deal with borrowers who wish to maintain confidentiality with respect to their activities. The monitoring and enforcement function would explain lending to smaller firms, confidentiality would be more relevant for explaining lending to larger firms that could issue marketable securities on their own.[16] Moreover, the fixed money value of deposit liabilities appears to be consistent with the need to create appropriate incentives for agents to carry out effective monitoring and enforcement. In the earlier discussion of these functions it was noted that each of these activities could be provided for in a contract between ultimate borrowers and ultimate lenders. Such a contract would incorporate both a fixed payment by the ultimate borrower which would be independent of the investment outcome and a commitment of wealth by the borrower such that the lender would be assured that any commitment would be met. By itself, the monitoring and enforcement activity explains the form of the contract between lenders and borrowers. While it is conceivable that the ultimate lenders and borrowers could reach the same contractual arrangements on their own as they could through an intermediary, other factors may cause a preference for an intermediary.

The ability of the ultimate borrower to commit his wealth to the project as a substitute for monitoring and enforcement effort on behalf of lenders depends on the amount of the borrower's wealth and on his willingness to risk it. If the borrower's wealth is insufficient to assure lenders that they need not spend resources to monitor and enforce the contract, then a role may exist for deposit-taking intermediaries. For example, if some part of the costs of monitoring and enforcement is independent of the number of investment projects that are supervised, intermediaries who supervise numerous investments would have a cost advantage over individual investors. In addition, as suggested by Leland and Pyle (1977) and Fama (1985), the fact that deposits with intermediaries are a major means of payments gives these intermediaries an inherent advantage in monitoring the activities of its customers.

The introduction of social risk together with monitoring and enforcement costs also increase the probability of the emergence of a pure deposit-taking intermediary. Without the need for monitoring and enforcement, the risk-transfer function by itself explains only an institution that passively accepts the return and risk of marketable securities supplied by the market. When the investment requires monitoring and enforcement, the issue by a financial institution of liabilities that depend on its monitoring and enforcement effort and the performance of the underlying investment requires supervision on the part of its holder, especially to the extent that another claim-holder earns a residual claim. In this case, any misspecification of the return on investment by the residual claimant would distribute wealth away from the other claim-holder to the benefit of the residual claimant. The offering of a fixed-claim deposit by the residual claimant may be mutually beneficial to both the depositor and the residual claimant in that the depositor can save the resources required to monitor and enforce the outcome of the investment. This arrangement requires the residual claimant to bear more risk than would be optimal in the absence of transactions costs. The savings by the depositor from the reduced need for supervision together with the value of not bearing any risk must be sufficient to compensate the residual claim-holder for the additional risk he must bear.

The introduction of private risk also makes the monitoring and enforcement functions more likely to be performed by intermediaries. In order to diversify or reduce their risk, ultimate investors want to supply funds to a variety of borrowers. In isolation, they would incur multiple costs of supervision because they invest in more than the minimum number of projects. An intermediary can as a consequence limit the supervision expenses by investing on behalf of a number of investors in multiple projects and then committing its own wealth to a degree that is sufficient to allow the investors to reduce the resources they use for supervision.

Implications of alternative models of intermediation

The present analysis suggests that deposit-taking institutions and their major characteristics cannot be explained adequtely by any single set of factors. Nevertheless, delegated monitoring and enforcement appear to be essential elements of any theory in order to explain the concentration of non-marketable securities by deposit-taking institutions. This approach recognises that deposit-taking institutions actively manage and shape risks rather than just adapt passively to risks that face them.

The monitoring and enforcement view of financial institutions is relatively new and many of its implications have not been fully worked out. Much of the existing literature on the theory of financial intermediation contains more complete development of theories designed to explain the portfolio behaviour of intermediaries than theories explaining the existence of and functions performed by intermediaries. This imbalance poses the danger that theories of portfolio choice developed for intermediaries do not adequately reflect the functions performed by those intermediaries. In some cases the separation of theories explaining behaviour from theories explaining the existence of particular features of the economy may not matter in that the behaviour stands independently of the source of the feature. In other cases the separation of the explanation of behaviour from the explanation of function may come at some cost.

The behaviour of deposit-taking institutions in response to market changes is modelled typically on the basis of the Tobin–Markowitz model of portfolio selection.[17] As Santomero observes:

> The Tobin–Markowitz asset portfolio models are used for quantity choice in a perfect market. The results follow directly from the finance literature and add little more. Their insights and they are many come from the realization that the bank asset problem is a special case of the standard portfolio choice model (Santomero, 1984, p.590).

The choice of this model depends implicitly on the assumption that intermediaries serve mainly the risk-transfer function between investors on the basis of differences in their willingness to bear risk. Even in this context these models fail to incorporate the transactions costs required to explain the existence of intermediaries. More fundamentally this modelling fails to capture the essential elements of deposit-taking intermediaries to the extent that their existence depends on advantages in monitoring and enforcement as well as in risk transfer.

Whether the typical portfolio model is suitable for analysing the behaviour of intermediaries depends on the degree to which it gives appropriate predictions. The monitoring and enforcement approach suggests that these functions serve to explain both the existence of deposit-taking intermediaries and their specialisation relative to others in the holding of non-marketable securities. What difference does the presence of a monitoring and enforcement role make in explaining the behaviour of an intermediary? There are a number of possibilities.

First, much of the literature that tries to explain bank behaviour has little relevance to an institution whose existence purports to be explained by transfer of risk alone. The customer-relationship literature (Hodgman, 1963, and Fama, 1985) suggests that it is mutually advantageous for banks and their customers to make decisions taking into account their continuing relationship. Similarly literature on credit-rationing stresses the informational problem faced by banks and their customers (Stiglitz, 1985). Neither of these issues appears relevant to a deposit-taking institution that derives its rationale solely from portfolio diversification or risk-transfer motives

Second, the monitoring and enforcement explanation gives an interpretation to the problem of bank capital that differs from arguments based on diversification or risk-shifting. In these latter theories the bank-capital problem can be viewed as part of the optimal portfolio choice made by bank shareholders on the basis of expected returns risks and their attitudes towards risk. In contrast the monitoring and enforcement explanations of deposit-taking institutions suggest that bank capital creates confidence among depositors so that they are willing to place their deposits with the institution permitting it to perform its specialised functions. The difference between the two approaches can be illustrated by the predictions of the consequence of an exogenous shock that increases the riskiness of shareholders' capital in a bank. The portfolio model suggests that shareholders might rearrange their portfolios so as to hold less of the risky bank capital and more of the safe asset. Theories emphasising monitoring and enforcement would suggest that the bank's owners may have to subscribe more capital to assure depositors that their claims could be met.

Finally the monitoring and enforcement explanation leads to predictions in areas where portfolio explanations would not. For example, financial intermediaries would be expected to be more important relative to total financial market activity in developing as opposed to developed economies. In developed economies more enterprises could be expected to have reached a stage at which they can effectively convey information directly to potential lenders.

4 The Operation of Financial Markets

K. ALEC CHRYSTAL

It does not take too much research to identify the most topical issue concerning the behaviour of financial markets. The question crops up in some form on the financial pages of the newspapers every day. The question, of course, is the extent to which financial markets are too volatile when left to themselves and, consequently, the extent to which the authorities should intervene to change the situation.

Notice that I have referred to 'volatility' and not to 'inefficiency'. One of the interesting questions is the degree to which volatility reflects inefficiency, but I shall have more to say about that below. Notice also that the central question is probably not one which can be answered purely by reference to empirical evidence. The evidence is relevant, but it is usually impossible to say how alternative systems would have coped with particular events. Most importantly, students who are relatively new to the study of markets should be aware that debates for and against free markets have been going on for a very long time – in fact, as long as markets have existed. We should not, therefore, expect a quick resolution of the issue, but neither should we forget that much as been learned from previous rounds of the debate. (See Alt and Chrystal, 1983, ch. 2 for a brief summary of the historical debate.)

Much of the literature prior to the 1980s was concerned with markets in general and tried to explain why there appeared to be booms and slumps in real activity. Could some method of central government intervention improve the situation – the most extreme form of such intervention being central planning? Dramatic evidence on this question has recently been provided by the collapse of central planning regimes in Eastern Europe. These countries have decided to adopt market economies as quickly as possible and to introduce a full range of financial markets. Thus the overwhelming benefits of a market economy over a planned economy are clearly demonstrated.

However, the failure of 'command' economies does not establish that market economies work best with a total absence of government intervention. Indeed, in contrast to the enthusiasm for free markets expressed in Eastern Europe, there is still a widespread suspicion of unbridled market forces in most Western economies. This is especially true in relation to those financial markets which have proved to be the most volatile. In many aspects of financial-market regulation there are ongoing debates about restrictions on trading activity which may make the market outcome 'better'. The grounds for interference differ from area to area, but there is a common theme based upon market 'failure' of some kind.

This chapter will first outline the argument for greater intervention as it has come up in three different areas of the financial system – foreign-exchange market, stock markets and retail financial markets. The detail is slightly different in each case but the issue is basically the same – can the market be left alone or do we need intervention? I shall then argue that in almost all cases government intervention makes things worse not better. The one exception to this is the foreign exchange market where it is arguable that an acceptable solution may be to do away with foreign-exchange markets entirely.

FOREIGN EXCHANGE MARKETS

In the years just after the Second World War, it was widely accepted that governments should stabilise exchange rates by active intervention in foreign exchange markets (though see Friedman, 1953, for a statement of the case for floating exchange rates). The experience of the inter-war years had been of severe cycles in real activity and it seemed obvious that devaluations and exchange-rate instability had contributed to that instability.

Accordingly, it was agreed at the Bretton Woods conference in July 1944 to set up a global system of pegged (but adjustable) exchange rates. This involved the creation of the IMF as a monitoring (and short-term credit) agency, but the main feature was the commitment by member-governments to maintain their currency values within plus or minus 1 per cent of their 'par values' against the dollar. For its part, the dollar was pegged to gold at $35 per ounce.

The system was maintained for a time by means of import controls and foreign-exchange controls, but in 1958 the major industrial countries adopted current-account convertibility. This meant that foreign exchange could be purchased freely for the purchase of imports. However, most countries maintained capital controls for much longer. These prevented people from holding foreign-currency bank accounts, purchasing foreign property and investing in foreign securities. The UK abolished all its exchange controls in October 1979. Many countries (particularly smaller ones) continue to have such controls in place.

The cracks in the Bretton Woods pegged-exchange-rate system began to show by the mid-1960s. There were traumatic devaluations by the UK and France and a revaluation by West Germany. In March 1968, the USA partly abandoned its commitment to peg the dollar to gold. The privilege of buying gold at the official price was maintained for other central banks but the private-sector gold price was floated. Finally, in August 1971, the USA 'closed the gold window' entirely and the dollar was temporarily floated against all other currencies. In December 1971, it was agreed at the Smithsonian Conference to repeg all the major exchange rates at new parities, but this patch-up job lasted only a short while. Sterling was floated in June 1972 and the other major currencies floated in the spring of 1973 (though most small countries remained tied to the currency of a larger country or to a currency basket) and so the fixed-rate system had effectively collapsed.

Economists expected that the early days of floating would see exchange rates somewhat volatile but that they would soon settle down as market participants came to comprehend the new system. There was a good deal of volatility of nominal exchange rates in the early days but there turned out to be no tendency for this volatility to settle down. Nonetheless, since the trends in exchange rates seemed to conform to those which at least some versions of theory would suggest, many commentators thought the system was working reasonably well (see Frankel, 1979, for a study which finds the behaviour of the dollar–DM rate easy to explain in the early period of floating).

Right from the beginning of the floating era there were some countries which were not happy with floating and opted for regional pegging arrangements – the European Snake and its successor, the ERM, is an obvious example. However, a more general disillusionment with floating grew in the early 1980s. This was a result of hard-to-explain swings in real exchange rates. (The 'real exchange rate' reflects the relative competitiveness of one economy compared to others). Sterling appreciated strongly from 1976 until 1980 and the dollar appreciated from 1980 to 1985. The behaviour of the latter was a special cause for concern, given the key role of the dollar in the world economy. Perceived misalignments of the dollar gave grounds for coordinated intervention by G7 finance ministers in the foreign-exchange markets. Two important episodes were associated with the Louvre Accord and the Plaza Agreement (see Artis, 1989). A general feelings of dissatisfaction with the performance of floating exchange rates had clearly emerged by the late 1980s and 'policy coordination' and coordinated intervention by the major governments (in order to attempt to influence the course of exchange rates) became the fashion.

Are foreign-exchange markets efficient?

In the theoretical literature there is an ongoing debate about the extent to which foreign-exchange markets are 'efficient' (for a recent survey of the issues see Levich, 1989). This is an important literature, but there is a danger that its significance will be misunderstood. The central question asked is 'Do prices fully reflect all available information?' Or alternatively, 'Are there any unexploited profit-making opportunities?' It is very clear that all riskless arbitrage opportunities are eliminated very quickly indeed (hence the opportunities to profit from covered interest arbitrage or triangular arbitrage are few and far between). Accordingly, the efficiency literature has concentrated on the question of whether a profit can be made from speculation in forward foreign-exchange markets. (A profit would arise if the forward rate were predictably different from the future spot rate on average.)

Early studies could not reject the hypothesis that the forward rate was an unbiased predictor of the future spot rate. However, a host of studies in the 1980s (e.g. Baillie *et al.*, 1983) have found clear rejections of the speculative efficiency of the forward rate. There are two possible reasons for this rejection. The first is that these markets are inefficient. The second is that market participants may be risk-averse. The latter is the presumption that most of the literature has adopted and hence the search has been for measures of the 'risk premium'. The details of this discussion are not relevant here, but it is important to note that efficiency could be rescued by changing the underlying hypothesis about the way market participants behave. As Levich (1989) has pointed out, this means that we are always testing a joint hypothesis – we have to say 'efficient relative to what?' Efficiency can only be defined in the context of a specific theory of how exchange rates are determined in the first place. Empirical rejections of efficiency may just mean that we do not have the right underlying theory. Hence even this narrow concept of speculative efficiency of forward markets must remain an open question.

One important result in the empirical exchange rate literature was that of Meese and Rogoff (1983). They found that none of a series of exchange-rate models could out-perform a random walk in out-of-sample forecast tests. (A 'random walk' implies that the future price is equal to the current price plus a random change.) At first sight, this seems very depressing for all efforts at exchange-rate modelling. However, in reality, it is a fairly clear indication that foreign-exchange markets are very efficient (in some sense) and in no way does it imply that our theoretical models of exchange-rate determination are thereby proved to be useless. On the contrary, suppose we all knew for sure what the correct model was. The current exchange rate would immediately reflect fully all that is known about the relevant determining variables, not only in the past and present, but also in the future. Hence, changes in the exchange rate could only be the result of events which were totally unexpected – 'news'. Such events are by definition random (otherwise they could be forecast). This means that the mere fact that exchange rates bounce about in response to new information is not itself evidence of inefficiency. On the contrary, the approximation to a random walk is consistent with a specific concept of efficiency.

There is a further problem with accusing foreign-exchange markets of being too volatile and that is that the volatility of foreign-exchange markets may in part result from inefficiencies *elsewhere in the economy*. This is most clearly demonstrated in the Dornbusch (1976) 'overshooting' model. In this model prices in foreign-exchange markets adjust instantaneously to new information, while goods prices adjust slowly. The latter causes exchange rates to overshoot their long-run equilibrium for just as long as it takes goods prices to catch up. When shocks hit the economy it is the exchange markets which react first, because they are the most flexible and provide the escape valve for the pressure. Hampering this adjustment would presumably divert the pressure elsewhere but it would not necessarily stop it having an impact somewhere. Hence, while exchange rates may well deviate from their long-run equilibrium value for quite significant periods, this is not sufficient to prove that it would be 'better' to restrict them in some way.

Nonetheless, there is a case for re-examining policy towards exchange rates, especially in the light of the ongoing discussion of the design of monetary institutions within Europe. We shall return to this argument below. The case for intervention is much weaker in the other two areas to be discussed and it is to these that we now turn.

STOCK MARKETS

There are two levels of argument about the inefficiency of stock markets. The first concerns the excess volatility of prices – this is a similar (though not identical) argument to that applied in foreign-exchange markets. Another way of thinking about the same issue is to ask whether equity prices reflect 'fundamental values'. The second concerns the fundamental misallocation of resources which allegedly occurs because of the reputed inadequacies of the stock market as an institution for channelling savings into investment. 'Short-termism' is the phrase which encapsulates the latter set of arguments. It is claimed that pressures from institutional investors (or rather their fund managers) are such that firms cannot adopt appropriate long-run investment strategies.

There are some important differences between stock markets and foreign-exchange markets which arise because stock markets trade in a much wider variety of securities. Issues about inside information and the lack of liquidity in the markets for shares in small companies are important, but we shall not have space to discuss them here. Rather, our central concern is the role of the market mechanism in the determination of prices of shares in the major companies.

The question of whether stock markets reflect fundamental values has been controversial for many years. On the one side are those who believe in efficient markets. For them the current stock price is the market valuation of the present value of an expected future income stream. New information will change this valuation. Indeed, there is no reason why the current price cannot be extremely volatile for quite 'correct' reasons. 'News' may radically alter the current assessment of the future prospects of a company. As new information accrues more or less randomly, there will be a random element to the stock-market valuation. In this respect, volatility may be supportive of 'efficiency' rather than the reverse.

Those who criticise the efficient-markets view would nonetheless accept the critical role of expectations. However, they would give a dominant role to abnormal waves of optimism and pessimism which are not justified by fundamentals. Keynes talked about 'animal spirits' shortly after having lived through the events of 1929, and Shiller (1981) provides some empirical evidence that equity prices do deviate substantially from those prices which appear justified by fundamentals.

More recent work suggests a fairly simply reconciliation of these two extreme positions (see, for example, Mills, 1989). Short-term movements in stock prices appear to be dominated by short-term money-market conditions – interest rates, exchange rates, and other short-term macroeconomic indicators. However, in the longer term (periods longer than about twelve months) the yield fundamentals (based upon profits and providing for sustainable dividends) turn out to be the dominant influence. Figure 4.1 illustrates the long-term correlation between stock prices and dividend yields. Hence, the fundamentals are the single most important influence on the long-term trend, but fluctuations about this trend are influenced by news and current events.

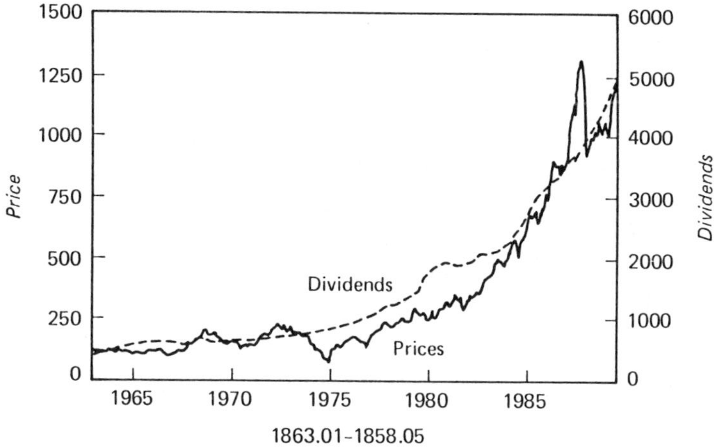

FIGURE 4.1 FT-Actuaries 500: price and dividend indices

If this interpretation of the evidence is correct, the natural follow-up question is: Does the noise matter? Certainly there is some harmful effect owing to the fact that managers of quoted companies cannot ignore their share price. Undervaluation of shares is often perceived by managers as a vote of 'no confidence' by the financial markets. Funding through equity issues and the potential for takeover are seriously affected by the phase of the market. Capital is hard to raise in a bear market but at the same time companies become vulnerable to takeover (because market valuation understates true asset value). In contrast, during bull markets it is often too easy to raise new capital and firms may end up with over-optimistic expansion plans.

Those who are convinced of the irrationality of share-price movements often recommend that speculative activity should be restricted in some way. Keynes recommended a 'substantial transfer tax . . . with a view of mitigating the predominance of speculation over enterprise . . . ' Tobin (1978) has suggested a tax on international capital flows that would 'Throw sand in the works of the international financial system.' Others have proposed 'circuit-breakers' to stop panics getting out of hand. Following the Brady Report into the 1987 crash on Wall Street, a maximum daily movement in the Dow-Jones Index was introduced. The intention is to make participants pause, rather than force further sales on a falling market. The logic of this is that it is intended to halt a wave of irrational selling. At the same time it also puts a halt to any automatic process of 'computer trading' whereby a flood of stop-loss orders is executed simultaneously. (A 'stop-loss' order is a prearranged order to sell as soon as the price falls to a specified level. This enables the investor to get out of a position before the price falls too low. The alleged bad effect of such orders is that they add sales to an already falling market.)

Do circuit-breakers make a market better? The answer is not known, as it partly depends upon what is meant by 'better'. However, it is important to note that circuit-breakers bring costs as well as benefits. Once a market has closed after a limit has been reached no further trades can take place. This is true even if the market has been moved by 'fundamentals'. Where trading activity is arbitrarily prevented, even temporarily, an explicit inefficiency is created which would not otherwise have existed. Trades may move to other markets and confidence in the trading system may be reduced. A great deal more research will be needed in order to determine whether circuit-breakers create an improved market. Suffice it to say that the alleged benefits are currently unproven.

A further issue relates to the relevance of modern computer technology in the market outcome itself. The *bête noire* of computer trading has already been mentioned. In this context the term 'computer trading' usually refers to the automatic execution of stop-loss orders. Santoni (1988) claims that computer trading cannot be blamed for the 1987 stock-market crash. Indeed, similar selling strategies are possible without computers. However, there is a wider issue. Do markets behave differently when they are executed by computer systems, as in the post-Big-Bang International Stock Exchange, as compared with face-to-face or open-outcry markets? The answer is, again, unknown. Nonetheless, it is clear that modern telecommunications have had one demonstrable effect in linking markets in diverse parts of the world much more closely. This means that issues of market structure can no longer be decided at a local level and whatever 'shocks' do occur tend to be transmitted from one market to another very quickly. In this context, regulators in one country have much less freedom to affect market forces than if their country were operating in isolation of the world markets.

A final point worth noting on the question of stock-market volatility is that much of the 'news' which makes markets move is about the erratic behaviour of governments. The two biggest uncertainties which affect stock markets in the short run are those relating to potential changes in government and potential changes in policy stance of an existing government. At the time of writing, the international political uncertainty resulting from the Gulf situation has had a strong negative effect on stock markets world-wide. Similar (or even worse) stock market declines were caused by oil-price shocks in 1973 and 1979; both of these events had clear political causes. Hence, at least some of the blame for market instability must be attributed to the instability of the political environment rather than to any intrinsic fault of the market mechanism.

The arguments about 'short-termism' need not detain us too long as they are usually fairly superficial. There is certainly some truth to the line that banks take a shorter-term view than their corporate customers, but that is because the equity markets provide long-term finance while banks (in the UK and the USA at least) have traditionally concentrated on providing finance at the short end.

The most common form of the short-termism argument is based upon the supposition that fund managers are concerned only with their fund performance for the quarter or the year, while firms have to invest over a much longer horizon. These perspectives are not inconsistent, of course, if market valuations correctly reflect present values of future income. But do firms behave any differently because analysts are breathing down their necks? A CBI survey in 1987 found that only 4 per cent of industrialists thought that pressure from analysts was of major significance. In contrast, 77 per cent thought that such pressures were of no significance in making long-term strategic choices. Indeed, the argument could equally be turned on its head. A German economist has recently argued that the *strength* of the top British firms relative to their German rivals owes a great deal to the fact that they are disciplined by exposure to outside analysts. Managers are, thereby, kept on their toes and the company develops a healthy competitive advantage.

In short, the interaction between financial markets and industry is symbiotic. The general well-being is furthered by each seeking the best terms from the other. There is, certainly, no reason to believe that governments or regulators can improve economic efficiency in these markets by interfering in a major way.

RETAIL FINANCIAL MARKETS

For better, or worse, governments have a very heavy regulatory presence in retail financial markets. The reason is that the participants in wholesale markets can be presumed to be professional, well-informed and competent to judge their own self-interest. In retail markets, the customer is 'Joe Public' and wherever the public acts the politicians will claim to be able to defend their interests. Such claims will nearly always be unfounded. However, finance is a classic case where politicians' attempts to protect the public are in danger of inflicting incalculable damage (and have done so in the past).

We are not concerned here with the legal framework which defines legitimate behaviour of financial institutions. Some such framework is always necessary. Neither are we concerned with measures associated with aggregate monetary policy, though the macroeconomic and the microeconomic cases are often confused. Rather, the concern is with the argument that consumers cannot be 'trusted' to make sensible decisions for themselves and, therefore, need some protection or help in running their financial affairs.

One of the problems that has had to be faced in the 1970s and 1980s in the UK is how to unwind all the post-war restrictions on retail financial markets. These include foreign-exchange controls, hire-purchase restrictions and bank-lending ceilings. It could be argued that, since all these restrictions have been swept away, there is a transitional problem of educating people to use productively the new financial opportunities open to them. There is certainly an important role for economic education and there always will be. However, there are loud voices (see Chrystal, 1990, for explicit quotations) calling for retrenchment in the process of financial-market liberalisation – especially at the retail level, the reason being simply that too many people are getting too deeply in debt. It is claimed that this is the result of excessively aggressive marketing of loans (in various forms including credit cards) by financial institutions. Indeed, the increase in gross personal debt is often taken as a self-evident sign of economic and even moral decline. 'Live now and pay later' is an attitude to be discouraged and condemned. Such concerns have led to the creation of a new 'Code of Practice' for banks which, among other things, puts restrictions on the marketing of loans – even though the problem (if it exists at all) is mainly with the non-bank financial sector.

There certainly are some very real problems associated with personal financial debt, but the significance of these is usually overstated. What is seldom if ever commented upon is the large number of people who have benefited enormously from the freedom to borrow at certain times in their lives. Those who do get into serious trouble, in the vast majority of cases, have suffered from unexpected changes in circumstances – like the loss of a job or the death of a spouse. In cases like these, however, debt is not the prime problem but merely a symptom of problems elsewhere. Further, there is a danger of confusing 'debt' and 'poverty'. People with low incomes are always going to have problems making ends meet, simply because their incomes are insufficient to cover the costs of even the most basic housing and essential goods. However, the people on lowest incomes are not normally those with the biggest debts to financial institutions. The latter do not distribute loans randomly. Rather they make every effort to check that the customer is capable of paying the loan back.

Borrowing money is a totally rational thing to do if you are purchasing a durable good (such as a house) the services of which will be consumed over a long period of time. It makes sense to spread the payments over time too. The biggest debt which most people have is a mortgage which is used to buy a house over, perhaps, a twenty-five-year period. Young couples starting out on married life typically have the largest debts (relative to their incomes) and as a result the media coverage tends to suggest that the younger generation is increasingly indebted. They may well have debts but they have assets also and the vast majority have an increasing net worth – much more so than if restricted from borrowing. Hence the overwhelming majority have gained substantially from the freedom to borrow.

Any reintroduction of restrictions on the availability of credit would hurt most those it is intended to protect. Rationing of credit would give implicit priority to those individuals who already have the highest net worth and are, therefore, the least risky. The relatively rich will, thus, be least restricted in their ability to borrow. Profitable opportunities will thereby go begging for the less-well-off and their wealth-accumulation prospects will thereby be diminished.

In short, while calls for credit controls to reduce personal debt burdens are well-meaning, they are entirely misguided. The main effect of such restrictions would be to limit the opportunities of those thereby excluded. Indeed, like many other arbitrary market interventions, it hurts most those it is intended to help. Far from solving debt problems, credit controls can make them worse, both by driving the needy into the hands of loan sharks and by forcing rapid adjustment to crises that might otherwise be manageable. (The ability to borrow buys time for adjustment to a new set of circumstances.) It is far better to let markets work and to let people learn from their own mistakes.

MONETARY STANDARDS

The case we have been putting above is not an especially controversial one. It is that governments should not attempt directly to interfere with the working of financial markets. Such arguments have, of course, been around since at least the time of Adam Smith. However, we mentioned above that there was an issue surrounding exchange rates which made the case for floating exchange rates far more complicated than when we are talking about the market for a specific product or service. This topic forms the subject matter of Charles Goodhart's chapter in this volume. However, I still wish to draw out some implications for foreign-exchange-market intervention, as it makes a big difference to the appropriate application of market principles to these markets.

The existence of foreign-exchange markets is not fundamental to the existence of an efficiently working economy. Foreign-exchange markets are an arbitrary artifact of the currency structure of the world monetary system. Suppose, for example, that the entire world had the same currency. Would the world economy be less efficient? So long as this currency was of stable value, the answer would have to be 'no'. On the contrary, the real economy would be far more efficient as there would be no noise in the price mechanism and the information efficiency of the world economy would be considerably greater.

Foreign exchange is not a product demanded for its own sake. It is a product of wider choices about monetary standards. The choice to float a local currency is really the choice to have an independent monetary standard. Fixing the exchange rate to an external currency is a decision to be tied to that external monetary standard. The choice between these two options – and, indeed, the third option of having the same currency – is not a simple matter of avoiding intervention in markets, and so the same arguments do not apply.

The real issue at the back of this question is the institutional structure within which the monetary standard gets determined. Some people argue that there should be no government involvement at all in the issuance of money (see, for example, Dowd, 1989). However, within the current institutional structure it makes no sense for the government to argue that the value of a currency must be market-determined. This is because that government is the monopoly supplier of that currency and so it is primarily the central bank's behaviour which determines the value of the currency. The question is 'How should it behave in order to control the value of its liabilities?' Constraining itself to maintain convertibility (at a fixed price) against another currency is a perfectly sensible objective under many circumstances. Of course, the rest of its monetary policy will have to be subordinated to that goal, but this is not an interference with real market forces in the same way that trying to peg the price of potatoes would be.

The bottom line is that the case for not interfering with market forces does not necessarily apply to exchange rates. Indeed, a liberal economic environment may be enhanced by an exchange-rate constraint, since this may be the most effective practical way of guaranteeing a low inflation rate. Indeed, for many small economies there is no effective choice but to peg to a larger country, as their exchange markets would be highly volatile and disruptive to trade in the absence of such a policy. Some commentators would like to return to the days of a commodity standard (such as the gold standard) whereby convertibility of paper currency into something of relatively fixed supply would restrain overissue. Restrictions (or disciplines) such as these may be justified as *supportive* of the working of the free-market real economy rather than obstructive.

CONCLUSION

Financial markets may not be perfect, but it is hard to think of ways in which intervention can improve things. As a general rule it is harmful for governments to interfere with markets. They rarely achieve their intended goal and normally succeed only in reducing the efficiency of the economic system. However, this logic cannot be applied to foreign-exchange markets. On efficiency grounds alone it is plausible to argue that they should be abolished in favour of a single world currency. Within Europe, the best we could do is to install a single low-inflation currency (though a single inflating currency would be worse than the present multi-currency system). Pegging is certainly difficult for a central bank which does not have full control over the growth of its liabilities. But this is precisely why central banks should be so constrained, so that they cannot debauch the currency at will. There may be other ways of achieving the same goal, but some such constraint there must be.

5 Financial Innovation: Causes and Consequences

DANIEL L. THORNTON and COURTENEY C. STONE

INTRODUCTION

A number of significant changes have taken place in domestic and international financial markets over the past two decades. The introduction of a host of new financial products, an influx of numerous and more diversified types of financial firms and expanding use of computers and communications technology have combined to produce a revolution in financial services. As with all revolutions, there is considerable interest in what caused this one and what changes it has produced.

Analyses of the causes and consequences of financial innovation mirror the analytical dichotomies that exist between microeconomics and macroeconomics on the one hand, and between finance and economics on the other.[1] There have been considerable effort and reasonable success in analysing the causes and assessing the consequences of financial innovation at the microeconomic level; a similar effort, however, has led to less success or, at least, much less agreement about its macroeconomic consequences.

In this chapter, we focus primarily on the macroeconomic 'mysteries' of financial innovation rather than present yet another extended discussion of its generally accepted microeconomic 'facts'. Accordingly, the first section offers a succinct summary of the history and microeconomic implications of financial innovation in the USA over the past twenty years. The second section examines perhaps the most puzzling mystery in monetary economics – the 1980s 'breakdown' in *M*1 velocity in the USA. We focus on this specific puzzle because of *M*1 velocity's former macroeconomic and monetary policy importance and because financial innovation is widely perceived as the primary cause of its breakdown. In the third section, we summarise some evidence linking financial innovation and the *M*1 velocity puzzle.

MICROECONOMIC ASPECTS OF FINANCIAL INNOVATION

Financial innovation has been so extensive over the past twenty years that it is impossible to draw up a complete list of its manifestations. This is due in part to the fact that the process of financial innovation continues essentially unabated: new forms and varieties of innovation emerge almost daily. Table 5.1, for example, represents on attempt to list the major financial innovations that took place in 1985 alone. A similar list for 1990 would reveal at least as many innovations; included among these would be the new LIBOR and Nikkei futures contracts traded on the Chicago Mercantile Exchange and the accelerating competition to establish global automatic teller machine (ATM) networks.

Another difficulty in drawing up the definitive list of innovations is that analysts disagree about which are significant; consequently, lists of key financial innovations often differ substantially. For example, Table 5.2 shows some financial *product* innovations that took place in the 1980s. His list, however, ignores innovations in financial *processes* (e.g. electronic securities trading and funds transfers) that others (Silber, 1983, and Van Horne, 1985) consider to have been significant.

Similarly, lists of important innovations differ depending upon the specific financial markets being studied. Table 5.3, for example, focuses on innovations associated solely with deregulation of the deposit-taking activities of commercial banks and thrifts from 1970 to 1986; as a result, it includes few of the innovations shown in Table 5.2.

Despite these differences, however, there is general agreement about the economic and regulatory influences that combined to produce financial innovation in all its guises over the past two decades and about its microeconomic consequences. Table 5.4 lays out the primary causes of the financial innovations that took place from 1970 to 1982. More recent surveys of financial innovation (Wenninger, 1984, and Van Horne, 1985) have generally followed this format and focused on these specific factors with only slight modifications. Thus, while they can be combined in a variety of ways, three major factors are generally credited with having produced financial innovation:

(a) the increases in risk (or uncertainty) that took place in financial markets in the 1970s and 1980s;
(b) the regulations that severely constrained the ability of US depository institutions to compete effectively with firms that offered new or repackaged financial services;
(c) a potpourri of legal (e.g. tax-law changes), technological (e.g. computers and telecommunications advances) and other factors (e.g. development of theoretical asset pricing models).

Increased financial risk and uncertainty

Tables 5.5, 5.6 and 5.7 illustrate a well-known fact about the past two decades – they were marked by increased price volatility across financial markets worldwide when compared with prior years. Table 5.5 shows the rise in the standard deviation of monthly nominal corporate bond yields that occurred since 1974 in five Western nations compared with similar yields in the 1960s; Table 5.6 shows the corresponding rise (except for West Germany) in the standard deviation of monthly stock returns for these countries over the same periods. Finally, Table 5.7 shows the rise in volatility (measured by the coefficient of variation) in selected month-end to month-end exchange rates during the 1970s and 1980s when compared with the two previous decades. While some increase in exchange-rate volatility associated with the adoption of flexible exchange rate is not surprising, Table 5.7 indicates that the rise in volatility across the major currencies was substantial.

A somewhat different way to illustrate the extent of the increased financial risks in the past two decades is shown in Figure 5.1, which contains quarterly *ex post* real-interest rates for 90-day

TABLE 5.1 Financial innovations in 1985

Instrument	*Description*
International markets	
Floating-rate coupon securities	
• Capped	Upper limit on coupon reset rate
• Mini/max	Upper and lower bounds set
• Mismatched	Coupon reset and coupon payment occur at different frequencies
• Partly paid	After initial payment for first part of an issue, purchaser must subscribe to future tranches
Non-dollar FRNs	Introduction of Deutschmark- and yen-denominated FRNs
Non-dollar zero-coupon bonds	Introduction of Deutschmark-, Swiss-franc-, and Japanese-yen-denominated issues
Shoguns	US dollar bonds issued in Japan
Sushis	Eurobonds issued by Japanese entities that do not count against limits on holdings of foreign securities
Yen-denominated Yankees	Yen bonds issued in US market
ECU-denominated securities	Increased utilisation in US markets; introduction of issues in Dutch and Japanese markets
Dual-currency yen bonds	Interest paid in yen, principal paid in other currency at a specified exchange rate
'Down-under' bonds	Increased utilisation of Euro-Australian dollar and Euro-New Zealand dollar bond issues
Domestic markets	
Variable-duration notes	At coupon payment date, holder elects to receive either coupon or an additional note with identical terms
Zero-coupon convertible	Zero-coupon bond with option to convert to common stock
Collateralised securities	
• Multifamily pass-through	Pass-through collateralised by multifamily mortgages
• Lease backed	Collateralised by lease on plant and equipment
• Automobile backed	Collateralised by automobile loans
• Revenue indexed	Mortgage-backed security in which interest payments are suggested by a percentage of issuer's gross earnings
Commercial real estate	
• Finite-life real estate	Portfolio of real estate equities with a specific date by which the portfolio must be liquidated

• Commercial mortgage pass-throughs	Pass-throughs collateralised by commercial mortgages
• Cross-collateralised pooled financing	Pooled securities allowing recourse to other mortgages in the pool
• Rated, pooled nonrecourse commercial mortgage	Publicly rated non-recourse real-estate-backed bonds
Tax-exempt securities	
• Daily adjustable tax-exempt securities	Puttable long-maturity bonds with coupon rate adjusted daily
• Zero coupon	Zero-coupon tax-exempts
• Capital appreciation bonds	Zero-coupon bonds sold at par or better
• Stepped tax-exempt appreciation on income-realisation securities	Zero-coupon bonds for an initial period, after which they are converted to interest-bearing securities
• Municipal option put securities	Puttable bonds with detachable puts
• Periodically adjustable rate trust securities	Participant certificates based on tax-exempt commercial mortgage loans
Futures and options	
Municipal bond contract	Introduction of futures contract to tax-exempt market
Options on Eurodollar futures	Introduction of exchange-traded options on futures to the short end of yield curve
Options on Treasury note futures	Introduction of exchange-traded options on futures to intermediate section of yield curve
Japanese government yen bond futures	Introduction of Japanese financial futures contracts
ECU warrants	Introduction in Europe of publicly offered and listed options on ECU
European-style options	Introduction in USA of options that can only be exercised at expiration; in addition, currency strike prices are in European rather than American terms
Range forward contract	A forward-exchange contract that specifies a range of exchange rates for which currencies are exchanged on the expiration date
US dollar index	Introduction of a futures contract on the dollar's trade-weighted value
Options of cash five-year Treasury Notes	Introduction of options to this sector of the yield curve.

Source: Kaufman (1986) pp.24–26.

TABLE 5.2 Financial product innovations

Market Instruments	*Mortgages*
CDs – variable rate, zero coupon, indexed	Adjustable-rate mortgage (ARMs)
Sweep account – cash management accounts	Shared appreciated mortgage (SAM)
Money market deposit accounts	Reduction option loans (ROLs)
Market index deposit accounts	Early ownership mortgage (EOMs)
	Home equity loan
Notes	
YCAN – yield curve adjustable notes	*Financial Features*
Medium-term notes	Interest rate futures – Treasury bills, bonds, and notes, municipal bonds
PIN – portfolio income notes	
Step-down floating notes	Stock Index futures – S&P 500 major market index, NYSE
Deferred-pay notes	
Extendible notes	
	Options (Registered Exchanges)
Bonds	Equity options
Variable rate bonds	Index options – S&P 100, S&P 500, major market index
Original-issue high-yield (junk) bonds	Subindex options – various industry sectors
Original-issue discount bonds – zero coupon bonds	
Zero-coupon treasuries – STRIPS, TIGRs, CATS	Corporate loans
Event risk-protected bonds – poison pill bonds	Syndicated loans
Exchange rate linked bonds	Swaps – interest rates and currency
Puttable bonds	Interest protected loans – floors, caps, and collars
Pay-in-kind bonds – PIKS	
Insured bonds – credit enhanced bonds	*Preferred Stock*
Defeased bonds	Variable rate
Asset backed bonds – CARs and CARDs	Convertible adjustable
Zero coupon convertible – (LYONs)	Auction rate

Mortgage Backed Bonds
Pass-throughs
Collateralised mortgage obligations (CMOs)
Real estate mortgage investment conduit (REMICs)

Mutual Funds
Municipal bonds funds
High-yield bond funds
Select industry stock funds
International funds – bonds and stocks
Option funds
Country funds
Money market funds
Commodity funds

Equity
Unbundled stock units
Americus Trusts – primes and scores
Stock index participation certificates
Stubs

Notes: *LYONS, TIGRS and CATS*: These are deliberately cute acronyms given to zero-coupon US Treasury-derivative securities by the investment houses that initiated them. Essentially, they bought US Treasury securities, had a bank act as custodian for the securities and issue zero-coupon securities based separately on the coupons and principal of the underlying Treasury securities. Merrill Lynch called their issues '*T*reasury *I*nvestment *G*rowth *R*eceipts' or TIGRs; Salomon Brothers labeled theirs '*C*ertificates of *A*ccrual of *T*reasury *S*ecurities' or CATs; etc.

'*Defeased bonds*'. These are corporate bonds that have been effectively removed as a liability from the firm's balance sheet (and the associated interest payments removed from the firm's income statement) by the following 'trick': the firm assembles and places into an irrevocable trust a portfolio of Treasury notes and bonds (or TIGRs or CATS) whose cash flows match exactly and are dedicated to covering the interest and principal payments of the outstanding debt. This allows the firm to 'improve' its debt measures and financial ratios and, depending on the cost of assembling the portfolio, to achieve a one-time increase in its reported earnings.

Source: Klemosky (1989) p.11.

TABLE 5.3 Selected measures deregulating deposit-taking activities, 1970–86

Effective date	*Measure*
June 1970	Reg. Q ceilings suspended on large-denomination negotiable certificates of deposit (CDs) with maturities of 30–89 days
September 1970	Federally chartered savings and loan associations (S&Ls) permitted to make pre-authorised transfers from savings accounts for household-related expenditures
June 1972	State-chartered mutual savings banks (MSBs) in Massachusetts began offering negotiable-order-of-withdrawal (NOW) accounts
May 1973	Reg. Q ceilings suspended on large-denomination negotiable CDs with maturities of 90 days or more
January 1974	All depository institutions in Massachusetts and New Hampshire authorised by Congress to offer NOW accounts
November 1974	Commercial banks permitted to offer savings accounts to state and local government units
April 1975	Member banks authorised by Federal Reserve to make transfers from a savings account to a demand deposit on customer's telephone order
November 1975	Commercial banks permitted to offer savings accounts to business
February 1976	All depository institutions in New England authorised by Congress to offer NOW accounts
May 1976	State-chartered S&Ls and MSBs in New York authorised to offer cheque-accounts
June 1978	All insured banks and thrifts authorised to offer 6-month money market certificates (MMCs) with minimum denomination of $10 000 and ceiling rates related to that on 6-month Treasury bills
October 1978	Depository institutions in New York authorised by Congress to offer NOW accounts

(continued)

(continued)

November 1978	Commercial banks and MSBs authorised to offer automatic transfer service (ATS) from a savings account to a cheque-account
July 1979	Commercial banks and thrifts authorised to offer small saver certificates with no minimum denomination but with minimum maturity of 4 years and ceiling rates somewhat below that on 4-year Treasury securities
January 1980	Minimum maturity of small saver certificates reduced to $2\frac{1}{2}$ years, with ceiling rates somewhat below that on $2\frac{1}{2}$ year Treasury securities
December 1980	Commercial banks and thrifts nationwide authorised to offer NOW accounts; maximum rate payable set at $5\frac{1}{4}$ per cent; no minimum denomination
December 1981	Commercial banks and thrifts authorised to offer ceiling-free individual retirement accounts (IRAs) and Keogh accounts with maturities of $1\frac{1}{2}$ years or more and fixed or floating rates; no minimum denomination
May 1982	Commercial banks and thrifts authorised to offer ceiling-free accounts with minimum maturity of $3\frac{1}{2}$ years and no minimum denomination
	Commercial banks and thrifts authorised to offer 91-day time deposits with ceiling rate related to rate on 3-month Treasury bills and minimum denomination of $7500
September 1982	Commercial banks and thrifts authorised to ofer 7–31 day accounts with ceiling rate related to rate on 3-month Treasury bills and minimum denomination of $20 000
December 1982	Commercial banks and thrifts authorised to offer money market deposit accounts (MMDAs) – ceiling-free accounts with no minimum maturity but with $2500 minimum balance and limited transaction features

(continued)

Table 5.3 (continued)

Effective date	*Measure*
January 1983	Commercial banks and thrifts authorised to offer Super NOW accounts – ceiling-free transactions accounts with $2500 minimum balance
	Minimum denomination on 7–31 day accounts, 91-day time deposits, and 6-month MMCs reduced to $2500.
	Rate ceiling removed for 7–31 day accounts
April 1983	Rate ceilings removed for time deposits at commercial banks and thrifts with maturities of $2\frac{1}{2}$ years or more
October 1983	Rate ceilings removed for time deposits at commercial banks and thrifts with maturities of more than 31 days and for shorter-term deposits with minimum balance of $2500
January 1985	Minimum balances for MMDAs, Super NOWs, and 7–31-day accounts reduced to $1000
January 1986	All minimum balance requirements removed
	Rate ceilings and other regulatory limitations on NOW accounts removed
April 1986	Rate ceiling on passbook savings accounts removed
	Authority of federal regulators to set deposit rate ceiling expire

Source: Burns (1988) pp.65–7.

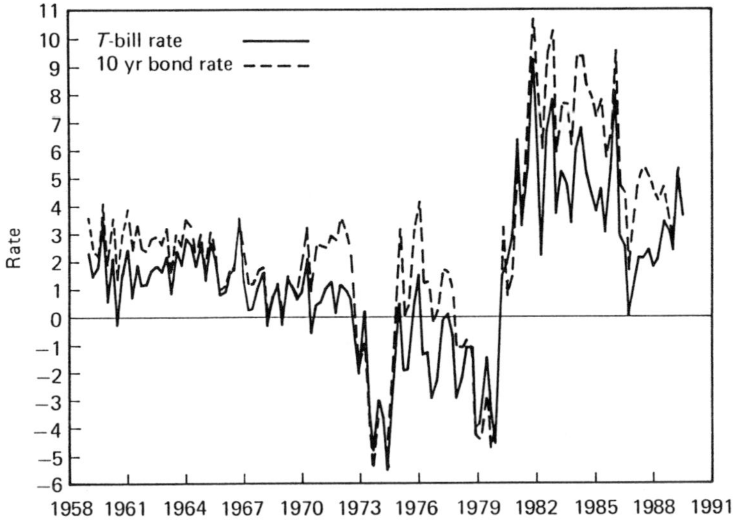

FIGURE 5.1 Ex post real rates, 1959.1 to 1989.4

treasury bills and US government 10-year bonds (calculated as the difference between their nominal yields and the consumer price index) from 1959.1 to 1989.4. The swings in the real rates are much more pronounced in the 1970s and 1980s then they were in the 1950s and 1960s. More importantly, the negative real-interest rates throughout much of the 1970s and the unusually high positive real rates in the 1980s suggest that US financial-market participants' inflation predictions were considerably less accurate than they had been previously.

This rise in financial risk, common to virtually all financial markets, spawned increased demands for new financial products and services that permitted greater hedging or specialised risk-bearing opportunities – and a plethora of such products and services were developed; many of these are listed in the tables previously discussed. While technological advances and research in asset-pricing models contributed to the sheer abundance of these innovations, their primary impetus came from the significant increase in the volatility of financial asset prices during the past twenty years.

TABLE 5.4 Financial innovations: 1970–82

Types	Exogenous causes: Inflation: Level of interest rates	Exogenous causes: Inflation: General price level	Exogenous causes: Inflation: Tax effects	Volatility of interest rates	Technology	Legislative initiative	Internationalisation	Other
A. Cash Management								
1. Money Market Mutual Funds	x							
2. Cash Management/Sweep Accounts	x		x					
3. Money Market Certificates	x			x				
4. Debit Card	x		x					
5. NOW Accounts	x							
6. ATS Accounts	x		x					
7. Point of Sale Terminals					x			
8. Automated Clearing House					x			
9. CHIPS (Same Day Settlement)					x			
10. Automated Teller Machines					x			
B. Investment Contracts								
(i) Primary market								
1. Floating Rate Notes				x				
2. Deep Discount (Zero Coupon) Bonds	x		x	x				
3. Stripped Bonds	x		x	x				
4. Bonds with Put Options or Warrants	x			x				
5. Floating Prime Rate Loans				x				
6. Variable Rate Mortgages				x				
7. Commodity Linked (Silver) Bonds				x				
8. Eurocurrency Bonds	x							
9. Interest Rate Futures				x			x	
10. Foreign Currency Futures								

11. Cash Settlement (Stock Index) Futures						x	x	
12. Options on Futures				x		x		
13. Pass-Through Securities						x		
(ii) Consumer-type								
1. Universal Life Insurance				x				
2. Variable Life Policies		x						
3. IRA/Keogh Accounts			x			x		
4. Municipal Bonds Funds			x			x		
5. All-Saver Certificates	x					x		
6. Equity Access Account		x		x				x
C. Market Structures								
1. Exchange-traded options								
2. Direct Public Sale of Securities								
Green Mountain Power Co.				x				
Shelf Registration				x		x		
3. Electronic Trading								
NASDAQ					x			
GARBAN					x			
4. Discount Brokerage						x		
5. Interstate Depository Institutions					x	x		
D. Institutional Organization								
1. Investment Bankers/Commodity Dealers	x			x				
Salomon/Phibro, Goldman Sachs/J/ Aron, DLJ/ACLI								
2. Brokers/General Finance								x
Shearson/Amex, Bache/ Prudential, Schwab/Bank of America	x			x		x		
3. Thrifts with Commercial Banks								x
4. Financial Centres (Sears Roebuck)								

Source: Silber (1983) p.91.

TABLE 5.5 Standard deviations of monthly corporate bond yields, 1960–90

	1960–70	*1974–90*
France	0.31	0.49
Germany	0.14	0.19
Italy	0.22	0.44
UK	0.19	0.36
USA	0.09	0.25

Source: Kupiec (1990).

TABLE 5.6 Standard deviations of monthly stock index return, 1961–89

	1961–70	*1974–89*
France	4.83	5.66
Germany	3.94	3.52
Italy	5.08	5.43
UK	3.68	4.32
USA	3.10	3.43

Source: Kupiec (1990).

TABLE 5.7 Coefficient of variation of month-end to month-end exchange rates, 1950–87

	Volatility, %			
Period	*Can$*	*UK£*	*DM*	*¥*
1950–59	4	0*	0*	0*
1960–69	4	6	2	0*
1970–79	6	13	21	18
1980–87	6	21	18	21

* Less than 0.5 per cent
Source: Levi (1990) p.11.

Innovation and the rise of non-bank sources of funds in credit markets

One of the most significant consequences of financial innovation has been the sizable decline in the role of US commercial banks in major credit markets in recent years and the rise of alternative sources of funds.[2] Table 5.8 shows several key sources of funds raised in credit markets by US non-financial corporations over the past three decades. Two opposing trends in corporate debt financing stand out clearly in the table. First, there has been a steady decline in the share of funds raised directly from US banks. Instead, during the 1970s and 1980s, corporations have raised funds directly in commercial paper and bond markets or from foreign sources. During the 1960s, about 44 per cent of US non-financial corporate-debt-funding come from these three sources; in the 1980s, however, they supplied more than 62 per cent of the funds raised in debt markets by US corporations.

TABLE 5.8 Sources of funds raised in debt markets by US non-financial corporations, 1960–89

	1960–69	*1970–79*	*1980–89*
US banks	34.8	25.9	23.1
Commercial paper	2.8	4.1	5.6
Notes and bonds	40.9	49.3	56.5
Foreign sources	0.0	0.6	5.1
Other	21.5	21.1	9.7
	100.0	100.0	100.0

Source: Federal Reserve Board, Flow of Funds Accounts.

The relative decline in the role of US banks in credit markets has generated additional concern beyond simply worrying about the future of the US banking industry. Many analysts believe that monetary policy actions influence the economy chiefly by affecting the supply of bank reserves and, thereby, the supply of credit to the economy. A number of recent articles have suggested that the shrinking role of banks in credit markets has seriously weakened the ability of the Federal Reserve to influence the economy.[3] The following sections examine the macroeconomic effects of financial innovation in more detail to determine whether some innovations may, indeed, have had such an impact.

MACROECONOMIC EFFECTS OF FINANCIAL INNOVATION

At the present time, our knowledge of the macroeconomic effects of financial innovation, is unfortunately, speculative. While there are theorectical reasons for believing that certain financial innovations potentially could, and perhaps even should, have had important implications both for the macroeconomy and for policy-making, few empirical studies have been able successfully either to document these impacts or to tie them directly to financial innovation. In this section, we discuss the theoretical issues; the empirical evidence is reviewed in the following section.

Four aspects of financial innovation should be considered in assessing its potential macroeconomic influence. First, some innovations have altered both the absolute and relative costs of holding various financial assets as well as reducing the transactions costs associated with exchanging one financial asset for another; many of these appear in the tables shown previously. Second, some new financial assets created by innovation are close substitutes for the traditional 'media of exchange' assets included in M1; as a result, the elasticity of substitution for the latter assets should rise, thereby increasing the interest elasticity of demand for *M*1. Third, financial innovation has altered the traditional 'Balkanised' market structure facing financial intermediaries; the fundamental distinction between commercial banks and thrifts has all but disappeared and the important distinction between depository and non-depository financial institutions has been eroded severely. Fourth, financial innovation may have altered the money supply process itself and, thereby, affected the monetary authority's ability to control the various monetary aggregates.[4] These aspects all come into play when the puzzling breakdown of *M*1 velocity in the 1980s is examined.

Financial innovation, money demand and monetary policy

It is widely believed that the single most important macroeconomic effect of financial innovation has been the sharp decline in the US income velocity of *M1* in the decade of the 1980s. Figure 5.2 shows the abrupt 'breakdown' in *M*1 velocity that occurred in the early 1980s after more than 35 years of relatively stable velocity growth.

The specific financial innovation frequently cited as having produced the shift in *M*1 velocity was the nationwide introduction of NOW accounts in January 1981.[5] Because NOW accounts pay interest rates similar to those paid on savings deposits, individuals are presumed to have shifted funds from their savings accounts into their NOW accounts. This, in turn, is believed to have altered the 'moneyness' of cheque accounts by introducing a significant savings component into *M*1.[6] This aspect of the financial innovation hypothesis asserts that savings balances are now commingled with the traditional transactions balances in *M*1.[7]

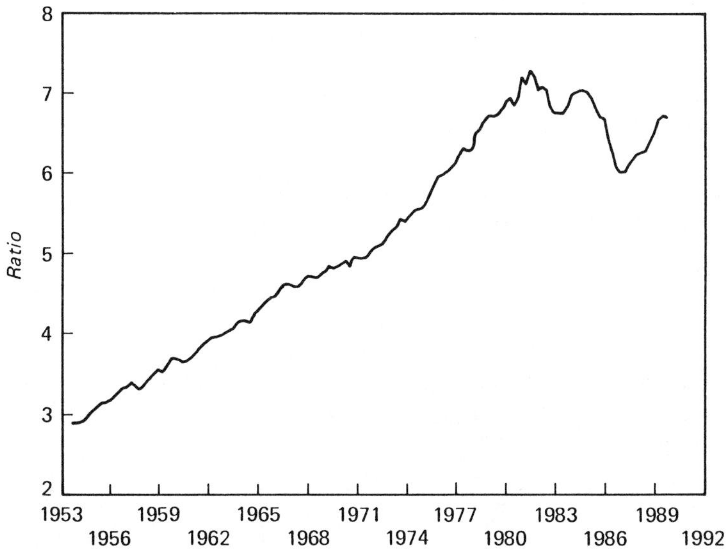

FIGURE 5.2 The income velocity of M1, 1954.1 to 1989.4

If the introduction and widespread use of NOW accounts has actually 'blown up' measured cheque account balances relative to nominal GNP, measured *M*1 velocity should have declined significantly. Moreover, if the savings balances allegedly flowing into *M*1 have altered its responsiveness to changes in income or interest rates, the behaviour of *M*1 velocity should have been altered permanently as well. In particular, if the interest elasticity of saving balances in *M*1 is significantly greater than that for *M*1's transaction balances, there should be a discernible change in the interest elasticity of *M*1 velocity.

This effect would be exacerbated if yet another innovation, savings accounts with limited transactions characteristics – such as money market mutual funds (MMMF) and money market deposit accounts (MMDA), has reduced the demand for transactions balances in *M*1 and increased its interest elasticity as well. Other things the same, the elasticity of demand for any good increases ith the number and closeness of its substitutes. Because Regulation Q interest rate ceilings were lifted only gradually – with the last vestige of such regulations expiring on 31 March 1986 – the observed interest sensitivity of *M1* should have *increased* after the introduction of these new deposit accounts.[8]

Financial innovation and the demand for money

The above discussion can be illustrated more formally by considering the following demand function for *M*1:

$$(M1/P) = f(y, i), \tag{5.1}$$

where $(M1/P)$ and y are real money balances and real income, respectively, P is the price level, and i is the nominal interest rate. Equation (5.1) is usually rewritten as

$$(M1/P) = yf(i) \tag{5.2}$$

or as:

$$(M1/P)/y = f(i)^9 \tag{5.3}$$

Equation (5.3) is the reciprocal of the income velocity of $M1$, i.e.,

$$y/(M1/P) = f^{-1}(i) = v(i) \tag{5.4}$$

Suppose that the demand for real savings balances can be written similarly, i.e.,

$$s = g(y, i) \tag{5.5}$$

where s is real savings balances, but the demand for s is related to y in a different way than is the demand for real $M1$. Specifically, assume that equation (5.5) can be written as

$$s = y^n g(i) \tag{5.6}$$

where $n = 1$. Equation (5.6) can be rewritten in terms of income velocities by dividing both sides by y and inverting the equation to yield:

$$y/s = g^{-1}(i)/y^{(n-1)} = v'(i)/y^{(n-1)} \tag{5.7}$$

Suppose that, due to financial innovation, a 'new' $M1$, designated as $M1^*$, has been defined as equal to old $M1$ plus some proportion θ of saving balances, S, that had not been formerly included in the old $M1$ measure. That is:

$$M1^* = M1 + \theta S \tag{5.8}$$

Given these assumptions, the demand for $M1^*/P$ can be written as:

$$M1^*/P = f(y,i) + \theta g(y,i) \tag{5.9}$$

and $M1^*$ velocity can be written as

$$v^* = Py/M1^* = 1/[f(i) + \theta y^{n-1} g(i)] \tag{5.10}$$

If $\theta = 0$, financial innovation has no *direct* effect on the income velocity of $M1^*$.[10] However, financial innovation can have an effect on the interest elasticity of $M1$ if $f^{-1}(i)$ changes due to financial innovation.

If $\theta \neq 0$, the interest elasticity of $M1^*$ velocity will differ from that of $M1$ velocity.[11] Furthermore, the income velocity of $M1$ will change with the level of income if $n \neq 1$: the higher is the level of income, the lower (higher) income velocity will be if $n > 1$ ($n < 1$).

Monetary policy implications of financial innovation

If financial innovation has affected the income velocity of $M1$, it has important implications for both the conduct and potential success of monetary policy. To see why, we must reconsider why velocity 'matters' for monetary policy.[12] In its most general form, velocity is usually written as:

$$yp/M1 = v(z) \tag{5.11}$$

where z represents the factors that determine velocity.[13] Because y is not constant, it is useful to rewrite equation (5.11) in growth-rate form

$$M1 + v(z) = P + y = GNP \tag{5.12}$$

where the dots denote rates of change of the specific variables.

There is considerable controversy over what policy-makers can and should achieve with monetary policy. For this discussion, however, assume that policy-makers want both to stabilise the short-turn fluctuations in real output around its long-run growth path and to keep the rate of inflation 'low'. They believe that they can achieve their goals if they can stabilise nominal *GNP* along some desired path.[14]

However, if financial innovation affects velocity as described above, monetary policy-makers will find it more difficult to stabilise nominal *GNP* growth. To see why this is so, suppose that the money stock is completely under the control of the monetary authority (and, thus, monetary control is unaffected by financial innovation). From equation (5.12) we see that the monetary authority can achieve a specific target rate for *GNP* only if it can predict and offset the effects of changes in velocity, $v(z)$. For

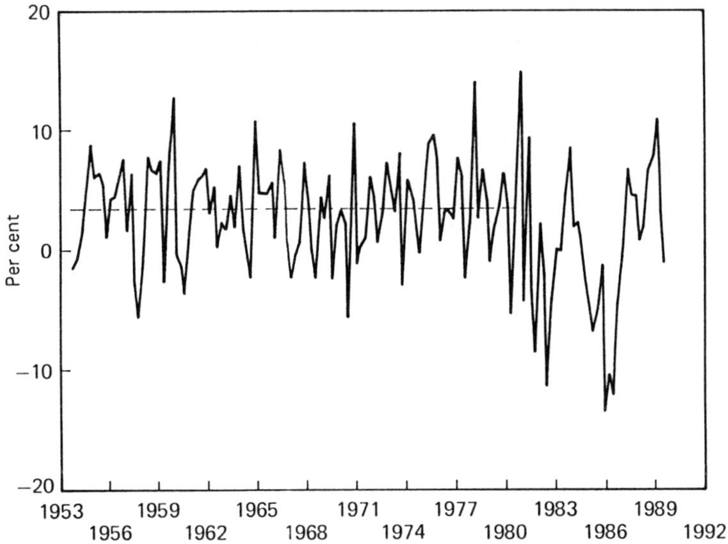

FIGURE 5.3 The growth of M1 velocity, 1954.1 to 1989.4

example, if $v(z)$ rises, the monetary authority must reduce $M1$ to keep GNP constant.

There are two very different aspects involved in predicting $M1$ velocity. First, both its level and growth were always difficult to predict over short-run periods (e.g., quarter-to-quarter).[15] Second, $M1$ velocity grew at a relatively constant rate of about 3 per cent per year for about 35 years prior to the early 1980s. Figure 5.3 shows the growth rate of velocity from 1954.1 to 1989.4; it indicates that $M1$ velocity growth displayed considerable short-run variation around a fairly stable mean until the early 1980s. It also suggests that, while monetary policy-makers may have been unable to predict $M1$ velocity well enough to use monetary policy to stabilise nominal output growth in the short run, $M1$ velocity could have been used as a long-run guide for monetary policy prior to the 1980s. For example, suppose that real-output growth is independent of money growth in the long run and its 'trend' is about 3 per cent; in addition, let the desired long-run growth of inflation be zero. In this case, the long run growth of GNP would be stabilised at around 3 per cent if the long-run growth of M1 was maintained at around zero per cent.

In the short run, money growth could be varied for any number of plausibly valid economic or political reasons with little harm to the economy. As long as policy-makers achieved a zero rate of money growth over longer-run periods, they would be able to achieve their goal of a zero long-run inflation rate.

If financial innovation altered both the level and the growth rate of the income velocity of *M*1 as discussed above, velocity would be considerably less useful for monetary policy attempts to stabilise nominal *GNP* growth over any time-horizon. Indeed, one of the most intriguing policy implications of financial innovation is that, by strengthening the effect of policy actions on velocity and, hence, nominal *GNP*, financial innovation reduced the usefulness of nominal *GNP* or *M*1 as an intermediate policy target. For example, if financial innovation has increased the interest elasticity of the demand for *M*1, *M*1 velocity will be more responsive to changes in the interest rate as well. However, if money-supply changes affect interest rates (either through the so-called 'liquidity effect' or through inflationary expectations), it now becomes more difficult to determine the precise monetary policy response required to achieve a specific nominal *GNP* target.

Suppose, for example, that policy-makers increase the rate of growth of the money supply to offset a decline in the growth rate of velocity and that, just for the sake of illustration, this action reduces interest rates and causes velocity growth to fall even more. Thus, to stabilise nominal *GNP* growth around some desired rate, monetary authorities must correctly anticipate the initial decline in velocity growth, the consequences of their actions on interest rates and the subsequent effect on velocity growth as well.[16]

The same basic analysis applies for the effects of money growth on real output. For example, suppose that changes in money growth initially affect real output growth, but only affect inflation with some lag. Therefore, an increase in money growth intended to offset a decline in velocity (occurring for other reasons) will produce a smaller (larger) than anticipated change in both real and nominal *GNP* if velocity falls (rises) as output rises. The fundamental point, once again, is that financial innovation could make monetary policy actions subject to considerably greater uncertainty.

If both real-output growth and real-interest rate are independent of monetary policy actions in the long run, a change in the output or interest elasticity of velocity, *per se*, should have no effect on the long-run policy usefulness of $M1$. Nevertheless, nominal *GNP* growth might vary more around its long-run desired path as a result of financial innovation.[17]

Of course, the inability of the monetary authority to predict velocity in the long run accurately would affect $M1$'s usefulness for policy purposes. This outcome could occur, for example, if the real-interest rate were unstable in the long run and if the interest elasticity of velocity changed in response to financial innovation. In this case, velocity would move unpredictably with the real-interest rate. This same result would also occur if financial innovation made velocity dependent on the level of output itself. Using the example developed earlier, if $n > 1$, velocity would decline secularly as output rose over time. The ability of the monetary authority to determine the trend in velocity growth could be hampered further by cyclical movements in output around its trend rate. Until the monetary authority could establish a new 'trend' in velocity growth, it would be difficult to determine the rate of $M1$ growth that would stabilise the price level in the long run.

Financial innovation and monetary control

Financial innovation may have also complicated the monetary process further by reducing the monetary authority's ability to control the money stock.[18] This result could occur through the effect of innovation on the k-ratio in the monetary multiplier. The k-ratio, which is the ratio of the currency component of $M1$ to total chequeable deposits, is the most important component of the monetary multiplier. It is unlikely that financial innovation has had any appreciable direct influence on the demand for currency; the nominal rate of return on currency, which is zero, has been unaffected and innovation has produced no new close substitutes for currency.

As mentioned earlier, however, innovation may have increased the demand for total chequeable deposits. If so, the k-ratio would have declined as funds flowed out of savings into other chequeable deposits (OCD); moreover, the k-ratio would also vary with the level of output. These changes would make it more difficult for the monetary authority to control the level and growth of $M1$.

EMPIRICAL EVIDENCE FOR FINANCIAL INNOVATION'S IMPACT ON VELOCITY

The Federal Reserve has frequently cited financial innovation as the principal reason for its de-emphasis of $M1$ targeting and for its broad eclecticism in examining various potential intermediate targets for conducting monetary policy.[19] Yet, whether financial innovation actually affected $M1$ velocity in the ways discussed earlier and, consequently, the usefulness of $M1$ targets for monetary policy, remains an open question. While the lack of such evidence is understandably annoying, it really should not be surprising; after all, financial innovation is an ongoing evolutionary process that has spanned several decades.

However, as noted earlier, perhaps the most significant innovation for determining the impact of financial innovation on the income velocity of $M1$ and the conduct of monetary policy in the USA was the introduction of nationwide NOW accounts on 1 January 1981. These new interest-bearing cheque accounts were included in $M1$ along with currency and the previously existing non-interest bearing demand deposits. And, not too long after nationwide NOWs were introduced and defined as part of $M1$, there was an abrupt change in the behaviour of the income velocity of $M1$. Not surprisingly, this observation has loomed large in studies that have sought to demonstrate the crucial impact that financial innovation has had on the economy and on policy-makers.

Initially, the observed decline in $M1$ velocity following the introduction of nationwide NOW accounts was taken by many analysts as *prima facie* evidence for financial innovation's impact on a key economic and policy variable. The extremely close timing between the new accounts and the sharp drop in $M1$ velocity was often so compelling that, at least to some analysts, empirical investigation seemed superfluous. Moreover, the reason for the decline in $M1$ velocity was supported by anecdotal evidence indicating that some depositors were shifting funds from their savings accounts into NOW accounts; it seemed only too obvious that the addition of these savings balances were artificially raising $M1$ balances and depressing $M1$ velocity.

The validity of this explanation was strengthened further by the marked increase in the interest elasticity of $M1$ velocity in the

1980s.[20] As illustrated in Figure 5.4, there was little correspondence bewteen *M*1 velocity and the 3-month Treasury bill rate prior to the 1980s (the vertical line is drawn at 1980.4). Since then, however, there has been a discernible positive relationship between them as implied by the financial innovation hypothesis.[21]

Recently, however, several studies have raised doubts that financial innovation is actually responsible for the abrupt change in *M*1 velocity growth in the early 1980s – at least, as far as nationwide NOWs are concerned.[22] Rasche (1987), for example, has noted that neither *M*1 velocity's decline *per se* nor the rise in its interest elasticity closely matches the timing of the nationwide introduction of NOW accounts. Income velocity peaks in the third quarter of 1981, not the fourth quarter of 1980 as the financial innovation hypothesis would seemingly suggest. Furthermore, there is considerable uncertainty over when the initial rise in the interest elasticity of velocity took place.

However, it should not be too surprising that the precise nature of the expected timing of the change in velocity and increased interest elasticity under the financial-innovation hypothesis is so difficult to determine. Certainly, the initial portfolio shifts follow-

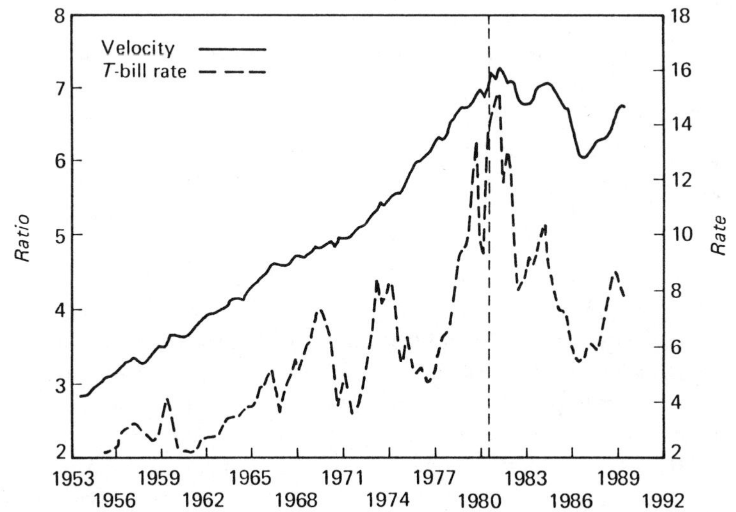

FIGURE 5.4 M1 velocity and the 3-month T-bill rate, 1954.1 to 1989.4

ing the nationwide introduction of NOW accounts were from traditional non-interest-bearing demand deposits into new interest-bearing cheque accounts; these shifts should have little or no discernible effects on the level of velocity or its interest elasticity.[23] If the shifts from savings balances into NOW accounts (or the increase in balances held in such accounts due to the pricing of NOW accounts) occurred later, there would be no reason to expect that the velocity decline and increased interest elasticity should correspond exactly with the January 1981 nationwide NOW innovation.[24]

The other problem with which critics of the financial innovation hypothesis must contend is that, if the 1980s velocity puzzle is not due to financial innovation, precisely how can it be explained? Unfortunately, the empirical support for alternative explanations is at least as weak as that used to support the financial innovation hypothesis.

Financial innovations and the supply of money

There is some evidence that suggests that the *k*-ratio has been affected by financial innovations. Tatom (1990) found a statistically significant relationship between his financial innovation variable and the *k*-ratio. In addition, the interest elasticity of the *k*-ratio appears to have increased significantly in the 1980s. This is illustrated in Figure 5.5, which shows the *k*-ratio and the money multiplier (based on the monetary base) from 1959.4 to 1989.4. The figure shows several points of interest for monetary control purposes. First, movements in the *k*-ratio explain much of the short-run and long-run movements in the monetary multiplier. Second, the behaviour of the *k*-ratio changed markedly in the early 1980s. After rising secularly, the *k*-ratio levelled out and then declined; moreover, it has become considerably more volatile.

Furthermore, much of the variation in the *k*-ratio is associated with variation in total chequeable deposits, which, in turn, is associated with movements in short-term interest rates. Consequently, as illustrated in Figure 5.6, movements in the *k*-ratio have been more highly associated with movements in short-term interest rates in the 1980s than they were previously.[25]

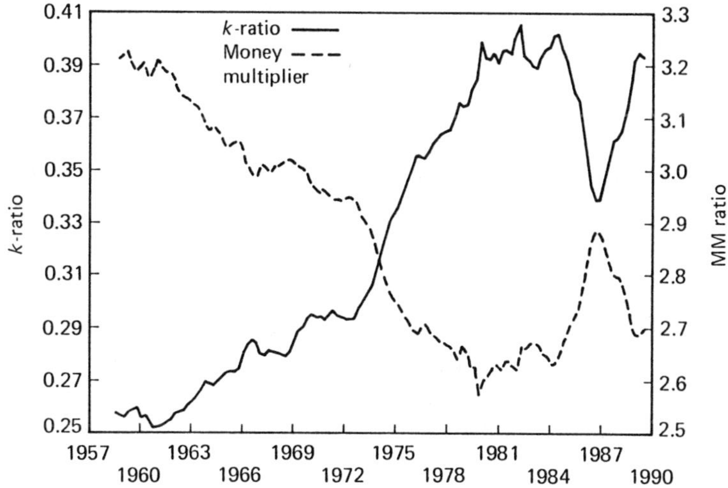

FIGURE 5.5 The *k*-ratio and the money multiplier 1959.1 to 1989.4

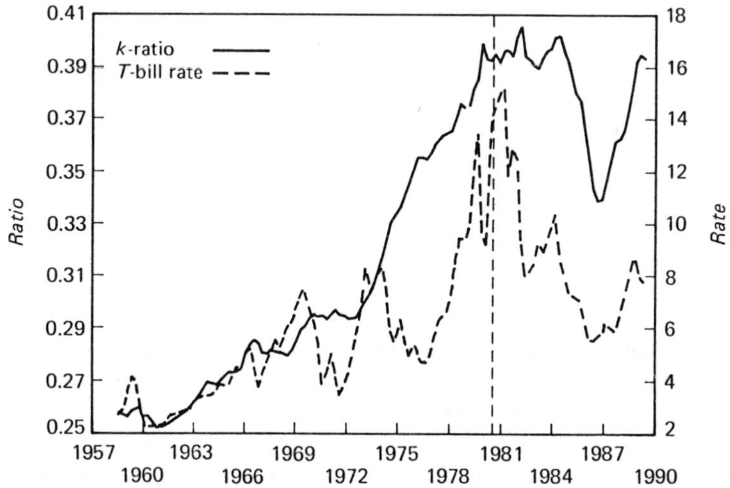

FIGURE 5.6 The *k*-ratio and the 3-month T-bill rate, 1959.1 to 1989.4

CONCLUSION

There are two distinctly different perspectives from which to view the impact of the financial innovation that has taken place over the 1970s and 1980s. From a microeconomic perspective, the reasons for the vast majority of changes that have taken place in the financial markets can be explained relatively easily and their consequences are generally predictable. The chief causes of financial innovation were:

1 the increased uncertainty and the corresponding increased volatility in prices (rates of return) in all financial markets;
2 regulations on many traditional financial firms, especially banks, that provided the opportunity for new unregulated firms to develop innovative financial products and services in response to the increased financial uncertainty.

The chief consequences have been the gradual erosion of many financial regulations and the declining significance of banks as sources of funds in credit markets.

From a macroeconomic perspective, the causes of innovation are understandable but the consequences are still uncertain. Increased financial and real economic volatility has been produced, at least in part, by more erratic macroeconomic policies in the 1970s and 1980s. In that sense, the underlying source of financial innovation may have been simply the market's response to erratic and uncertain macroeconomic policies.

It has also been argued that financial innovation itself has affected the demand for money and, hence, the ability of the monetary authority to influence the economy in the short run and perhaps in the long run. Certainly, it appears that the longer-run relationship between money and nominal spending, and hence money and prices is more tenuous. As a result, it is more difficult to achieve long-run objectives for inflation by specifying long-run objectives for money growth.

Furthermore, the monetary authority's ability to control the money stock appears to have eroded following the nationwide introduction of interest bearing NOW accounts. Once again, however, the evidence that financial innovation brought about this result is tenuous.

It is clear that over the past two decades, financial innovation has wrought dramatic changes in the organisation, scope and functions of financial instruments, institutions and markets. While the potential theoretical effects of financial innovation for the demand for money are straightforward, and some observed behaviour of monetary aggregates is consistent with these implications, there is still considerable disagreement about its overall impact on the demand for money. However, 'something' has significantly impacted on the demand for and supply of money in the USA during the 1980s. If not financial innovation, what?

6 Banking Reform

GERALD P. O'DRISCOLL Jr[1]

If the US economy has performed so remarkably for seven years, its banking system has surely been an embarassment. How can an economy that has grown consistently for more than seven years have a banking system in such disarray? In 1988, the sixth year of an expansion, the economy generated 3.6 million new jobs – over 300 000 each month.[2] In the same period, 200 commercial banks failed – a post-war record. Concomitantly, 12 per cent of the nation's savings and loans were insolvent according to generally accepted accounting principles. The nation's thrift industry is being all but nationalised in the process.

In this chapter, I offer a diagnosis of what went wrong with the US banking system and examine some proposed remedies. Only by understanding the present situation can one appreciate why so many banking reform proposals have recently been offered. Many deal only with symptoms and not causes, attempting to stop a financial haemorrhage with a policy of Band-Aid. In the first part of the chapter, I focus on proposals that identify and address the causes of the banking crisis. Nonetheless, these take for granted most institutional features of the monetary and banking systems. In the second part, I examine some even more fundamental reforms that have been suggested. I begin with an examination of the thrift crisis that currently grips the USA. The crisis encompasses all of the problems plaguing banking, but exhibits them to a heightened degree.

THE THRIFT CRISIS

It is difficult to exaggerate the magnitude of the problems in the US thrift industry. President Bush proposed and Congress implemented a $157 billion bailout of insolvent thrifts, previous efforts having conspicuously failed.

The Financial Institutions Reform, Recovery and Enforcement Act of 1989 (FIRREA) makes explicit what has long been implicit: the necessity for the taxpayer to underwrite the losses accruing from successive public policy failures in the thrift industry. The new law removes the thrift crisis from the status of a regional problem to a national one. For these and other reasons, FIRREA is laudable.

Previous efforts at dealing with the thrift crisis were predicated on misconceptions and were, in any case, underfunded. By the early 1980s, the Federal Savings and Loan Insurance Corporation (FSLIC) confronted a substantial number of thrift organisations rendered insolvent by high market-interest rates. Before the decade of the 1970s, thrifts had survived on the profit derived from borrowing short-term money and using the proceeds to fund fixed-rate mortgages. In the inflationary 1970s, the profits turned into losses as the money-market rates rose above the average return on existing assets. The losses rapidly eroded the capital of many thrifts. FSLIC had two options: to close the insolvent thrifts, or to subsidise their losses and keep them open. The first option often required a comparatively large up-front cash disbursal to provide for insured depositors. The second option was clearly more expensive in present-value terms because it permitted the institution to continue haemorrhaging losses.

FSLIC tried merging smaller, insolvent institutions, into larger ones (the 'phoenix' programme). The policy was predicated on the belief that one larger insolvent institution is more easily managed and disposed of than a number of smaller ones. FSLIC found it difficult, however, to extricate itself from the mega-institutions it had created (Kane, 1985, pp.5–6).

FSLIC realised it needed to acquire additional funds. The new programme, called the Southwest Plan, was woefully underfunded.[3] The $10.8 billion provided by Congress was inadequate to resolve the insolvent institutions in Texas alone.[4]

The FIRREA is a decided improvement because it envisions closing insolvent institutions and greatly increases funding. It does have the potential, however, for misdirecting policy-makers' attention and, possibly, sowing the seeds of another financial crisis.

As constituted, the plan suggests that money is the solution to the thrift crisis. Certainly, an injection of funds must be an element in any plan. But lack of money, specifically capital, is not the primary *cause* of the current crisis. The savings and loan industry dissipated billions of dollars of capital that it once had. Understanding how individual institutions could not only permit their capital to dissipate, but also move deeply into the red is fundamental to any permanent solution. That understanding has yet to take hold among policy-makers. It requires insight into how federal deposit insurance operates.

Before discussing the role of deposit insurance, I offer a perspective to non-American readers. Focusing on deposit insurance may strike you as parochial. But deposit insurance is only the peculiarly American form that blanket financial guarantees of the banking systems have taken. Any policy that effectively underwrites banking losses produces moral hazard and invites American-style banking problems. As Europeans look to 1992, they need to consider the incentives generated by their public policy toward banking. Among other things, they need to learn to allow insolvent banks to fail. US-style public policy towards banking is one American idea that should be discarded, not imitated.

DEPOSIT INSURANCE

In the simplest terms, insurance constitutes an intertemporal exchange between the insured and the insurer. The insured trades a fixed loss or outgoing each period (the premium) for a promise that he will be indemnified against losses of a stated kind (up to a maximum value) for the life of the insurance contract. The insured gains because he forgoes a small sum in return for protection against a potentially greater loss. The insurer gains because, by pooling risks of many insureds, he can earn a profit. Though the basic principle is quite simple, provision of insurance is a complex matter. Many of the provisions of an insurance contract are designed to specify the exact risks covered and the amounts of the coverage. Other provisions are designed to constrain the insured's behaviour in the future, because possession of insurance establishes perverse incentives. Having insurance reduces the incentives for the insured to avoid the risk against which he has been insured. Such behavioural change, by increasing the frequency of occurrence of the risk, would alter the probability of calculus underlying the insurance contract. What would have been a profitable transaction for the insurance company might become unprofitable (Arrow, 1971, p.142).

Fire insurance provides a readily understandable example. A home-owner covered by fire insurance will, on the margin, take fewer precautions than he would were he exposed to the entire risk of loss due to fire. Notice that I am not assuming that he will deliberately increase the risk of fire. (Such behaviour might, however, occur if the house were insured for more than its value.) Risk is something that individuals must incur costs to avoid. Being insured against a particular risk reduces the return to risk-avoidance. Insured individuals will, therefore, reduce their effort at the margin to avoid the risk. Consequently, risky outcomes increase.

A situation in which opportunistic behaviour will result in greater risk is called moral hazard. Sound insurance is structured to avoid moral hazard, or offset its effects with countervailing incentives. In the case of fire insurance, underwriters will both prescribe and proscribe certain behaviour so as to reduce the probability of loss. The insurance contract will normally include a deductible amount, so the insured bears some of the cost of opportunistic behaviour. The presence of such features is essential to the viability of insurance as a commercial product.

Since 1933, the US government has provided for insurance of bank deposits.[5] Initially set at $2500 per deposit, the insured amount has risen over the years. In 1980, Congress raised the coverage from $40 000 to $100 000, and individuals are covered for up to that amount at each depository institution. Since there are approximately 14 000 separate commercial banks in the USA, one individual could theoretically hold $1.4 billion in insured deposits at commercial banks. Additionally, there are the nation's thrift institutions, savings and loans, as well as credit unions. Furthermore, by holding joint accounts and accounts in trust for others, an individual can multiply several-fold the insured deposits in each bank.[6]

Federal deposit insurance has always been provided in an unsound fashion. Specifically, the premiums charged are unrelated to the riskiness of the bank's portfolio. Thus provided, deposit insurance skews the choice in favour of incurring additional losses. An investor can generally increase the probability of earning higher returns if he is willing to incur additional risk of loss (Short and O'Driscoll, 1983, pp.14–15). A rational investor weighs the expected returns against the risk of loss, and decides whether an investment's expected returns compensates for the probability of loss.

Normally, various market signals are sent to an investor undertaking a risky activity. If he has purchased insurance protection for the activity, he will face rising premiums as the risk increases. The higher premiums will tend to restrain risk-taking by increasing its cost. In the case of banking, this channel is blocked, and, it turns out, blocking this channel also interferes with the transmission of other important market signals.

Creditors of my hypothetical investor will ordinarily make the same risk-return decision as the investor. As the risk of his investment increases, his creditors will demand higher returns. Accordingly, the riskier the proposed investment project, the higher the interest rates the investor will pay. We observe the phenomenon in a wide variety of contexts. Well-established firms in predictable lines of business pay less to borrow than start-up firms in new and untested business ventures. B-rated bond issues pay a higher return than A-rated issues.

Historically we have not observed the relationship in banking – certainly not to the same degree. While riskier banks have had a higher cost of funds, the differential has tended to emerge not when the risk was taken, but only after problems developed. To be an effective price signal, any premium must affect risk-taking *ex ante*. Moreover, the magnitude of the differentials in bank's funding costs have historically not approached those for non-financial corporations (Short, 1987).

Because of mispriced deposit insurance, the deposit market does not adequately constrain risk-taking by banks. The market for deposits is the most important one for pricing risk in banking because banks enter it daily. By contrast, banks issue new equity shares or subordinated debt infrequently. In the USA, most banks are small and will never issue either debt or new equity once established. If the deposit market does not work, then banks will not receive timely market signals as they alter their risk exposure. Consequently, they will tend to incur too much risk (given the expected return).

Depositors are not irrational. The same individuals who ignore a bank's risk of failure carefully investigate the risk of their non-bank investments.[7] The incentives generated by deposit insurance explain the apparently inconsistent behaviour. *Depositors behave as if they are not at risk because they normally are not.* Deposits at insured banks have no risk or loss so long as their account balances are within the insured limits. At large banks, deposits of any size can be held risk-free. This is because of the 'too big to fail' doctrine that protects large banks from failure. In an ominous development, regulators have in one instance – Continental Illinois National bank – indemnified all *creditors*, depository and non-depository, of a failed bank.[8] *Blanket guarantees of safety anaesthetise credit markets, dulling the senses to risk.*

Many factors can generate losses on bank portfolios. The relevant policy question, however, is why so many bank managers have permitted losses to mount, eroding capital and threatening the viability of their institution. And, if managers have allowed this to happen, why have depositors funded the losses? In other words, what is the *systemic* cause of the current banking problems in the USA?

Mispriced deposit insurance has played a critical role in the emergence of these problems. Insolvent banks are currently open for business and attracting deposits. And attract funds they must, because they are using insured deposits to cover daily operating losses. Institutions known to be insolvent can attract funds only because deposit insurance immunises the depositor against loss. The depositor is effectively depositing his money with the government, not the bank.

Not only do insolvent institutions garner funds in competitive deposit markets, their stock trades at a positive price. This makes no sense in ordinary accounting terms, unless one realises that the stock trades with a put option on the deposit insurance fund. For a firm to be insolvent means that its liabilities exceed its assets. Accordingly, its equity value ought to be negative. A positive share price, however, implies positive equity value. The equity markets clarify what accounting practices obfuscate – deposit insurance guarantees are an unbooked asset on the balance sheets of depository institutions. Indeed, Kane (1985, p.23) has estimated that the US government is 'the leading supplier of equity funds to deposit institutions'.

Put in the most straightforward way, deposit insurance constitutes a blanket guarantee against losses to depositors. By doing so, deposit insurance also insulates stockholders and managers against the *near-term* effects of excessive risk-taking. Managers are free to engage in strategies that 'bet the bank' on particular outcomes. If they win, managers book the profits. If they lose, the deposit insurance picks up the tab for any losses in excess of bank capital.

Critics point to the low level of capital, particularly equity capital, in US depository institutions. Some see this as the cause of current difficulties. Consequently, many have called for tougher capital standards. There is no question that bank capital has eroded in recent years and that a healthy dose of capital would strengthen depository institutions. But actions to improve the capital positions of banks will not address the fundamental problem of incentives. With deposit insurance, who needs capital? It is a wonder that banks have any at all. Mispriced deposit insurance encourages the substitution of public capital (deposit insurance) for private capital.

Uncovered creditors (for example, holders of subordinated debt) will insist that the bank have some equity capital. In recent years, the demands have become more insistent as these creditors have watched the rising bank-failure rate. Most US banks are too small to issue any subordinated debt, however. To a significant extent, banks are holding as much capital as they do only because of regulatory pressure. Where that pressure has been relaxed and supervision lax – as in the savings and loan industry – capital levels are lower than in the rest of the banking system.

If incentives are not changed, compelling banks to hold more capital may just be increasing the amount to be dissipated by risk-taking. True, more capital lengthens the period in which regulators can identify problem institutions. But the regulatory record does not make one sanguine that regulators will avail themselves of the opportunity. Several factors contribute to the problem.

First and foremost, the incentive structure militates against the ability of regulators to constrain bankers' behaviour sufficiently.

Bankers stand to capture the gains from financial innovations that circumvent regulations. For every form of risk-taking constrained, bankers have found two new ways to take on more risk in the search for higher returns. The lure of higher profits will always make it feasible for banks to pay inventive employees more than regulatory agencies can compensate methodical examiners. If an examiner comes along who outmanoeuvres the best and brightest products of the nation's business schools, a depository institution will probably lure him away.

Second, regulators judge bank solvency according to acounting principles that value assets at cost or book value, but the economic solvency of a bank depends on market values. The discrepancy between historical or accounting value, and economic or market value, can be quite large. It is certainly large enough to permit a bank to stay within regulatory standards, but be utterly insolvent if its assets and liabilities were marked to market. If taxpayers are to be protected against future losses, a market-valued accounting system must be introduced.

Third, as a practical matter, it is impossible to supervise adequately the number of depository institutions in the USA. Commercial banks alone number approximately 14 000 and the kind of close supervision necessary to prevent loss to the insurance fund is beyond the resources conceivably available to the supervisory agencies. The situation is different, of course, in Great Britain and the Continent. This may justify the Bank of England's greater reliance on supervision and capital levels. The Bank of England's regulatory approach cannot be readily imported, however, into the USA.

Finally, supervisory responsibilities are divided between federal and state governments. (This division is what is meant by 'dual banking' in the USA.) It would be naive to expect the federal and state bureaucracies to keep at all times in as close contact as would be necessary to adequately supervise banks. Additionally, the interests of federal and state banking regulators do not always coincide. State regulators generally take a position as more of an advocate for the interests of the banks they supervise than do their federal counterparts. More importantly, the federal deposit insurance agencies are more attentive to the effects of public policy on their funds than are the other regulators. Unfortunately, under the US system, the various state and federal agencies find themselves competing to regulate banks. This situation is not conducive to a system of effective supervision and regulation.

All things considered, it is too much to expect any system of supervision and regulation to offset perverse incentives established by financial safety nets like the present deposit insurance system. The only way to straighten out the mess is for policy-makers to get the incentives right, but that seems to be just what the political system seems least capable of doing. If the pessimistic assessment is accurate, then the present crisis has the potential to be repeated – probably within the next decade. And each repetition brings greater federal government involvement and further moves to *de facto* nationalisation of banking in the USA (Kane, 1985, p.13).

Other factors have also contributed significantly to the current thrift crisis. Previous regulation of savings and loans can only be described as lax – at both the state and federal levels (Kane, 1989). When savings and loans experienced losses, the Federal Home Loan Bank Board engaged in 'capital forbearance', which relaxed capital standards. To put it bluntly, regulators allowed the industry's actual capital position to determine the capital regulations, rather than the other way around.[9] Now the taxpayer will be paying the piper.

In summary, one must be very careful not to confuse cause and effect. The existence of deposit insurance leads banks to lower capital below what it would otherwise be. Additionally, mispriced deposit insurance results in excessive risk taking that often erodes what capital there is. Increasing capital requirements, is thus no substitute for altering the incentives set up by deposit insurance.

DEPOSIT INSURANCE REFORM

Virtually every major public policy problem in US banking derives from the existence of mispriced deposit insurance. If deposit insurance is not actually the cause of the problem, it is the chief obstacle to reform. Only recently, however, has the deposit insurance system become the focus of banking reform proposals. That it has done so is testimony to the suddenness with which the consensus on the deposit insurance system has changed.

In their monumental work on banking history, Friedman and Schwartz (1963, p.434) concluded that:

> federal deposit insurance of bank deposits was the most important structural change in the banking system to result from the 1933 panic, and, indeed in our view, the structural change most conducive to monetary stability since state bank notes were taxed out of existence immediately after the Civil War.

In other words, deposit insurance was seen as a government programme that worked – even from a classical liberal's perspective. Friedman and Schwartz's statement accurately summarised economists' views at the time and shaped them for years to come.

Besides deregulating deposit liabilities and broadening asset powers for thrifts, the Garn-St Germain Act Depository Institution Act of 1982, mandated that the deposit insurance agencies re-examine the insurance protection afforded commercial banks, savings and loans, and credit unions. This produced a flurry of studies at the various federal bank regulatory agencies.[10] The studies, though well done, languished. The moral hazard inherent in the deposit insurance system was evident to many, but it was not the time to act politically.

It is now apparent to nearly all that the deposit insurance system is in trouble (Garcia, 1988). Up to the end of 1988, there have been 878 commercial bank failures in the 1980s for an annual average of 98. In 1989, 207 banks insured by the Federal Deposit Insurance Corporation (FDIC) failed. Meanwhile, 262 savings and loans are being operated under FDIC supervision.[11] These figures compare with an annual average of six commercial bank failures in the period 1946–79. Recorded failures undoubtedly understate banking problems. If assets and liabilities were valued at market rather than historical prices, additional banks would surely be revealed to be insolvent. FSLIC went broke and now the FDIC's fund is strained.

Suddenly, substantive reform of deposit insurance is a serious possibility. Once again, the regulatory agencies are studying the question, and the topic appears on almost every banking programme. Yet virtually all the proposals accept the political impossibility of completely abolishing federal deposit insurance.[12] Consequently, in one way or another, each proposal involves compromises.

Benston *et al.* (1986, pp.304–14) advocate a fairly typical reform package for FDIC insurance. First, the authors recommend establishing risk-related premiums for deposit insurance, and joining this with a system of risk-adjusted capital standards. Next, they suggest several alternatives for reducing insurance coverage. These include a selective rollback of the *de jure* coverage from \$100 000 to 50 000 or \$25 000. Finally, they argue that premiums should be collected based on the riskiness of the entire portfolio of the bank holding company. They reject the idea that the risks of non-bank activities can be functionally isolated from banks in a holding company.[13]

In an earlier article, Short and O'Driscoll (1983) proposed a plan designed to facilitate a transition to competitive provision of deposit insurance. They proposed that *de facto* coverage above statutory limits be eliminated, coverage limits be introduced, and some form of co-insurance developed. These proposals were each intended to address the moral hazard inherent in the current system. Additionally, they recommended a number of other actions to open the door to private suppliers of deposit insurance. These suggestions were based on the views that it would be practically impossible to price risk systematically without competitive markets. The FDIC could remain as a supplier of deposit insurance, but its monopoly needed to be eliminated.

Flannery and Protopapadakis (1985, p.8) advanced the critique of a governmental agency's attempting to price risk:

> Public institutions' decisions are subject to public scrutiny. Such scrutiny can involve lengthy debates, appeal procedures, and compromises between economic efficiency and political needs. Even the most well-meaning and efficient public institutions move with glacial speed compared to the rapid assessment of information and the continuous reassessment of risk that takes place in the financial markets.

Aside from the public choice critique, there are additional difficulties with reform proposals like those offered by Benston *et al.* Market forces are likely to undermine many of the suggested reforms that are instituted. For instance, there does not appear to be coverage low enough to prevent most depositors from securing as much insurance protection as they desire. Money-market brokers routinely place funds in lots as small as $1000, so with commercial banks and thrifts numbering thousands, financial markets could reallocate even large sums into many smaller insured accounts. To deal successfully with moral hazard, any successful proposal must also incorporate some form of deductible or co-insurance. Yet any such proposal would run foul of the political commitment to protect small depositors.

In fact, deposit insurance was crafted to protect not the small depositor, but a system of uneconomically small and undiversified banks (O'Driscoll, 1988b, p.2–5). Economic fact, however, cannot surmount the obstacle of the political mythology surrounding the small depositor. Unless the mythology is successfully countered, deposit insurance reform will be unsuccessful. Even the $150 billion cost (in present value terms) of the thrift crisis has not shaken the faith of the system's supporters. Perhaps only a second bill of similar size will awaken American taxpayers to the system's cost.

Other banking-reform proposals attempt to offset the effects of deposit insurance by performing more radical surgery on the banking system. Robert Litan (1986, 1987 and 1988) envisions highly diversified financial holding companies (akin to universal banks), which would consist of both traditional commercial banking services as well as a broad range of additional financial services. His plan defines a narrow subset of banking services that would be funded by insured deposits. 'The "bank" . . . would essentially be a money-market fund, permitted to invest in highly liquid "safe" securities, such as obligations of the United States Treasury and high-quality commercial paper' (Litan, 1986, p.10). The financial holding company's other activities could be funded by anything except insured deposits.

Litan's ingenious, if somewhat complex, plan testifies to the lengths to which reformers must go to offset the effects of deposit insurance. Viewed in isolation, the plan makes little sense. Why institute a legally separate institution for investing in very safe and liquid assets? The answer, the only answer, is the existence of a blanket guarantee for deposits. To render that system safe and sound, the assets purchased with the deposits must themselves be immunised against risk – Litan's plan would largely accomplish this task at the cost of potential inefficiencies in the financial system. The inefficiencies may be preferable, however, to the losses being generated under the current system.

One telling criticism of the Litan proposal can be made. The proposal suggests that deposit insurance only be offered on transaction accounts backed 100 per cent by highly liquid and safe assets. Yet the financial system has already developed a similar system: money-market mutual funds. (Litan even analogises his plan to these funds.) Notably, however, these accounts are not insured. In the USA, they have grown phenomenally, and now contain well over $300 billion in assets. The experience of money-market mutual funds suggests that deposit insurance would not be required in such a system. Further, if banks were compelled to provide such insurance on transaction accounts, they would be likely to lose even more market share to money-market mutual funds. The latter have consistently been lower-cost providers of funds. It appears, then, that Litan's proposal might be a case of overkill. If we could get banks to hold the appropriately safe asset portfolios, then deposit insurance would be unnecessary.[14]

Market forces and legislative changes at the state level are evolving a system of more diversified regional, if not national banks. These developments are to be applauded, as they may partially offset the effects of deposit insurance (O'Driscoll 1988a). Broadening bank powers to permit greater asset diversification would further strengthen the US banking system (Benston *et al.*, 1986, pp.127–59). It is unlikely, however, that the US banking system will be safe and sound until deposit insurance is eliminated or significantly changed.

Some banking reform proposals now go significantly beyond addressing deposit insurance. These proposals question basic features of the existing banking system. In the next section, I examine some of them and analyse the issues they raise.

BANKING REFORM

Robert Litan's plan constitutes a transition between reform proposals designed simply to deal with the moral hazard generated by the current deposit insurance system, and those proposals envisaging more far-reaching changes in the commercial banking system. Litan implicitly raises the question of whether substantial changes in the structure of the banking system are needed. What the proposals I now consider have in common is that they each provide an affirmative answer to the question.

All the proposals examined here advocate a highly deregulated financial system in which there is no role for central banks. Since Europeans are now debating whether to have a European central bank, the questions raised by the literature are particularly relevant today. White (1984) is the most influential recent work on the historical performance of free banking, specifically, Scottish free banking. In a series of articles, Rolnick and Weber (1982, 1983, 1984, and 1986) re-examined the American free banking experience.[15]

White (1984) argued that, judged by accepted criteria, the Scottish system of competitive and unregulated free banking performed well historically (1716–1844).[16] The banking system was safe and relatively stable. While there were bank failures, these did not generate uncontained runs or systemic failure. The Scottish banks compared particularly well with the unstable English banking system, whose source of strength was the Bank of England. White found the Scottish system to be stable despite (or, in his view, because of) the absence of a central bank.

In her important but neglected book on central banking, Lutz (1936) aptly described the American banking system as one of 'decentralization without freedom'. To this day, the American banking system reflects a public policy of an uneconomically large number of small banking units. In contrast, White (1984, pp.33–4 and 82–4) identified the system of nationwide branch banking as playing a crucial role in stabilising Scottish banks by immunising them against local downturns.

Additionally, in the US, regulators have traditionally prescribed and proscribed assets for bank portfolios. Particularly important in many states was the requirement that institutions chartered under the free-banking statutes hold state bonds as collateral for notes issued. Purportedly designed to ensure that notes were backed by safe assets, the requirements look more like a scheme designed to stimulate demand for the sometimes dubious paper of antebellum state governments. In some cases, new banks could acquire depreciated state bonds and deposit them with the state banking commissioner, who valued them at par. The banks then issued liabilities in the form of bank notes against the inflated value of the bonds. This policy effectively made the banks insolvent from their inception. In periods of rising interest rates, the gap between accounting and market values of the bonds increased. If a bank experienced a run, it would be unable to redeem all its notes. These characteristics of some state free banking system generated unsound banking practices and gave free banking its bad name among historians.

Rolnick and Weber thus dealt with a system of free banking more alike in name than akin in substance with the Scottish system. Yet they found that the system was not inherently unstable. That is, problems faced by free banks 'were caused by economic shocks that caused many banks to fail but did not lead to bank runs or panics' (Rolnick and Weber, 1986, p.878). Rolnick and Weber (1984) found that the role played by state bonds was significant. Yet the state bond programs represented bad public policy, not an element inherent to free banks (White, 1986, pp.891–5).

The recent work on free banking has generated a large and growing literature that reassesses free banking historically and theoretically. Lacking, however, are programmes for applying the insights to contemporary monetarty institutions. Advocates face the classic problem of getting from here to there. So it becomes a question of creating or evolving parallel institutions.[17]

In a separate strand of literature, a number of authors offer proposals for fundamental institutional change. Intellectual and historical priority in the literature is surely held by Black (1970). He imagined the future evolution of banking. It would be a world in which banks were free to offer any variety of depository liabilities and price them as they choose. In Black's world, banks cease to be institutions whose distinctiveness lies in their producing money. In this world, 'money' is an abstract unit of account and banks the place in which exchange of goods are registered. The unit of account is no longer a means of payment, and there is no longer any circulating medium. The unit of account is a kind of mnemonic for registering exchanges and entering loans and repayments in units of equivalent value. There is no reason to fear or restrict the creation of bank deposits – their supply is completely endogenous to real transactions. Reserve requirements would be absent, so there would be no reason for open market operations by a central bank. 'In such a world, it would not be possible to give any reasonable definition of the quantity of money. The payments mechanism in such a world would be very efficient, but money in the usual sense would not exist' (Black, 1970, p.9).

O'Driscoll (1985) argued that, both historically and theoretically, circulating money would not disappear. Largely unregulated banking systems have produced no observable tendency for circulating money to disappear. Moreover, Black's banking system is theoretically incomplete. Any banking system requires something constituting final settlement between banks. By its nature, the good constituting final payment cannot itself be a liability of one of the banks. What the good is has varied over time, but it constitutes the base money of the system. We can perhaps contrive a world without circulating currency, in which debit cards substitute for currency and coin, but we cannot conceive a banking system without a means of settlement (i.e. banks' reserves or base money). Thus, the limitation on the supply or quantity of bank deposits is not a contrivance but a natural phenomenon.[18]

Black's article had a significant influence on subsequent authors. Though clearly derivative, Fama (1980) further developed Black's vision of an unregulated payments system. Greenfield and Yeager (1983) constitute a genuine extension. They present a blueprint for implementing a Black–Fama payments system. They advocate the system because of what they view as the poor macroeconomic performance of fiat money, whose supply is unresponsive in the short run to changes in money demand. There is no stability of value in our current monetary system, because purchasing power is only what the demand and supply of money fleetingly accord to a dollar, pound or franc.

Complicating the problem is the fact that money has no market of its own. Consequently, monetary disequilibrium must be worked out in *all* markets. Further, prices are inflexible in the short run. 'Under these realistic circumstances, failure to keep the quntity of money correctly and steadily managed can have momentous consequences' (Greenfield and Yeager, 1983, p.309). They conclude that monetary authorities are not up to the task of so precisely managing a fiat money supply. They view Black's vision as implementable and desirable.

Key to their proposal is that the government should define a unit of value, just as it does units of weight and measurement. They suggest a unit of value encompassing a broadly representative bundle of tradable commodities. The commodities chosen, however, need not be either stored nor storable, as there would be no convertibility. In fact, the authors point to the lack of convertibility as one of the system's chief benefits. 'The value unit remains stable in terms of the designated commodity bundle because its value never did depend on direct convertibility into the bundle or any specific commodity. *Instead, its value is fixed by definition*. It is free of any link to issues of money that might become inflated' (Yeager and Greenfield, 1983, p.306; emphasis added).

No one other than the authors seems to understand how value can be effectively fixed *by definition*. A great deal of the literature that has developed around the original article (including responses and additional contributions by Greenfield and Yeager) deals with this issue. The critics have not been able to understand the point, and the authors have supplied no satisfactory explanation. To be more precise, Greenfield and Yeager have specified no market mechanism maintaining the equivalence of defined values and actual prices. Under certain circumstances, convertibility could accomplish this, but they have ruled out this mechanism. It would be fair to say that the reader is being asked to take their proposal on faith.

One can approach the issue from another perspective. Yeager and Greenfield (1983, pp.307–8) allow for the development of debt instruments denominated in units of account. What is to keep these instruments from trading? In the *laissez-faire* system they propose, they could be no basis for a prohibition. Experience tells us, however, that tradable debt instruments easily become circulating media, like bills of exchange once were. The final stage in the evolution of circulating currency comes when issuers realise that market dynamics will allow them to issue non-interest-bearing notes (O'Driscoll, 1985, p.28). Now we have the market dynamics for a classic case of overissuance of circulating media. An issuer can trade non-interest-bearing currency for interest-bearing debt. He will want to do so *ad libitum*. In Greenfield and Yeager's system, we not only have the potential for money's re-emergence but for instability of prices in the extreme. Actual monetary systems typically placed limits on the expansion process, but there is no limiting mechanism in Greenfield and Yeager.

One must conclude that Greenfield and Yeager contains a basic error. Price stability cannot be attained simply by definition.

Further, though they believe that they have rid their system of circulating money, the system contains the incentives to reintroduce it. Moreover, in their system there would be no central bank or market constraint on overissuance of fiat currency. The classical criticism of unregulated fiat money remains intact. Such systems require some anchor for nominal values, whether provided by a central bank or otherwise.

CONCLUSION

It has been said that bad monetary practice produces good monetary theory. Theories are not developed in a vacuum, and pressing economic problems often stimulate sound economic analysis. Recent banking difficulties in the USA have stimulated a host of policy proposals. Many focus on the critical role played by deposit insurance in the recent wave of bank failures. While perhaps seeming to be a peculiarly American problem, the bank failures reveal the powerful effects that bad public policy can generate. As Europe develops a comprehensive banking policy, the Community surely wants to avoid the policy traps that have lead to the banking problems in the USA. Most importantly, policy-makers must avoid actions that hide banking risk and insulate risk-takers from the consequences of their actions.

The cumulative monetary and banking problems of the 1960s, 1970s and 1980s have also generated broader and more far-reaching recommendations for changing the banking system. Because they are more removed from immediate public policy problems, these plans tend to be more abstract than deposit insurance reform. Nonetheless, they raise important and interesting questions that merit further development and debate.

7 Deregulation and Monetary Policy

KEVIN T. DAVIS and MERVYN K. LEWIS

7.1 WORLDWIDE FINANCIAL CHANGE

Financial deregulation is one part of the current surge of change in financial markets world-wide. Global financial change is nothing new. It was as prominent in the nineteenth century as it is today. Then nearly half a century of structural change saw the decline of bimetallism and the establishment of the gold standard, a switch from note issue towards the use of chequeable deposits and, finally, the rise of limited liability banking, which transformed banks in Europe from small regional partnerships into major national and multinational institutions. For much of this century, by contrast, it seemed that the forces of change had been muted. The structure, practices and technology of banking seemed to change little from the late nineteenth century until the 1960s. Multinational banking declined, and as late as 1967, R. S. Sayers could record in his book *Modern Banking* that 'banking organisation does not easily straddle national frontiers' so that 'the banking business of the world is organised in the main on national lines' (Sayers, 1967, p.16).

Matters are very different today. Over the intervening years, banking and financial markets have been transformed by the rise of Eurobanking, wholesale banking, liability management, multinational banking, multiple currency loans, 'securitisation', secondary mortgage markets, multi-option facilities, interest rate and currency options and swaps, and financial futures. Credit cards, debit cards, automated tellers, cash management accounts, electronic fund transfers and point-of-sale terminals are also part of this worldwide process of change which began in the 1960s, has sustained itself for over two decades, and continues to reshape the nature of banking and financial markets.[1]

So strong have been the competitive forces in a number of countries in the 1980s that it is tempting to attribute much of the change to a spontaneous outbreak of competition. Deregulation has been an important proximate factor spurring greater competition, but decisions about deregulation do not occur in a vacuum. Deregulation both influences and is influenced by the economic and financial environment, and is responsive to pressures from firms in the regulated industries. The interplay of a number of forces has thus contributd to financial change.

One of these forces comes from developments in the 'real' sector which have led to demands for some new types of financial services. The growth of multinational business corporations has prompted banks to follow suit. With world trade and development proceeding apace, the evolution of financing demands has prompted a response which includes syndication of loans and Eurobonds. the rediscovery of international and multinational banking has integrated markets internationally. Integration of domestic markets has occurred through the development of new instruments, such as money-market funds, which straddle previously segmented sectors and fill in gaps in financing demands. As a consequence, financial innovation has been rapid in terms of markets (e.g. Eurocurrency and Eurobond markets, secondary asset markets, swap and futures markets), instruments (cash management accounts, variable rate lending, leveraged buyouts) and technologies (ATMs, data processing). The microeconomic and macroeconomic aspects of financial innovation were explored in Chapter 5 of this volume.

Developments in information technology have also played an important role in underpinning the process of financial change. Many of the financial assets on offer today, such as money-market mutual funds, rely on being able to mark asset values to market continuously and compute instantaneously the value of the liability for withdrawal purposes. Without modern computing technology the costs involved in producing these assets could be prohibitive. By reducing costs, technological advances can also give individuals and business firms direct access to previously inaccessible markets, so hastening along the 'securitisation' trend now underway.

The influences identified above depict structural change as being prompted by forces external to the financial sector, such as technological advance, changes in attitudes to regulation and changes in the types of financial services demanded. However, it is important not to forget the role of inventiveness emanating from within the financial system as a consequence of the ongoing competitive struggle. Indeed, deregulation sometimes comes about as a means of validating supposedly prohibited activities of financiers which the authorities give up trying to control.

Deregulation, inventiveness, innovation and technological progress thus interact with each other in complex ways, and it can be very difficult to disentangle them and sort out the *causes* and *consequences* of deregulation from the other factors affecting financial markets. However, deregulation differs from the other forces making for change in that it is the outcome of a political process. In seeking to explain this process we shall draw upon the theories of regulation which integrate economic and political aspects of behaviour in terms of 'public interest', 'private interest' and 'political-support-maximising' models. This is the subject matter of sections 2 and 3. Sections 4 and 5 examine the *effects* of deregulation upon banking markets and the economy. The final section then looks at some longer-run implications of deregulation for the nature of monetary controls.

7.2 FINANCIAL REGULATION AND DEREGULATION

Deregulation has not been confined to banking and finance. There has been a major alteration in attitudes to government controls and regulations across a number of countries and in a number of activities. These have included airlines, transport, communications and various public utilities as well as financial services; so many, in fact, that one group of writers have called the 1980s the Age of Regulatory Reform.[2] Regulatory reform is a better description than deregulation which implies the complete abandonment of regulation instead of a shifting emphasis and selective removal.

What is regulation? The *New Palgrave Dictionary* defines it as 'governmental actions to control price, sale and production decisions of firms in an avowed effort to prevent private decision-making that would take inadequate account of the "public interest" '[3] However, all governmental actions impinge upon one or more of these aspects. Usually the description 'regulation' is reserved for the use of methods such as the setting of entry conditions, product restrictions, price control, safety standards, and market barriers. Stigler (1971) provides an alternative definition of regulation as 'any policy which alters market outcomes by the exercise of some coercive government power'. His definition focuses on the way 'market outcomes' are achieved, and emphasises in particular the role of coercion *vis-à-vis* incentives. Yet by effectively excluding taxation and subsidies from his definition of regulation, Stigler may have made it too narrow for our purposes: reserve ratio requirements and devices such as the 'corset' (supplementary special deposits) can be viewed as taxation equivalents (see Artis and Lewis, 1991) yet they are perceived in British circles as being direct regulatory controls over banking and not as market (dis)incentives.

On either definition, extensive regulation remains in most countries. Entry into banking is supervised. Business is restricted by a number of asset-composition guidelines. Output is constrained by capital gearing ratios. Safety standards are set and rules govern banks' relationships with other institutions. Insurance companies must meet statutory requirements. Stock Exchanges are regulated, and so on.

Nevertheless, important changes have taken place. Table 7.1 summarises aspects of the financial regulation in selected countries. Controls over interest rates have been either removed or lightened. Selective controls upon consumer instalment credit and lending directives are little used. Long-standing barriers between banking and other financial institutions are coming down. Barriers to the participation of foreign financial firms in domestic markets have been lowered. Exchange controls and restrictions upon capital movements have been eased, although cross-border constraints upon insurance and pension-fund portfolios remain. Access of foreign borrowers to national capital markets is much freer, and less administrative 'guidance' is offered over Eurobond issues. The EEC also aims to create a completely open market in financial services by 1993.

In most countries the controls removed go back forty or so years and have their origins in attitudes shaped by the experience of the

TABLE 7.1 Aspects of financial regulation in major industrial countries

	Interest rate controls	*Credit controls*	*Product barriers*	*International barriers*	*Market barriers*
USA	None on over 30-day maturities; otherwise abolished for individuals in 1983	None	Separation of commercial banks, savings banks, and securities firms; and restraints on interstate banking but impact reduced	No controls since 1974; easy foreign entry	Wide range of well-developed markets in CP, CDs, future options, FRNs, etc, with few restrictions
Japan	Time deposits over $2m phased out, MMC minimum reduced to about $200 000	*Ad hoc* 'window' guidance	Separation of banking, securities, trust, and insurances; also of short- and long-term lending	Controls eased in 1980–4; continuing portfolio requirements and difficult foreign entry	CDs introduced in 1979, BAs (1985), futures (1985), deep-discount bonds; no options; size and maturity limits on corporate issues
Germany	Abolished in 1967	None	Universal banks separate from regional savings banks, real estate banks and building and loan associations	Controls substantially eased in 1960s and abolished in 1980–1, eased foreign entry in 1985	Zeros and FRNs (May 1985), CDs (1986), swaps allowed but discouraged, no CP or MMFs
France	On demand, time and savings deposits	Abolished at end 1986	Universal banks separate from merchant banks, long-term credit institutions, finance and specialised institutions	Eased in 1986, and remaining controls removed in 1990; foreign entry easy in principle	CDs, CP with some restrictions on maturities and amounts (1985), futures (1985)
UK	Abolished in 1971	None since 1982	Eroding divisions among commercial banks, merchant banks and building societies	No controls since 1979, relatively easy foreign entry	Similar to USA with CP market new and relatively undeveloped

Italy	None	With varying degrees of formality	Separation of specialised banks, and short- and long-term credit institutions	Easing in 1986, remaining controls removed 1990; easy foreign entry	No futures or CP, undeveloped options and CDs markets; zeros possible
Canada	Abolished in 1967	None	Separation of chartered banks and securities dealers, under review	No capital controls; limitations on foreign entry and ownership of financial institutions	Wide range of well-developed markets with few restrictions
Switzerland	None	None	Universal banks separate from cantonal and local savings banks	Controls abolished in 1979–80; no SF Euro-bond market; foreign entry with reciprocity	Undeveloped money and short-term bill markets; no options, CP or CDs
Australia	Most removed in December 1980. Finally abolished in April 1986	Lending restrictions abolished in 1982, liquidity ratios in 1985	Restrictions on diversification by banks largely lifted, eroding divisions among institutions	Exchange controls lifted in 1983. Foreign investment relaxed in 1985–6	Wide range of markets in CDs, BAs, futures, options and CP equivalents with few restrictions
Sweden	Abolished in May 1985	Credit ceilings removed in Nov. 1985	Divisions remain between banks, insurance and brokerage	Exchange controls on transactions greater than 6 months, foreign-bank entry allowed	CDs (introduced in 1980). CP (1983), futures (1985), FRNs (1985), options (1986). No zeros.

1930s, and to the enthusiasm for centralised planning and detailed controls which grew out of wartime emergency powers. Considerable public interest attached to banking in this period. The Bank of England and Banque de France were nationalised, and controls were fashioned to ensure that banking policy, along with much other financing, accorded with government policy. While the primary impetus was in terms of macroeconomic policies, the standard microeconomic justifications for intervention in market outcomes have their parallels in banking and finance.

Traditional economic analysis distinguishes spillovers (externalities) and market power as sources of divergence from the competitive ideal (Bator, 1958). More recently, imperfect information has been emphasised as an additional source of market failure. Let us consider these in turn. First, externalities can exist between customers of a firm or between firms if there are knock-on effects in the industry and to the economy. There is the potentiality for both externalities to be present in banking. Negative externalities can exist between depositors, since one holder of a bank deposit can encash his or her balance but large numbers of depositors cannot do so at the same time without imperilling the bank itself. The failure of one organisation can erode confidence in other banks. There is thus considerable benefit to the economy as a whole in sustaining confidence in the financial system. Second, market power may arise if there are substantial economies of scale in particular activities, e.g. in the provision of a payments system or in the operation of a branch banking network, and if it is thought desirable to prevent takeovers of regional and local institutions. Third, information asymmetries lie at the heart of the problem of bank failure – a bank's management inevitably knows more about its balance sheet than even the best-informed depositors (and shareholders). More generally, inadequate information has been held to provide a case for investor protection and the policing of fraud where consumers cannot evaluate readily the information available, where the costs of mistakes are high (e.g. purchase of the 'wrong' pension scheme) and where available legal remedies, such as private court actions, are more costly than is regulation in the public interest.

Regulation can take a number of forms. Some public authority (e.g. the Securities and Exchange Commission) can do it, firms can regulate themselves (i.e. 'self regulation', the traditional pattern in the City of London) or regulation can take place within a statutory framework (as in the present arrangements in London). Regulation can be of either structure or conduct: in the former, rules are implemented determining the structure of the market (e.g. controlling entry); in the latter, regulation governs conduct in the market (e.g. capping either prices or rates of return). Kay and Vickers (1988) contend that much of what passes for deregulation is in fact a shift from structural regulation to rules guiding conduct, and such a switch is certainly evident in financial regulation. But, whoever performs it and however it is carried out, the traditional view is that regulation responds to perceived market failures and seeks to correct them – what Meltzer (1988) called the 'goodwill' or 'benevolent dictator' theory of government.

Public-choice scholars take a different tack. They argue that intervention often results from pressure brought to bear upon politicians and government officials by organised interests. Even regulation which begins in the public interest can be 'captured' to serve the interest of the firms and workers in the regulated industry. This idea of 'regulatory capture' is associated especially with Downs (1961) and Stigler (1964, 1971) and Stigler and Friedland (1962). Stigler asked what regulation achieves and who benefits from it, and found that regulation increases the economic well-being of the soliciting groups and is often antithetical to the economic interests of the general public. Downs's argument was that the political process in general will tend to over-supply private-interest policies, while those in the public interest will be under-supplied.

There is thus a basic distinction in the literature between the idea that regulation is motivated by the 'public interest', i.e. to promote macroeconomic stability, financial stability and social economic efficiency, and the notion that regulation really acts to serve various 'private interests', including the self-interest of the regulators themselves.[4] Somewhere in between these two is the political-support-maximising model of Keeler (1984), which emphasises the social consensus upon which regulation in the public interest relies. All these models make clear that regulation cannot remain static but must vary over time in response to changes in technology and market conditions, shifts in the distribution of benefits and gains from regulation, and public perceptions as to the benefits and costs of regulatory interference. Each, however, offers a different perspective on the factors which may lead to deregulation.

Under the public-interest theory, deregulation results from environmental or technological developments which erode industry boundaries and reduce the pay-offs to society from inherited regulatory techniques: existing controls have outlived their usefulness. There is an extra dimension when financial services are involved. For most industries, the choices open to the regulator usually do not include the ability to alter market prices across the whole economy as a means of influencing output. Central banks do have such instruments at their disposal. They can enter the bond market or the foreign-exchange market like any other transactor and buy or sell domestic and foreign assets. These market actions can be distinguished from the regulatory ones. Much deregulation consists of a change from regulatory to market actions (and, we might add, within the category of regulatory to market actions, from structural controls to conduct and protective measures). In this way, the authorities seek to strengthen monetary controls in an altered environment.

A feature of central banking in a large number of countries has been the employment of 'non-classical' techniques of policy. Fousek (1957), in a survey of techniques then in use, found thirty-three countries actively employing variable cash reserve ratios and twenty-five using variable liquidity ratios. These techniques were adopted to meet two special features of the local economies. One was the substantial seasonal and cyclical fluctuations in bank reserves which came from the balance of payments under fixed exchange rates. The other was the undeveloped nature of securities markets and the limited scope for open-market operations to be used to offset these fluctuations. It was only natural that these devices would be phased out as countries moved to more flexible exchange rates and as the capacity grew to conduct open-market operations.

An element of self-interest on the part of the regulators themselves might be traced in the speed, or rather the lack of it, with which this substitution of market-based techniques for direct controls occurred. Self-interest might also be seen in the alacrity with which regulators in most countries have moved to replace the dismantled monetary controls with prudential forms of supervision. But it is too easy to be cynical on both counts, for regulatory controls often perform a number of functions. Liquidity ratios, imposed mainly for monetary policy purposes, may have served to reassure depositors and thus bolster confidence in banks. Interest-rate ceilings were often used to facilitate the operation of monetary policy, but they also prevented 'excessive' competition for deposits of the sort which took place by US savings and loan associations in the early 1980s. Close quantitative restrictions over bank lending acted as a substitute for bankers' own prudence, so regulated banks were generally safe lenders (although bank subsidiaries and affiliates may not have been). In the new framework, capital adequacy ratios ostensibly reinforce bankers' caution, but also act as gearing constraints upon banks' balance-sheet expansion.

One of the major strands of the 'private interest' view of regulation is the capture of the gains from regulation by producer interests, tolerated by the regulators in return for their cooperation. Financial regulation in the UK and many other countries built upon and officially sanctioned an interest-rate cartel operated by a small number of private banks. Initially, regulation probably served the bankers' interest. In the aftermath of the 1930s, caution was most likely uppermost in their minds and competition subdued. Close cooperation with the authorities enabled banks to run capital reserves down to historically low levels. Only later, as memories of the crisis faded and a new generation of bankers came to the fore, was the erosion of market shares and benefits of enhanced competition stressed. On this view, regulation and deregulation emerges as a by-product of cycles of under- and over-expansion in the financial industry.

These 'public interest' and 'private interest' explanations of deregulation ignore the substantial shifts which have taken place in the attitudes of academic economists, business groups and private citizens to financial regulations. Administered interest rates, credit controls and the social direction of bank lending reflected an apparent distrust of market outcomes. The experts' renewed conviction in the advantage of the market must be seen as a factor of major significance behind deregulation. The 'political support' model of regulation sees deregulation as most likely to occur when there is also an increase in the cost of maintaining the framework of regulation which is so large as to shake widely shared conventions.

7.3 PRESSURES TO DEREGULATE

There is little doubt that 'regulation begets regulation, since private efforts to escape the effects of regulation engender pressure for further regulation'.[5] Examples abound in financial services. US bankers' attempts to evade product and geographic market restrictions by means of the holding-company formula led to the Bank Holding Company Acts. The 1980 Depository Institutions, Deregulation and Monetary Control Act extended and equalised reserve requirements across institutions. Erosion of external controls in a number of countries during the 1960s led to the introduction of a bewildering array of special-reserve requirements, deposit taxes, negative interest rates and dual exchange-rate systems to limit capital movements.

Over time, a complex regulatory web emerged in most countries in which one regulation was counterbalanced by another. Given that interdependence, there was little chance – short of making wholesale change – that individual regulation could be removed without rendering unstable the entire regulatory superstructure.

Whey then did deregulation of interest rates, credit controls and market barriers occur when it did, and in so many countries? Two factors stand out which combine elements of all three theories of regulation. Interestingly, both illustrate a characteristic which distinguishes financial from other regulation, namely, the potential for evasion of controls by way of product-substitution from domestic and external sources.

The application of regulatory controls to financial institutions seems likely to give rise to costs which must be borne by someone – depositors, shareholders or non-preferential borrowers. These costs are frequently difficult to discern and, so long as they remain so, may even receive the tacit approval of those upon whom they fall.[6] This social consensus regarding the distribution of benefits and gains from regulation may be relatively stable so long as a certain tolerance threshold is not breached. If it is, and the extent of the wealth transfer through the regulatory process is revealed, the 'political support' crumbles and the pressure for a change can build up quickly.

Experience with interest-rate ceilngs in the USA illustrates the process.[7] For all of the 1970s, what Karėken (1984) called 'forced disintermediation' was a fulcrum of monetary policy in the USA. Banks and thrift institutions were subject to interest-rate ceilings on deposits. Certificates of Deposits (CDs) were exempted, allowing the banks to offer the wholesale market a deposit instrument bearing market-related yields. Opportunities for the retail sector were limited while access to the securities markets were circumscribed by minimum denominations and high transaction costs on small lots. Nevertheless, there appeared to be wide support for stable interest rates and the regulations which seemed to bring them about.

By allowing market rates of interest to rise relative to the ceilings, the authorities could lever deposits from both banks and thrift institutions. Controlled disintermediation could continue to work so long as (a) inflation remained subdued and (b) the retail segment of the financial system was divorced from securities markets. The problem was that inflation in the USA increased rapidly after 1978 and market interest rates soared. This change in the environment, from low inflation and low and stable interest rates to high inflation and high and unstable interest rates had a profound impact on all areas of the capital market. While yields on Treasury Bills rose about 10 per cent per annum, banks and thrifts were constrained by regulation to offer 5 to 5.75 per cent per annum. A gap was created which was too large not to be filled.

Securities firms such as Merrill Lynch did so. *Money market mutual funds* are a textbook example of a financial innovation which fills a niche when the time is ripe. They enabled institutions on behalf of individuals to carry out a 'size intermediation' function. Retail-sized deposits were aggregated to take advantage of the higher interest rates in wholesale markets. It was a short step from the money-market mutual fund to the *cash management account*, which tied together a money fund, an automatic overdraft privilege, a cheque book with a conventional commercial bank, and a credit card.

Introduced in 1970, the funds were little used until 1979. By the end of 1979, the total funds exceeded $50 billion and by the end of 1981 they exceeded $180 billion, as households withdrew balances from savings accounts. Regulations designed to protect banks and thrift institutions from excessive competition amongst themselves prevented them from competing with the money funds. The legislators were thus spurred into action.

The importance of the money funds as a *catalyst* for change is difficult to overstate, in that they:

1. forced the legislators to abolish interest-rate ceilings and to allow banks to provide interest on transactions accounts;
2. eroded the earlier segmentation between the relatively unregulated wholesale and closely regulated retail sectors of the capital market;
3. broke down the barriers between institutions, and sparked off the competitive surge which has sustained the deregulation process.

Much the same scenario was played out in Canada and Australia.

In the UK, the gap between wholesale rates of interest and retail bank-deposit rates was due more to the discriminatory pricing practices of the banks than to any regulatory inertia. While the gap was smaller and thus took longer to fill, the process of change in the 1980s was similar nonetheless. Unit Trust managers teamed up with merchant bankers to offer cheque-account facilities with market-related interest rates. Building societies and the smaller banks followed suit. This concerted attack upon the major banks' retail deposit base saw them respond by introducing interest on transactions balances. Banks in turn invaded housing finance, long the preserve of the societies, and this competition led to revised legislation which greatly widened the societies' powers, in much the same way as happened in the USA with the savings and loan associations.

As a result of these developments, part of transactions balances and the great bulk of the broadly defined money supply now bears interest, and it is increasingly the case that the interest is related to market trends. This has completely altered the character of monetary assets, and we shall discuss some of the implications of this alteration shortly.

These developments also illustrate an important feature of financial services: the fungibility of finance. This has been greatly aided by the dramatic improvements in information technology. It has been estimated that data-processing costs have declined at the rate of 25 per cent per annum over the past 25 years,[8] while communications costs have declined by about 15 per cent per annum. The enhanced tradability of financial services which has resulted has given deregulation an important international dimension. An ever-increasing number of international banking services probably fall into the category of what Bhagwati (1986) calls 'long-distance' services, capable of being supplied by means of modern microelectronic technology and telecommunications equipment without there being any physical proximity between the user and the provider. Low comparative production costs, low transportation costs and less costly regulatory requirements in other nations encourage the production of banking services to be shifted overseas, especially to the Euromarkets.

In the locales to which banking has shifted, Eurobanking offered a ready illustration of the opportunities denied by regulation. In the UK, for example, the developments of the Eurocurrency markets brought an influx of foreign banking firms to the City and the formation of parallel markets for banking and finance. Pressure to deregulate both banking and securities markets came from the contrast between the heady growth of the parallel markets and the relative stagnation of the traditional markets. 'Competition and Credit Control' in 1971 began the process of deregulation and represented the first attempt to bring the two banking systems closer together by enabling the primary banking system to engage in Eurocurrency banking and liability management. Later the focus shifted to the securities markets and to the contrast between the domestic markets and Eurobond and Euroequity markets. A major structural change was needed if London was to emulate them and meet the competition of overseas markets, and this led to the 'Big Bang' of 1986. That, in turn, put pressure on the Continental European markets, and deregulation there of stock exchanges and rules restricting derivative markets (e.g. futures, options) has followed, notably in France, Spain, Belgium and Germany.

The move of banking and other financial business to the Euromarkets created a persistent pressure for a lightening of domestic regulations to forestall the emigration of more of the regulated firms' business. Attempts to extend the regulatory domain to the Euromarkets have proved to be impractical. In 1979, the Board of Governors of the Federal Reserve System and the Bundesbank sought the cooperation of other central banks to apply reserve requirements to Eurocurrency deposits. The US–German proposal failed to gain support from other central banks,[9] and especially from the Bank of England, which was able to argue persuasively that the correct solution was for the USA and Germany to reduce the 'heavy-handedness' of their regulation, rather than extend it internationally and interrupt the process of international financial intermediation. The Bank of England's solution, by and large, is what has occurred. International banking facilities have been established in the USA (enabling US banks to conduct Euro-business on-shore), and domestic regulation in the USA has been lightened (with the removal of Glass–Steagall and reductions in reserve requirements being recent examples.)

7.4 DEREGULATION AND BANK INTEREST RATES

We now consider the implications of deregulation for bank interest rates. Monetary analysis has long taken as its starting-point the assumption that monetary assets bear no interest. With this assumption, 'the' rate of interest of monetary theory represents both the level of market interest rates and the difference between the interest return on money and non-money assets. When monetary assets themselves bear interest, it is that differential which must adjust to restore asset-market equilibrium following a change in market conditions. If bank interest rates are regulated, relative interest rates between bank deposits and other assets can be readily altered simply by changing market rates. With deregulation, it becomes a matter of how bank deposit rates are determined.

Consider the following representation of the market for bank deposits:

$$D(r_d, r_a, r_k; b_d)\, W = D^s \tag{7.1}$$

Here D^s is the supply of deposits, and the demand for deposits, as a proportion of private-sector wealth, W, depends on r_d, the banks' deposit rate, r_a, the yield on 'securities', and r_k, the yield on capital assets. The term b_d, treated for the moment as a parameter rather than a variable, represents the non-pecuniary benefits flowing from holding deposits – such as liquidity and 'implicit interest' taking the form of subsidised cheque services and the like. Conventional price theory would presumably see the yield on deposits being determined by the interaction of demand and supply in the market for deposits. If so, an excess supply of deposits would to some extent be 'bottled up' in the deposit market via an equilibrating reduction in bank deposit rates. On similar reasoning, Tobin (1963, 1969) saw flexibility of the interest on 'money' as destroying the potential for discretionary monetary policy. He attributed the 'secret of the special role of money' to its fixed rate, forcing the whole adjustment onto other interest rates. His conclusion was that 'if the interest rate on money, as well as the rate on all other financial assets, were flexible and endogenous . . . there would be no room for monetary policy to affect aggregate demand' (Tobin, 1969, p.26).

Our own analysis (Davis and Lewis, 1982, 1983) proceeds along different lines. Payment of interest on bank deposits is possible because of the intermediation activities of banks whereby bank deposits are used to finance holdings of other assets. Competition between banks will ensure that the deposit interest rate is such that only normal profits are made in banking. Consequently, the deposit interest rate will be driven to equality with the average yield on banks' asset portfolios (less the resource costs of providing non-pecuniary benefits to depositors). When the banks are subject to a required reserve ratio, s, the deposit rate r_D is given by

$$r_D = (1 - s - e)r_A + s.r_s - c \tag{7.2}$$

where e represents the excess reserve ratio of the banks, r_s is the interest rate paid on required reserves, r_A is the weighted average yield on banks' asset portfolios and c is the constant marginal resource cost of deposits. In the absence of required reserves (effectively the position in the UK), setting $r_s = 0$, we have

$$r_D = (1 - e)r_A - c \tag{7.3}$$

In Figure 7.1 this relationship (which is best interpreted as the banks' desired supply curve given constant returns to scale and an infinitely elastic supply of reserves) is depicted for a given r_A(i.e. $r^o{}_A$) and a constant value of e as $S_0{}^*$. D_0 is the public's demand for bank

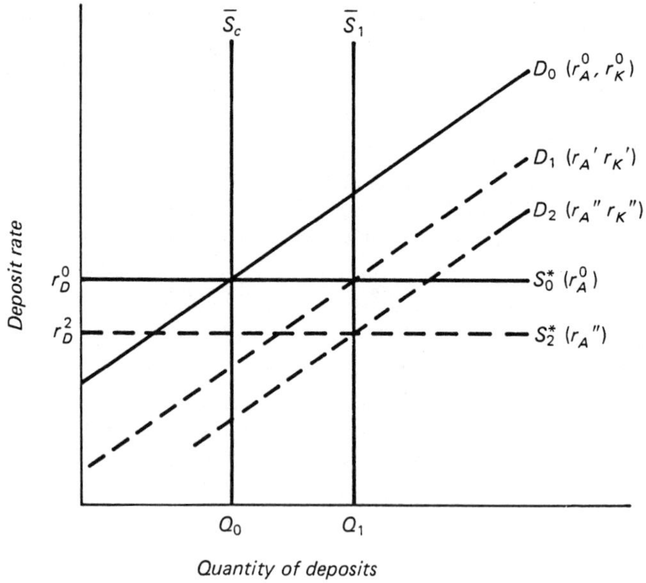

FIGURE 7.1 Deregulation and the deposit market

deposits, the position of which depends upon r_A (since these assets compete with bank deposits for a place in the non-bank sector's balance sheet), and is drawn for the same value of $r_A(r^o{}_A)$ as that underlying $S_o{}^*$. In addition, the position of D depends upon the value of r_k (given as $r^o{}_k$), the yield on existing real assets. (It is assumed that banks hold only financial assets.[10]) Finally, the stock of deposits determined by the manipulations of the authorities, for which individual banks are competing, is S_o giving initially equality between demand and supply at the deposit rate determined competitively under constant returns to scale.

Consider now an increase in the stock of deposits from S_o to S_1, which creates an excess supply of deposits at the prevailing interest rate structure. The excess supply, held but not demanded except as a temporary store of purchasing power, can then be dissipated in several ways – by purchasing securities and real assets, acquiring claims of non-bank intermediaries, and repaying advances. These attempts by holders of deposits to rid themselves of unwanted deposits will succeed only in reducing the yields on those other assets and thus the demand for deposits. In the first case when the deposit rate is fixed or adjusts only sluggishly to market rates, the adjustment occurs wholly on other yields. They must decline relative to the inflexible deposit rate r^{o}_{D} until the new equilibrium set (r_A', r_k') brings demand (D_1) into line with the new supply. In the second case when bank deposit rates fluctuate with market yields, the demand shift is accompanied by a fall in S^*. For equilibrium to result D must shift by more than S^*. This is given by the intersection of D_2, S_2^*, and S_1 at r^2_D. Comparing the two situations, the larger movement in the demand for money schedule needed to bring about asset equilibrium with flexible rates indicates the larger change in the level of interest rates (r_A'', r_k'' relative to r_A', r_k').

Far from losing its potency, it would seem that monetary changes are potentially more powerful. A fixed rate on money is not needed for monetary adjustments to fall upon other markets. That spillover comes about because of money's role as a temporary abode of purchasing power. Once the newly created money is accepted, removal of it requires a fall in the rate of interest on non-monetary assets *vis-à-vis* the rate on money. In the fixed-rate case this is achieved by a fall in the rate on non-monetary assets alone whereas in the flexible-rate case competition between banks means that the bank deposit rate follows market rates downwards. Thus, the variation in the level of interest rates which is needed to achieve a given change in relative yields is larger.

We have assumed for simplicity that the relevant transition is from a fixed interest rate to flexible bank interest rates. If, as in the USA and Australia, the change is from an interest-rate ceiling to removal of that ceiling an asymmetry operates between monetary restrictions and expansions. When the ceiling operates, bank rates may follow market rates downwards but cannot follow them upwards beyond the ceiling. Removal of the ceiling then implies more flexible bank interest rates, but mainly in an upward direction. Consequently, interest rates may be expected to be higher on average, as well as more variable.

These results presuppose that asset demand functions remain unaltered in the face of changes like the increased variance of bank deposit yields and increased covariance between bank deposit and other yields – about which more later. The results also assume that bank deposit rates are not already effectively market-determined because of bank competition via the payment of 'implicit' interest. When banks are prohibited from paying explicit interest on demand deposits and when ceilings constrain payment of interest on other liabilities, competition may encourage banks to evade the controls and pay 'implicit interest' – by providing transactions services without charge, expanding convenience services (e.g. branching), or by granting loans at less than market rates. If this implicit interest, reflected in the term b_d in equation (7.1), equalled the explicit interest paid after deregulation and responded as quickly to market forces, the effect of removing interest-rate controls would have more shadow than substance – except that *measured* interest rates would be higher. However, this seems unlikely. A study by Startz (1979) for US banks found that the implicit interest paid by banks did vary with market rates, but only by a factor in the region of 33–50 per cent, so that the short-term variability of bank deposit rates (in total) in the USA has indeed been limited by the prohibition of explicit interest rates.

7.5 THE EFFECTIVENESS OF MONETARY POLICY

The analysis in the preceding section, following Tobin, concentrated on asset-market adjustments to monetary changes. Ignoring the asymmetry implied by interest-rate ceilings rather than controlled interest rates under regulation, the argument can be translated into the familiar *IS*/*LM* framework to examine impacts upon the real economy. It implies an *LM* schedule which is less elastic with respect to absolute rates of interest, as the fluctuation of bank interest rates with market yields offsets to some extent the tendency of the demand for money to vary with 'the' rate of interest. An increase in the market-orientation of banks will have other impacts, too, upon the demand for money and the *LM* curve.[11] In total, four principal effects may be noted:

1. A re-intermediation into bank deposits seems likely to the extent that bank deposit returns were not previously market-determined by the payment of 'implicit' interest. Shifts into now higher-yielding financial instruments which form part of the conventional money supply will increase the demand for money.

2. Non-interest-bearing-transactions balances can be expected to fall, and the interest elasticity of the supply of deposits will increase, as yields become positive in real terms.
3. The sensitivity of money demanded to the general level of interest rates, in the longer term, is likely to decrease as bank deposit rates become more responsive to market rates of interest.
4. The income elasticity of the demand for (narrow) money is, however, likely to fall also, as deposits will be held as interest-bearing liquid assets, rather than simply to facilitate transactions.

The first two of these impacts seem likely to produce divergent trends in broad and narrow money and erratic movements of the *LM* schedule in the transition. The third, as noted, suggests a steepening of the *LM* curve while the fourth offsets to some degree the change in interest-rate elasticity on the *LM* schedule.

To the extent that a steepening of the *LM* curve results, several conclusions would seem to follow. First, other things being equal, changes in the money stock (which shift the *LM* curve by an equivalent horizontal amount in each case assuming no change in the income elasticity of money demand) will result in larger absolute fluctuations in interest rates in the flexible-rate world. Second, changes in the monetary growth rate will exert equivalently stronger effects on real activity in the deregulated environment. This comes about because the yield on existing real assets is among the yields which adjust to restore monetary equilibrium. Since yields in general change by more, a larger change in the yield on existing real assets (achieved by larger change in the market valuation of those assets) and a larger impact on investment decisions and economic activity can be expected. Third, the value is enhanced of maintaining control of the money supply in the face of disturbances emanating from the real sector, shown in Figure 7.2 as random shifts in the *IS* curve between IS_1 and IS_2. The chart illustrates the transition from regulated bank interest rates (LM') to unregulated bank rates (LM''), depicted in the limiting case of an *LM* curve rendered effectively vertical as the fluctuation of bank interest rates with market rates offsets the tendency for the demand for money to vary with 'the' rate of interest. This enables control of the quantity of money via money-supply targets (represented by the fixed position of the *LM* curves) to act as a more

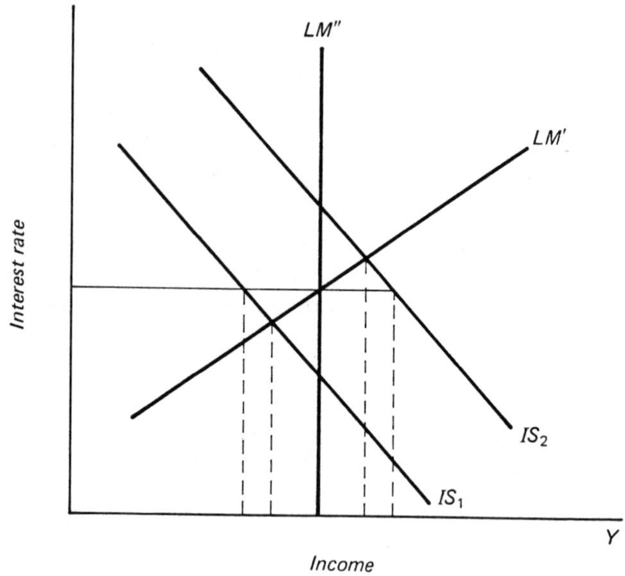

FIGURE 7.2 Interest-rate deregulation in the *IS*/*LM* framework

effective automatic 'stabiliser', reducing the variability of real income, at the cost of larger induced fluctuations in the general level of interest rates.

At the same time, however, conditions in the 'real' sector cannot be expected to remain unchanged in the face of these developments. Deregulation promotes competition and the decline in computation costs makes interest rate variation much cheaper: together, these developments reduce the incidence of credit rationing. In the UK, such effects, where not officially inspired, were promoted by inertial interest-rate adjustments in the building-society sector, resulting in significant 'credit-rationing effects' in the determination of dwelling investment. These effects, if not completely absent, are no longer obvious.[12]

In combination with some other developments, the following effects are suggested on the *IS* curve:

1. The spread of flexi-rate loan contracts and the development of private hedge markets for interest rate futures make it likely that it is the 'permanent' interest rate expected to rule over the

life of the loan contract which is relevant for investment decisions. Consequently, the *IS* curve may exhibit a reduced elasticity with respect to current short-term interest-rate movements, in so far as new expenditures are concerned.

2. Under the system of non-price credit-rationing, the flow of credit to some sectors was restricted, while others were sheltered from various interest-rate or price changes. Interest-rate changes will now affect most sectors directly.
3. Under the old system the impact of rationing and interest-rate increases fell heavily upon those borrowers seeking new accommodation from the banks. As flexi-rate loan contracts have become commonplace, all borrowers – existing and new – feel the brunt of monetary changes. For existing borrowers, the effect of higher interest rates operates much like a tax in squeezing discretionary income and depressing expenditures.
4. The removal of interest-rate ceilings will lead to a higher average level of interest rates. Interest costs will therefore form a larger proportion of total expenditure, and changes in the rate of interest could have a great impact on expenditure and budgets, although higher and more variable deposit yields have opposite effects.
5. Inflexibilities in other markets could increase interest-rate sensitivity. Borrowers are likely to be more sensitive to changes in interest rates if prices in product markets move more slowly.

The last four factors suggest a flattening of the *IS*, while the first suggests some possible offset. Overall, these considerations, together with the greatly increased financial exposure of the personal sector during the 1980s reflected in the rapid expansion of consumer debt, suggest that for the time being the transmission mechanism will bear more heavily on the personal sector than the corporate; but this is clearly not a long-run position. The personal sector may reduce its exposure and increasingly take advantage of hedging instruments and swapped contracts, especially if the policy-makers exploit the current position.

For the future, one of the consequences of financial change of the kind now in train is that the dividing line between banks and non-banks is becoming progressively more blurred. This development was anticipated and analysed by Fama (1980) and foreshadowed by Tobin (1963) and Gurley and Shaw (1960). As banks come to resemble other financial intermediaries (and *vice versa*) and even – as in the case of securitisation, come to resemble simply a bundle of contracts in a disintermediated capital market – the broader monetary magnitudes, originally consisting predominantly of 'bank' deposits, not unnaturally lose any substantive distinctive interpretation. One might as well look to still broader magnitudes, or to a narrower one which is not a 'bank' creation at all, such as the monetary base (or 'high-powered' money).

Part of the blurring of the dividing lines has been the reduction of the monopoly over money transmission services once enjoyed by 'banks'. Technology is changing here, too. Increasing use of credit cards reduces the demand for money to hold before settlement dates; newer developments promise instant debiting of bank accounts effectively reducing clearing times to zero. These changes affect the demand for money in the traditional transactions sense and seem all too likely to impart instability to the demand for monetary base. This leads us on to the question of the adequacy of monetary controls in the new environment.

7.6 THE EVOLUTION OF MONETARY CONTROLS

We noted in section 7.1 that the major elements of a modern banking system were in place by the late nineteenth century and the structure, practices and technology of banking seemed to change little from then until the wave of financial change and deregulation in the 1970s and 1980s. The developments in the nineteenth century can themselves be seen as the culmination of a process which began in previous centuries with the sovereign or government encouraging the growth of banks as a way of enhancing the State's credit,[13] and ended with the government sharing its money-creating powers with the banking system. The government's fund-raising ability was constrained by limited bases for taxation and undeveloped markets for securities. Also, reflecting their role as 'inside lenders' overcoming imperfect information in financial markets (Chapter 2), banks were in touch with borrowers and lenders in ways that the government was not. Once the government had become accustomed to relying upon credit from the banks it assumed a direct interest in bank solvency and this responsibility implied that it should have an influence over bank policies, and an entry to the banking industry.

Here we have the historical origins of two main motives for regulating banking and finance, and also the building blocks for a large body of monetary theory. One motive for regulation of banks (financial institutions generally) is to protect the money supply and the flow of credit to private- and public-sector capital formation from any systematic effects stemming from the failure of banks (bank runs) and loss of liquidity. The other is to achieve through monetary (and thus banking) policy various macroeconomic objectives, such as the control of inflation. Central banks took on the role of the guardians of bank liquidity and, with varying degrees of independence, that of a buffer and a constraining force upon money creation of both government and the banks.

Standard monetary analysis has developed from this foundation and it has been widely perceived as providing a justification for elevating the financial intermediation of banks to centre stage. The analysis begins with an account of the way that banks create money by intermediating between borrowers and lenders, and (typically by means of balance-sheet identities) determines how banks stand relative to the monetary authorities and the general public. With the money supply embracing elements of both outside and inside money, i.e. cash and bank deposits, this means that banks are effectively grouped with the monetary authorities as part of the 'control core'. Bank money is equated with fiat money, and both are assumed to bear interest rates set exogenously at zero. In this way the institution of money is inextricably tied to the institution of banking.

This is a not unrealistic description of how many national monetary systems looked before deregulation. A web of controls and directives was used to determine bank behaviour, and interest-rate ceilings and officially sanctioned cartels fixed bank interest rates. By means of moral suasion, directives and reserve constraint, monetary policy operated to a considerable degree upon output and prices through the availability of bank credit.

Prosecution of monetary policy has changed in the new deregulated environment, and is now implemented almost entirely by means of interest rates via markets. This may be thought in some ways to be a strange approach to the conduct of monetary policy. Suppose that we wished to control the production of a product like motor vehicles because of externalities of one sort or another created by excessive private supply. It is unlikely that the government would enter the market, buying up stocks of cars until price rose by enough to choke off private demand – which is the nearest equivalent to open-market operations. Rather, variations would be likely to be made in the rate of (sales) tax on motor vehicles. Yet when we come to monetary policy, a tax on banking is eschewed and market actions favoured.

Of course, analogies are never precise: although this one does borrow from an earlier one by Milton Friedman.[14] In this case, however, it is almost certainly predicated on a false premise – that premise being that the authorities want to control bank output. Rather the authorities are aiming interest rates at macroeconomic variables, such as the price level, and alterations to the balance sheets of the banks emerge as a by-product of that process rather than a necessary precondition.

Central banks were interested in controlling bank output when legal restrictions and regulations made banks and their liabilities 'special'. But in a number of ways, some concomitant with the removal of direct controls and lending directives and others a result of greater competitive forces in financial markets, banks have lost much of their specialness. They have lost their monopoly of the payments mechanism. They no longer have exclusive access to the discount window of the central bank. Banks are not the sole agents or dealers in foreign exchange. In some countries, bank deposits do not have full government backing. In a number of ways the distinctions between banks and other financial institutions are now blurred where once they were sharp, while 'securitisation' has eroded many of the barriers which separated market transactions from intermediate ones.

In effect, deregulation has led to a rearrangement of the earlier monetary control triad of government, central bank and the banking system. The monetary system is evolving towards a new structure in which banks can no longer be considered part of the 'core', but must instead be grouped with the other endogenously determined parts of the economy.[15] The area of policy control shrinks to the government and to the central bank, as its market agent and money issuer.

A system in which the banking sector's responses to monetary policy have become more 'endogenised' has consequences for the use of the money aggregates as intermediate targets of monetary policy. Benjamin Friedman (1975) and Bean (1983) have demonstrated in general terms the inferiority of using an endogenous variable as an intermediate target. The basic idea is that the information contained in the observations of the endogenous variable can be exploited better by transforming it from an intermediate target into an 'information variable'. All that matters when the money supply becomes such an information variable (i.e. indicator) is whether the observed movements provide information which helps predict future values of the macroeconomic variables such as incomes and prices; the question of whether or not the money supply causes the movements in income and prices loses the importance formerly attached to it. Something along these lines seems to have happened in British policy circles during the 1980s (Artis and Lewis, 1991).

There is then the question of whether, at an abstract level, a reliance upon market actions is sufficient for monetary stabilisation. Patinkin (1961) established the minimum prescriptions which must be set in order to assure the determinacy of the price level. In a general equilibrium framework, some 'important' nominal magnitude needs to be tied down or made in inelastic supply, and since with N assets only $N - 1$ rates of return are independent, some rate of return must also be exogenously determined. Usually, in monetary theory, the nominal quantity is conceived of as the fiat issue of 'money', used as the means of payment, and the interest rate exogenously set is the zero return on money. Since the money supply is cash plus bank deposits, banks are grouped with the central bank and their deposit rate is assumed to be fixed (at zero). In the new system, the fixed rate of interest becomes that on central bank money ('cash') set at zero. The 'important' nominal quantity which must be fixed is not the quantity of money but the amount of cash or the monetary base, determined by open-market operations.[16]

This is the theory, what of practice? After all, the monetary authorities are operating in the market much like any other transactor when buying and selling financial assets. Can those other transactors eclipse the transactions made by the central banks? Dow and Saville (1988) consider there to be an element of paradox in the fact that with so small a quantitative impact in the markets the Bank of England can exert such widespread effects on interest rates with many adjustments, e.g. in base rate, happening 'automatically'. They assign a major responsibility for this to the fact that because market rates are indeterminate within a range of their 'fundamental' values, the intervention of the authorities falls on especially receptive ground. The 'steer' given by the authorities thus becomes decisive. A closely analogous piece of reasoning may be applied to the intervention by central banks in foreign exchange markets. Here intervention is often trivial in relation to daily turnover but may provide a signal that the market craves.

Still in its domestic money markets a central bank is potentially much bigger than it is in the foreign exchange market. What seems to be a pure bootstrap effect may be alternatively viewed as the conclusion of a process of learning in which the driving force is the belief that the central bank could, if it wishes, persist in operations which will force the interest rate changes. Thus, the reason why the central bank's transactions are so important is that they are conducted with cash or central-bank money, and this asset can be produced by the government at virtually zero cost and in unlimited amounts for the purpose of market purchases. For market sales, the government is limited by the amount of securities it is willing to sell. In short, the key is that the central bank has a monopoly of the issue of central bank money in the face of demand which is relatively insensitive to interest rates.

Accordingly, the authorities' power as a market transactor hinges on two factors. One is the authorities' monopoly of the manufacture of cash. The second is the continued acceptability of cash in transactions: monetary policy does not require a stable demand for base money, but it *does* require *some* demand for the monetary base. Fortunately, from this perspective, the extreme of a 'cashless' society appears a distinctly unlikely prospect, and so the scope for monetary policy remains.

8 Credibility and Time-Consistency in Monetary Policy

KEITH BLACKBURN

8.1 INTRODUCTION

There is a strong presumption that policies work better when they are more credible. Impressive support for this is not difficult to find and one case in particular has received considerable attention of late. Consider a government embarking on a programme of disinflation. Such a programme might involve either a short period of severe monetary restraint (the 'cold turkey' approach) or else a less radical policy aimed at reducing monetary growth more slowly over time (the 'gradualist' plan). The relative merits of these schemes rest ultimately upon the speed of market adjustment. Regardless of which one is adopted, the success of either in bringing down inflation at little or no cost to the real economy depends crucially upon the programme being credible. If, for whatever reason, the public is sceptical about the policy, the economy will experience the familiar output-inflation trade-off, being plunged into a recession by high inflationary expectations. Only if the public has confidence in the programme will the danger of sliding down the Phillips curve be somewhat mitigated. Moreover, to the extent that inflationary expectations partly influence the actual inflationary process, a believable disinflation has the added bonus of contributing to the disinflation itself. This much, then, can be taken for granted: the greater the credibility of an anti-inflationary monetary policy, the less are the costs associated with it and the more powerful it is in actually establishing control over prices.

The scenario just outlined forms the basis of discussion in the present chapter. Policy credibility has often been talked about in the past but it is only recently that the construction of logically consistent models has provided an invaluable check against under-developed thought and poorly-formulated concepts. This research has progressed at a very rapid pace and I can give only a selective survey of it here. Like all conceptual advances, it has made one see not only old issues in a new way but also new issues altogether.[1]

Credibility can be influenced by a number of factors but one, above all, has received most notice. This is the extent to which policy makers can form binding commitments. Let me explain. According to the rational expectations hypothesis, agents (households and firms) make the fullest use of all relevant information when forming their expectations.[2] This means that their optimal forecasting rules respond systematically to changes in the economic, political and social environment. Stated alternatively, private behavioural relationships (for example, consumption, investment and demand for money functions) 'shift' when there are changes in the decision rules that policy-makers use. This fundamental insight is credited to Lucas (1976) and respects what traditional macroeconomics ignored – namely, the interdependence between centralised policy-making and private equilibrium behaviour. The point to note is that this interdependence produces situations not unlike those in a game, for which the relevant analytical framework is supplied by the concepts and methodology of game theory.[3] In the present context, the game can be imagined as between two players – a sovereign policy-maker (the government) and an intelligent forward-looking private sector. Given this, the issue of credibility can be allied to the strategic aspects of optimal policy design in the following way.[4]

Think of a government computing an optimal policy. This policy describes how the government will act both now and in the future. Suppose that agents believe this policy when it is announced. Then it can turn out that the policy may not actually remain optimal with the passage of time: that is, the government may have a standing temptation to renege (cheat) on its announcement. This difference between *ex ante* and *ex post* optimality was first identified by Kydland and Prescott (1977) and is known as the *time inconsisten-*

cy phenomenon.[5] Technically, an optimal policy computed at date t is time inconsistent if re-optimization at date $s > t$ implies a different optimal policy. The situation which gives rise to this can be likened to a Stackelberg game between a leader (the government) and a follower (the private sector).[6] Because of the incentive to cheat, an equilibrium of this game must involve precommitment. Only by somehow binding itself to the *ex ante* policy can the government make this policy credible (which is necessary if it is to be optimal in the first place). Without such commitment, the government has the freedom to deviate from what it promises to do. Since the private sector understands this, it would ignore any such promises and the government would effectively lose its leadership role. In this case, the relevant equilibrium concept is the Nash (or discretionary) equilibrium, being the only equilibrium that is *time-consistent* (and, therefore, credible).[7] Here, then, is where the problem lies – for this Nash equilibrium is generally inferior to that which obtains under precommitment. This problem is acute. Indeed, its very pervasiveness throughout public policy makes it both profound and disturbing. Even with the best will in the world, a government cannot help but face a potential crisis in confidence if it does not have the means to make binding commitments.

How does time-inconsistency arise in optimal monetary policy? What steps might society take to alleviate the problem? In the absence of commitments, are there other mechanisms that may do the trick? What are the implications of private information? Is the case for stabilisation policy qualified in a strategic environment? And under what other circumstances might credibility problems arise? These and many more issues are discussed in the following sections.

8.2 COMMITMENT AND DISCRETION IN MONETARY POLICY

To start making matters more precise, let me outline a simple model economy. The government is concerned about two outcomes – inflation and unemployment. The weights that it assigns to the objectives for these reflect its willingness to trade-off 'inflation prevention' for 'economic stimulation'. The outcomes themselves are related by a Phillips curve: unemployment deviates from its natural rate according to inflationary forecast errors. Thus, whilst inflation is disliked, it also yields benefits (reduces unemployment) if agents do not anticipate it.[8] To achieve its objectives, the government chooses the rate of monetary growth which determines the rate of inflation. This set-up, popularised by Barro and Gordon (1983a), is generally respected as a useful framework for thinking about problems of anti-inflationary management. Its implications are devastating and may well strike a chord with the reader.

Consider, first, the case in which precommitment is feasible. Under such circumstances, it follows that planned, actual and expected inflation (monetary growth) are automatically equal. Unemployment, therefore, is always at its natural rate. Given this, the government devotes monetary policy towards reaching its inflation objective. The resulting equilibrium is one in which inflation is kept low at no cost to the real economy.

Such an outcome, however, is unsustainable in the absence of commitment. In this second case of unrestricted discretion, the government is always tempted to 'ride the Phillips curve' – that is, to fool private agents by inflicting inflationary surprises in order to reduce unemployment. But agents understand this incentive and take it into account when forming their expectations. As such, both actual and expected inflation rise until the incentive to cheat vanishes. At this point, the economy becomes stuck at the natural rate whilst experiencing an inflationary bias. This, then, is an example of the time-inconsistency problem in optimal monetary policy. Whilst a low inflation strategy is optimal *ex ante*, it is not optimal *ex post* and consequently lacks credibility if the government is free to re-optimise. The upshot is an inferior (Nash) equilibrium, involving excessive inflation but no gains in output and employment.[9]

Before considering how this problem might be resolved, it is important to appreciate why it arises in the first place. Implicit in the foregoing argument is that the government dislikes the natural rate of unemployment. If this were not the case, then there would be no gains from inflationary surprises, no time-inconsistency and no inflationary bias. Evidently, therefore, this assumption requires some justification. This is supplied by appealing to various labour-market distortions which adversely affect voluntary supply decisions. These distortions might include income taxation and unemployment insurance which, by reducing incentives to work, generate an upward bias to the natural rate. Such considerations are usually taken for granted, though a few attempts have been made to model them explicitly.[10] Unless otherwise stated, I shall always be assuming that conditions are ripe for time-inconsistency to emerge. The question which then arises is how the problem might be overcome. It is to this that I now turn.

One set of proposals is concerned with strengthening the constraints on policy-making as a means of formally restricting a government's discretion. The most drastic of such schemes is the use of explicit legislation. Perhaps by making constitutional amendments, it might be possible either to force a government to abide by a statutory code of conduct (a legally-prescribed rule for money creation?) or else make it difficult and time-consuming to alter policy decisions. Apart from the risks of being arbitrary, cumbersome and wasteful of resources, however, restrictions of this sort may well do more harm than good if they also limit the scope for useful stabilisation policy. Implementing a battery of rules and regulations certainly creates a real danger of tying the hands of a policy-maker too tightly and preventing an effective response to unforeseen contingencies. In short, such a scheme is likely to be prohibitively expensive if it is to contain a full set of contingency plans.

A more compelling idea is that of (voluntary) *partial* commitment. Whilst a government may be unable to make all its plans binding, a commitment to some might at least be feasible. If so, then the constraints imposed by these commitments may be such as to enforce other actions. The best example of this is when a government decides to operate under a gold standard or fixed-exchange-rate regime. In doing so, it has to accept some degree of discipline on monetary policy. There is evidence to suggest that this sort of external constraint had much to do with making past attempts at eliminating hyperinflations so successful.[11] Nevertheless, governments are not always willing to surrender their sovereignty over domestic policies. In addition, and more generally, a question arises as to why some commitments are easier to make than others.

Failing any explicit restrictions, problems of discretion may be alleviated in another way. This is simply to alter the objectives of monetary policy. Rogoff (1985) has established the trivial result that the more conservative is a policy-maker (that is, the more weight is given to 'inflation prevention' relative to 'economic stimulation') the less is the inflationary bias when commitments cannot be made. One way of thinking about this is to see it as a proposal to make institutional changes and set up an autonomous monetary authority. There is a widely-held view, and one with empirical support, that democratically-elected governments are more prone to inflation than independent central banks.[12] This being so, a case can be made for de-politicising monetary policy by transferring responsibility for it to an apolitical institution. Some of the issues which arise from this are taken up later on. However, it is worth nothing here that such a scheme, whilst stabilising inflation, may destabilise the real economy by weakening the incentive to use monetary stabilisation policy. This is to say that there generally exists a trade-off between conservatism and flexibility.

I have outlined a few formal ways of dealing with credibility problems. The existing literature in this area seems to suffer from two main drawbacks. The first is that the models developed so far, whilst respecting microeconomic foundations, tend to rest upon a number of specific (possibly restrictive) assumptions which cast doubt on the generality of the results obtained. The second is that no theory is given as to how social institutions might actually evolve in response to time-inconsistency. These shortcomings offer considerable scope for further research. Yet a general resolution of the problem may already exist, having to do more with informal incentives and less with formal institutional arrangements. This resolution is the subject of the following discussion.

Agents are unlikely to forget how a government has behaved in the past. On the contrary, they are liable to use their experience as a guide to what may happen in the future. The government, in turn, must respect this when making its decisions. It must take into account that the way it acts now has consequences for the way it will be judged later on. I have so far ignored such considerations by implicitly assuming that the policy game is played only once. Realistically, however, the government and private sector are engaged in a *repeated* game (otherwise known as a *supergame*). The implication of this is that the government's incentive to cheat may be removed by the threat of being punished for such behaviour, in which case the discretionary equilibrium would never arise.[13] To see how this works, consider the case in which agents revise their beliefs according to the following rule: if actual inflation has been held down in the past, then expected inflation is held down currently; otherwise, if actual inflation has ever been raised, expected inflation is raised. This is an example of an *expectations trigger mechanism*. Faced with such a scheme, the government must optimise an intertemporal trade-off between the current gains and future costs of reneging. If the costs outweigh the benefits, there is never any temptation to renege, meaning that the *ex-ante* strategy of low inflation is credible. Whether or not this is likely depends upon the severity of the punishment implied by the trigger mechanism. This is determined by both the absolute value of the penalty and the length of time during which the penalty has to be endured. It is also influenced by the government's rate of time-preference – for since the costs of cheating are incurred in the future, they matter less if the future is more heavily discounted. This leads me to a well-known result of obscure origin – known as the Folk-Theorem – which may be stated here in the following way: the precommitment equilibrium of a one-shot game can be sustained as a Nash equilibrium of a repeated game provided that the government is not 'too' myopic.

The possibility that informal incentive schemes might substitute for formal commitments was first noted by Barro and Gordon (1983b). It is a comforting prospect and one that seems destructive of the time-inconsistency problem. Having said this it is as well to look a gift-horse in the mouth. The fact of the matter is that repeated games suffer from a chronic surfeit of equilibria. Indeed, so general is the Folk-Theorem that it is almost embarrassing, there being a multiplicity of trigger mechanisms to sustain good behaviour but no systematic criterion for discriminating between them. This problem can be partly resolved by appealing to a stronger concept of equilibrium, known as *subgame perfection*. Put simply, this has the effect of shrinking the set of possibilities by ruling out equilibria that rely upon non-credible threats. Being only a partial resolution there remains the important unresolved question of how a decentralised economy happens to coordinate upon one particular outcome. This is another potentially rewarding avenue for future research.

8.3 PRIVATE INFORMATION

I have been content up to now with brushing aside considerations of risk and uncertainty. It turns out, however, that these are responsible for some of the most interesting issues in the recent literature on credibility. Central to these issues is the idea that a government with more information than a private sector might be able to use its superior knowledge strategically – that is, by taking action to reveal, conceal or even misrepresent its information, it may be able to manipulate agents' beliefs towards its advantage. One new concept to note here is that of *reputation*. This is to be interpreted in a very precise way, being formally understood to mean a time-dependent state variable that measures the private sector's probabilistic assessment of a certain trait in the government's character. For example, it might be the probability that a commitment technology exists or that the objectives of inflation and unemployment have a particular form. Whatever the case, it can be likened to an asset which the government may seek to build up, maintain or run down and which evolves over time as agents learn optimally from experience. In what follows, I discuss more fully the role of reputational forces in determining equilibrium behaviour. I also extend the dicussion to a stochastic environment and consider some strategic implications for monetary stabilisation policy when the government has private information about exogenous shocks. Underlying most of the arguments is a complicated chain of reasoning that drives the decision-making process. In the first place, whilst agents may be ill-informed about certain matters, they will at least understand the government's incentive structure relating to information disclosure. As such, they will interpret the government's actions with some caution when forming their beliefs. This, in turn, must be respected by the government when making its decisions at the outset. And the whole process is inherently dynamic, with agents updating their beiefs as new information becomes available and the government having to solve a complex intertemporal optimisation problem. It is a great credit to the literature that all of this has been analysed with a striking degree of precision and completeness.

Backus and Driffill (1985) and Barro (1986) consider the following scenario. There are two types of government which differ according to their inflationary expectations: a type-1 (hard or strong) that always plays low inflation and a type-2 (weak or soft) that is tempted to create inflationary surprises. The private sector knows about these types but is uncertain which type it is actually facing. Under such circumstances, the type-2 has an incentive to conceal its identity for some time by imitating a type-1 (that is, by playing low inflation). This is because, by raising inflation, the type-2 reveals its true character and the economy ends up in the inferior discretionary equilibrium thereafter. By masquerading as a type-1, however, it can establish a reputation for itself until such time as this is not longer profitable. What happens, then, is that the type-2 government chooses its best strategy, given agents' beliefs and the effect of its current behaviour on future reputation. Agents, in turn, extract information about the government's identity by watching what it does, knowing full well that what they do observe may be nothing more than the dissembling actions of an imposter. Over time, new information is processed and beliefs are revised according to an optimal learning rule. In this set-up, therefore, reputation is understood to be the probability that the government is a type-1. The equilibrium is a *pooling* equilibrium, meaning one in which the actions of a government do not reveal its identity. The properties of this equilibrium are as follows.

For some period at the start of the game (e.g. when the government takes office), a type-2 government is sure to imitate a type-1. Throughout this period, reputation remains constant at its initial value since no information is conveyed by monetary policy which is certain to be the same for both types of government. The outcome here resembles that under precommitment. Following this, there is a period during which the type-2 is indifferent between masquerading and inflating. Both low and high inflation are now possible so that expected inflation (a probability-weighted average of the two) is raised to some intermediate value between these. Thus, if inflation turns out to be low, then reputation is enhanced but the economy experiences a recession; conversely, if inflation turns out to be high, there is a temporary boom but reputation is blown thereafter. Eventually, the type-2 is sure to inflate as the short-run gains from doing so more than compensate the subsequent costs of throwing away its goodwill.[15]

This framework has much to commend it. First and foremost, is the way that it comes to grips with the concept of reputation which, up to now, has not been well-defined in discussions of macroeconomic policy. Second are its implications for inflation and unemployment, the behaviour of which invites one to think of strategically-induced business cycles. And third are the insights which it yields into why policy-makers may wish to remain anonymous and why, as a consequence, monetary policy might be shrouded in secrecy. (The notion of a 'monetary mystique' is to start occupying a good deal of attention from here on.) There are, of course, a few questions outstanding:

1. What, for instance, is responsible for the initial beliefs of the private sector?
2. Are agents really so unforgiving that a government is never able to recapture a lost reputation?
3. Can one seriously believe that a period may exist during which monetary policy is determined by chance?
4. Might it not be in the interests of a type-1 government to somehow distinguish itself from a type-2?

The first of these questions remains unresolved, being of some concern given the importance of agents' priors in influencing how events unfold. The second and third questions are more specific to the assumption of only two types of government and Rogoff (1987a, b) has shown that extending the model to incorporate a continuum of types does little to alter the general conclusions of the analysis. The fourth question is possibly the most interesting and can be answered in the following way.

It is not just a type-2 government that suffers from being stuck with a bad reputation. A type-1 also loses out because of the recession which emerges when inflationary expectations remain high. Yet in order to establish a good reputation, each type is motivated to act very differently: while a high-inflation type wants to conceal its identity, a low-inflation type wants its identity to be known. It is conceivable, therefore, that the latter might take steps to signal its true character and separate itself from an impostor. For example, it may try to set inflation so low that imitating this is not profitable for a type-2. If successful, then observation of this inflation rate would signal a type-1 to be present whilst observation of anything other would signal a type-2. This leads to the notion of a *separating* equilibrium, meaning one in which the actions of a government are sufficient to reveal its identity. Driffill (1987) and Vickers (1986) have looked into this and come out with the following conclusions: whichever equilibrium (pooling or separating) obtains depends upon the extent to which the preferences of different government types diverge. In particular, pooling turns out to be more likely for relatively dissimilar types.[16] The reason for this is that a greater divergence between preferences implies greater potential gains for a type-2 if it can successfully masquerade as a type-1. As such, it is more difficult for the type-1 to find a rate of inflation that the type-2 has no incentive to mimic. Be this as it may, it is still possible to argue that the chances of pooling are somewhat overstated. A government does not have to rely solely upon the actual monetary policy that it implements in order to signal its inflationary intentions. It has other means as well for doing this which may also be more powerful and less restrictive. Consider, for example, the eagerness of politicians to engage in public debate and to confront their opponents with what they believe in. Consider, also, how a government's stand on a whole range of issues might be taken as indicative of its attitude towards economic objectives. And in thinking of these, never underestimate the importance that may be given to a government's ideological commitment.

Now let me look briefly at events in a stochastic economy. The issue of most concern here is that of optimal stabilisation policy. I have already mentioned the analysis of Rogoff (1985) which yields the conclusion that a trade-off exists between conservatism and flexibility. Of more interest, perhaps, is the following idea due to Canzoneri (1985). Behind this lies the assumption that a government (the character of which is known) has private information and exogenous shocks. Optimal monetary policy now displays an 'innovation-contingent' response, reflecting a stabilising feedback on random disturbances. Because of the informational asymmetry, agents face the problem of how to interpret observed changes in monetary growth. Such changes can come about for two reasons – the dynamic inconsistency of optimal policy and the government's incentive to respond to unforeseen contingencies. Given that neither of these is fully known to agents, the government has the chance of disguising one as the other. In particular, it could claim that a strategic monetary expansion was an act of stabilisation. Three implications of this are as follows:

(i) an apparently well-behaved government may not be so nice after all since there is always the risk that it has exploited its informational advances;
(ii) even a government that is well-behaved is faced with the problem that a genuine attempt at stabilisation may be misconstrued as an attempt to cheat;
(iii) because of all this, the task of designing suitable trigger mechanisms is made more complicated.[17]

One other contribution is also worth noting, if only because it goes some way towards generalisation. Driffill (1987) has studied the case where a government has private information about not only its character but also a control error in the setting of monetary policy. This control error means that the actual (realised) rate of inflation may differ from the government's desired (planned) rate of inflation. Under such circumstances, the reputational forces that induce a type-2 government to imitate a type-1 are weakened. The reason is that agents always assign some probability that a high rate of inflation is due to the imprecise control technology of a type-1 (i.e. the error in setting monetary policy). Thus, the type-2 stands a better chance of inflating without blowing its disguise.

What is one to conclude about the research surveyed in this section? A few critical observations are worth making first. Most obvious, perhaps is that the results obtained are extremely sensitive to apparently minor alterations in the information structure. The lesson, so it seems, is that almost anything can happen in a world of uncertainty. Next is that the issues involved here, to date, been formally analysed in only the very simplest of models. As such, there is a further question of generality to be raised. Finally, those matters which arise because of stochastic uncertainty seem rather unconvincing. Do policy-makers really have the edge over agents in identifying cyclical disturbances? And even if they do, what of the future when data eventually becomes available?[18] In spite of these remarks, it is difficult not to be impressed by this research which undoubtedly marks a fundamental breakthrough in understanding problems of credibility. Its strength lies not just in the questions that it faces but in the standards that it sets for answering these questions. By emphasising the role of information, and by seeking to model this role explicitly, it has led to conclusions more interesting and exciting than one could ever have anticipated beforehand. The theme that runs throughout these conclusions – secrecy in centralised decision-making – will continue to be present in much of the discussion that follows.

8.4 MONETARY POLITICS

Public policy is as much a part of politics as it is of economics. Decisions about it are reached through political institutions, whose job it is to aggregate the diversity of individual preferences into collective government action. In a representative democracy, this process of aggregation takes place via the electoral system: citizens indicate their preferences by voting for political candidates in regular, periodic elections. Considerable research is now being conducted into the role played by politics in determining credibility. Part of this research (I discuss another branch of it below) is related to the early work by Nordhaus (1975) and others on the theory of the political business cycle. This theory purported to show that democratically-elected governments are prone to use economic policy as a means of securing electoral gains. In doing so, they generate cycles in the economy that are synchronised with the timing of elections. The story goes something as follows: Prior to an election, a government expands the economy in order to reduce unemployment. Voters observe this but fail to realise the inflationary consequences. After the election, the government responds to the inflationary pressures by reversing its pre-election expansionary policies. Thus, given that this occurs at every election, cycles in inflation and unemployment are created. The assumptions behind this theory are questionable to say the least. They amount to an implausible description of government- and voter-behaviour which the new body of research redresses in ways that I outline below. References to note are Alesina (1987a,b), Alesina and Cukierman (1988), Alesina and Spear (1987), Rogoff (1987b), and Rogoff and Silbert (1988). As will become apparent, the relevance of all this for the issue of credibility stems basically from a difference between the pre- and post-election decision problems that a government confronts.[19]

The most objectionable assumption in the past was that of a myopic electorate which failed to realise the inflationary consequences of a pre-election boom. Indeed, so gullible were voters supposed to be in conventional models that governments, so it seemed, could systematically fool them into thinking that the good times before elections were there to stay. The new approach, by contrast, assumes voters who are rational and who are sure to see through an electioneering strategy. As a result, any electoral cycles that now manifest must be interpreted quite differently from those of old.

Another step forward has been the modelling of voters' preferences over rival political parties. This was ignored until recently, being further evidence of the lack of respect given to voters' behaviour. Nowadays, however, it is common to assume that decisions about voting are reached in much the same way as decisions about any risky prospect – namely, by a comparison of expected utilities under each of the uncertain outcomes. Thus, at least for those (floating) voters who have no strong political allegiance (and who are responsible for determining an election outcome), the relevant criterion is to vote for the political party, the policies of which are expected to yield the highest future stream of utility.

This brings me finally to the question of what it is that political parties are trying to achieve. The traditional approach here was to appeal to the Median Voter Theorem of Downs (1957). According to this, politicians seek power for power's own sake and not because it enables them to pursue other objectives. Their overriding concern, therefore, is to maximise their chances of election by maximising the number of votes cast for them. To do this, they tailor their policies towards those voters in the middle of the ideological spectrum who are open to capture by all types of political party. In a two-party system, and under certain conditions, the upshot of this is that the policies of parties will tend to converge as an election draws near, enabling the preferences of the median voter (the moderate majority) to be satisfied. There is some merit to this story and it is still appealed to widely.[20] To a large extent, however, it has been replaced by a more partisan view of economic policy. The presumption now is that different political parties have different objectives (or ideologies) that reflect the preferences of a 'core' set of voters to whom each party appeals.[21] Moreover, achieving these objectives is the reason why a party wants to gain office: power is now a means to an end and not an end in itself. This means that, in general, a trade-off exists between that policy which is closest to a party's ideology (the most preferred course of action) and that policy which maximises its chances of election. It also implies that the only credible pre-election announcement about a post-election policy is one that is consistent with a party's ideology: for once the party gains office, it is sure to implement its most-preferred strategy.

Evidently, there is no longer any scope for either policy convergence or electioneering behaviour. Or is there? To see how such events might now arise, the reader may find it useful to think in terms of the following example that is borrowed from the previous section. In this, the distinction between type-1 and type-2 policy-makers is understood to mean a distinction between two political parties (conservatives or Republicans and socialists or Democrats), each of which has its own ideology such that the former is more (less) averse to inflation (unemployment) than the latter. At the date of an election, uncertainty about which party will be elected means that expected inflation is a probability-weighted average of the rates of inflation that these parties will implement. Thus, if a type-1 (type-2) is elected, the economy experiences a temporary recession (boom) so that economic fluctuations are synchronised with the dates of election. This provides the clue about how policy convergence might arise: each party has an incentive to eliminate these fluctuations by coordinating with its rival on a common policy. And whilst each party is tempted to defect from this policy once it is elected, trigger mechanisms of the sort outlined earlier (in this case, the threat by each party not to cooperate at the next election) might remove this temptation. Notice, however, that policy convergence here is a *response to*, not a cause of, electoral cycles. To motivate consensual policies from electioneering behaviour, it is necessary to introduce imperfect information. Suppose, for instance, that voters are aware of a type-1's ideology but uncertain of the inflationary objectives of a type-2. Then the latter might be able to exploit this ignorance and move its policies close to those of the former. It may even be tempted to saddle itself with an imprecise control technology (i.e. to adopt a procedure for controlling the money supply which is subject to error) in order to make it more difficult for voters to figure out its preferences from its actions. All this sounds rather familiar but the new element, of course, is the idea that incentives to conceal information are allied to political considerations.

I indicated earlier that the literature on credibility and politics has another aspect to it, quite separate from the research discussed so far. This second line of inquiry goes more deeply into the decision-making process, paying more than merely lip-service to the notion that economic policy is best understood as a product of political bargaining. The basic contention is that any policy outcome should be seen as a consequence of pressures exerted by individuals and groups with conflicts of interest that are only partly reconciled by the existing system of power relationships.[22] Amongst those groups which influence monetary policy, the two most obvious are central bank officials and government representatives.[23] Conflicts between these may arise for a number of reasons, many of which have to do with inflation. It is commonly alleged that governments, especially, have a natural tendency towards monetary expansion. This may reflect such motives as the pursuit of short-run electoral gains from economic stimulation, the desire to reduce debt-service payments and the incentive to raise revenue by means of the inflation tax. Central bankers, on the other hand, being detached from such motives, and for other reasons as well, are normally regarded as being relatively conservative and paying greater respect to longer-run considerations, even if these imply policies that are politically unpopular in the short run.[24] It is possible, therefore, to view decisions about monetary policy as reflecting a compromise between advocates of 'economic stimulation' and advocates of 'inflation prevention'. Moreover, this compromise may shift over time as changes take place in the political composition of each group and the power relationships between them. Nothing in these conclusions is fundamentally altered by the degree of monetary autonomy. Central banks which seek to be free of governmental influence can never actually enjoy complete political autonomy. After all, it is the government (the political administration or congress) which establishes a bank's independence in the first place and which can take this independence away should the bank refuse to make at least some concessions on matters over which the government disagrees.[25] In general, therefore, the objectives of monetary policy can be seen as being subject to continual agitation by a wide range of political interests that vent themselves through the process of collective decision-making.

The verdict just reached does more than merely instance why agents may be imperfectly informed about monetary objectives. It also suggests that a monetary authority itself, whilst knowing its current preferences, may be somewhat uncertain of these in the future. Several implications of this have been revealed by Cukierman and Meltzer (1986a,b,c) who model the arguments above in terms of a serially-correlated stochastic process for the trade-off between 'inflation prevention' and 'economic stimulation'. Agents are never sure of this trade-off and, instead, draw inferences about it from observations of past inflation. These inferences are noisy because inflation fluctuations reflect transitory control errors in the setting of monetary policy as well as persistent shifts in preferences. For the same reason, it is optimal for agents to adjust their expected inflation only partially to changes in actual inflation. The monetary authority, meanwhile, is aware of all this but lacks information about its future objectives. It must predict these, however, because what it does currently affects what it can do in the future by affecting the private sector's future inflationary expectations.

One prediction of this framework is that when policy-makers become less concerned with 'inflation prevention' (for example, the 1960s and early 1970s), the sluggishness in expectations adjustment offers scope for monetary policy to reduce unemployment; conversely, periods characterised by conservative policy-makers (for example, the 1980s) are likely to display the features of a recession. Credibility here is defined as the speed with which the public realises that a shift in preferences has occurred. This turns out to be a decreasing function of the variance of monetary control errors, and the greater the precision of control procedures, the less are the costs of disinflation. A noisier control technolgy tends to complement a shift towards 'economic stimulation' by slowing down agents' recognition of this shift. Here, then, lies another explanation for why monetary objectives may be shrouded in secrecy: by keeping them ambiguous, the policy-maker enjoys greater flexibility in the timing of inflationary surprises.

Several other results emerge from this framework but let me turn, instead, to a few issues that are left outstanding. All of these have to do with the shifts that may occur in policy-makers' preferences. The first point to note is that such shifts are often associated with other important developments, not least amongst which are developments in economic theories and changes in the *operating procedures* of monetary policy. Consider, for example, the predominant concern with full employment in the 1960s, the neo-Keynesian consensus at that time and the corresponding use of interest rates as the main instrument of monetary policy; compare this with the growing concern over inflation throughout the 1970s, the accompanying increase in monetarist research activity and the eventual adoption of monetary targets at the beginning of the 1980s. A second observation is that changes in objectives are unlikely to arise from the pressures exerted by any single individual or group. Rather they are likely to reflect a widespread shift of opinion throughout the policy-making hierarchy. If so, then they would surely be more apparent to the public than the foregoing analysis implies. Third, and finally, changes in preferences do not just occur exogenously but often amount to an endogenous response to changes in economic conditions. Consider, again, the rising inflation during the 1970s and the subsequent shift towards anti-inflation objectives.

All this suggests considerable scope for further research. This would involve specifying more fully the channels of influence on monetary objectives and the bargaining process that is used to solve the problem of whose preferences to satisfy and to what extent. As for the link between politics and secrecy, one particular line of inquiry immediately comes to mind. This has to do with the issue of monetary independence and the theory of bureaucracy in central banking.[26] Briefly, this theory contends that central bank behaviour is best understood by seeing central banks as political institutions that are mainly concerned with their own self-esteem and self-preservation. To achieve these objectives, they are motivated to find ways of protecting themselves from outside interference and critical investigation. By securing such immunity, they are able to publish selective pieces of information which magnify their successes and minimise their failures. This is all familiar to long-term observers of central bank practice who have frequently argued that such institutions have a natural propensity to engage in covert methods of operation and deliberately create a 'monetary mystique'.[27]

The degree of monetary independence has much to do with the final issue that I consider. Any survey of this sort can never be complete without attending to the fiscal, as well as monetary, aspects of an overall macroeconomic programme. The main reason for this is as follows.[28] Fiscal policy reflects decisions about public expenditures, taxes and transfers which can normally be regarded as being under the close supervision of democratically-elected government. Monetary policy, however, might be the responsibility of a quite separate institution – an autonomous central bank. If so, then a real problem of policy coordination exists, the resolution of which is crucial for giving credence to a programme's coherence. The source of coordination (and credibility) problems lies in the interactions between monetary and fiscal policies summarised by the government's budget constraint. By integrating this constraint forward in time one obtains a solvency condition which, loosely translated, states that the government cannot live beyond its means. This condition imposes severe restrictions on the viability of a non-inflationary financial policy. Such a policy, being meant to avoid the monetisation of fiscal deficits, requires the issue of government debt which stores up future outlays in the form of interest payments. If the government is to remain solvent without resorting to monetisation, it has to run an appropriate stream of budget surpluses – otherwise, it would not be able to pay off its outstanding debt. (The government could, of course, repudiate its debt but then no debt would be held if agents were to anticipate this.) In the absence of a fiscal correction, agents are sent a clear signal of the inflationary consequences of debt-financing: for the only way to ensure a non-explosive path for government debt is to switch over to a money financing policy.

With the foregoing in mind, it is easy to see how the separation of monetary and fiscal management can lead to credibility problems. Suppose, for the reasons discussed earlier, that the central bank is keen to pursue a tight monetary policy whilst the governmetn wants to implement an expansionary fiscal policy. Then the composite macroeconomic programme is not credible because it is simply not feasible. One policy has to 'give way' to the other and it matters considerably for inflation which of them does so: if concessions are made on the fiscal side, the economy is kept under a tight monetary rein; otherwise, the prospect of persistent fiscal deficits must be met by monetisation. Such coordination problems create uncertainty for agents and invite speculation over how and when the conflict between fiscal and monetary policies will be resolved. They have been used to explain both recent and not-so-recent episodes of anti-inflationary management.[29] In short, then, the credibility of monetary policy does not depend upon monetary policy alone but also upon the macroeconomic programme in its entirety.

8.5 CONCLUSION

In this chapter I have given a fairly broad and critical survey of the literature on credibility and time-consistency in monetary policy. This literature has been one of the most exciting developments in monetary economics in recent years. Empirical work in the area is still very much in its infancy. Progress on this is probably the most important of all future research programmes.

9 International Monetary Policy Coordination

R. C. BLADEN-HOVELL

9.1 INTRODUCTION

A conspicuous feature of the post-war period has been the sustained tendency for the international economy to become increasingly interdependent. The general reduction in trade barriers and the almost complete removal of capital controls have resulted in highly integrated production activities, trade and financial flows with dramatic consequences for domestic-demand management. Persistent trade imbalances together with recent large-scale fluctuations of the major trading currencies have highlighted the international character of the linkages between domestic policy implementation and the economic performance of the main industrial nations, and many would now argue that these international links have become so strong as to impose severe limits on the degree of control and the scope for independent policy action on the part of individual governments.

These considerations became particularly acute for the USA by the mid-1980s. The administration of the time identified the increasingly serious misalignment of the dollar as arising, at least in part, from the uncoordinated nature of the monetary and fiscal policies being pursued throughout the world. The principal concern was that either currency speculation in the foreign-exchange market or a sudden loss of confidence in the dollar would trigger a so-called 'hard landing' in which a rapid fall in the dollar and a sharp rise in US interest rates, would precipitate a major global recession. These fears received formal recognition in the Plaza accord signed in September 1985, where it was agreed that a gradual decline in the dollar would be achieved by coordinating the monetary policy actions of the Group of Seven (G-7) nations, That coordination itself was seen as an important component of this policy response was further demonstrated by the fact that each subsequent economic summit has taken the opportunity to reaffirm its commitment to coordinated policy action. For example, the G-7 meeting in January 1991 reasserted a commitment to monetary cooperation: countries promised to strengthen cooperation and to monitor developments in exchange markets. By the beginning of the 1990s, therefore, international policy coordination appeared to be established as a backcloth against which domestic demand management would be set.

These practical policy considerations have stimulated an extensive theoretical and applied literature. Three strands of analysis are commonly identified in this literature. The first is based upon the strategic, or game-theoretic, treatment of policy formation within the international economy. Here a number of authors, most notably Hamada (1974, 1976, 1979, 1985), Miller and Salmon (1985) and Currie and Levine (1985) have all drawn attention to the possibility that policy spill-over effects and the associated externalities derived from non-cooperative behaviour, might lead to solutions that are inferior to those generated when all parties act cooperatively.[1] Such spill-over effects arise for a variety of reasons including the trade and financial links that transmit the effects of policy-induced disturbances from abroad on to key macroeconomic variables within the domestic economy. In this context, policy coordination is simply identified with the vehicle which internalises these externalities within the decision-making machinery of individual nations. The second strand examines how large these gains might be. This empirical work, has examined the performance of alternate strategies in the policy game. To anticipate the subsequent discussion, however, the general finding of this and many other empirical studies, is that the potential gains from coordination may be quite small.

By comparison, the third strand is of a more speculative nature and concerns recent proposals for possible reform of the international monetary system. Three key proposals are usually considered. These correspond to the symmetric gold standard of

McKinnon (1984, 1988); the extended target zone proposal of Williamson (1985) and Miller and Williamson (1988) and, finally, the proposal by Artis and Ostry (1986) which favours the use of an episodic form of coordination based around a regulator economic summit. In each case the coordinating framework is designed around a set of mutually agreed 'rules of the game' that establish the priorities and appropriate response of policy-makers in each country.

This chapter reviews this literature and considers its relevance for real-world policy coordination. Specific proposals for reform of the international monetary system are largely ignored in the survey except insofar as they relate explicitly to the theoretical or empirical literature, but the interested reader is referred to Artis (1989) for further detail. The remainder of the chapter is organised in four main sections. Section 9.2 examines the conventional wisdom adduced for policy coordination within a static, one-period framework. Here the focus is firmly centred upon the potential need for coordination where policy targets and instruments conflict. This naturally leads to a discussion of the strategic issues relating to coordination and raised initially by authors such as Hamada. Dynamic and expectational issues are considered subsequently in section 9.3 where particular attention is directed towards the problem of time-inconsistency and the role of reputation in international policy coordination. The major finding here is that, in the absence of any internationally binding legal arrangement, cooperation without reputation may be counter-productive insofar as it relaxes the constraint on the monetary authorities' ability to renege on policy commitments. The empirical evidence adduced to policy coordination is examined in section 9.4. As noted previously, the general conclusion of this section is that the gains from coordination seem to be quite small. Finally, the chapter is completed by a summary of the main results and conclusions.

9.2 POLICY COORDINATION IN A STATIC FRAMEWORK

Broadly defined, international policy coordination occurs when a group of nations, each recognising the importance of their economic linkages, undertake to modify their domestic-demand-management policies in what is intended to be a mutually beneficial manner. In this context coordination goes far beyond the degree of cooperation that might be implied, for example, in normal levels of assistance or transfers of information between governments. Each of these activities might form a component of any successful coordination package but does not on its own constitute coordination in the generally accepted sense of the word. Instead coordination requires both a willingness and an ability on the part of sovereign states to amend their existing demand-management policies and, where necessary, to adopt new policy proposals for reasons other than their own immediate well-being. The arguments in favour of policy-coordination, therefore, are essentially those based upon the need to assess policy performance from a global perspective rather than from the viewpoint of an individual nation.

Expressed in this way the basic rationale for coordination becomes clear. Where the economic behaviour in individual countries is interdependent, domestic-policy formation undertaken independently by one nation imposes significant spill-over effects upon the performance of other countries. These policy spill-over effects of externalities, together with any feedback they may provoke, represent a powerful means by which the economic performance of individual nations may be adveresely affected. A simple example of such interaction may be observed in policy-induced movements of the exchange rate. If the dollar appreciates as a result of fiscal policy in the USA this implies that all other exchange rates must depreciate with respect to the dollar. Other things remaining equal this depreciation will adversely affect the inflation prospects for the rest of the world. By internalising these externalities within the decision-making process of individual countries, policy coordination simply provides a vehicle whereby the world economy can be moved closer towards an optimal outcome.

The existence of spill-over effects has, of course, long been recognised in international economics. Indeed the small-country assumption so often invoked in open-economy macroeconomics is essentially designed in order to avoid the complications that such spill-overs introduce. Where all countries are small, the policy actions undertaken by any one will have no effect whatsoever upon the economic performance of any other. Only with the introduction of a large country together with the prospect that individual behaviour will influence the international terms of trade, does it become necessary to consider the role that spill-overs may play in the transmission of policy effects around the world.

Spill-over effects may occur through a variety of channels. The most obvious involves the trade balance: expansionary monetary or fiscal policy in one country benefits another country's exports and thereby provides a demand stimulus for the rest of the world. Moreover, in a world where capital is internationally mobile and exchange rates are fixed, a monetary expansion in one country will be transmitted positively via the capital account as well. Furthermore, this second channel will only be completely eliminated under flexible exchange rates provided that wages and prices are completely free to vary in both countries. In the absence of such wage and price variability, flexible exchange rates raise the prospect that monetary disturbances will be transmitted negatively throughout the world, a monetary expansion at home requiring a real depreciation of the exchange rate and a consequent fall in exports by the rest of the world.

Interdependence also takes the form of binding structural relationships between nations. For the world as a whole, for example, the sum of each country's balance of payments must be equal to zero.[2] As a result it is clearly impossible for all countries to run a balance-of-payments deficit (surplus) simultaneously even though all may wish to do so. At least one country must be prepared to accept an offsetting surplus (deficit) position and part of the global macroeconomic adjustment process will occur to ensure that this condition holds at all times. In the absence of coordination, however, this requirement will usually imply that in a world of N countries, only $N - 1$ can ever succeed in achieving their independently determined balance-of-payments target: the position of the remaining country being given by the accounting condition that, at the global level, these targets must sum to zero.[3]

A corollary to the problem of target compatibility is the issue of instrument redundancy. Even if all countries manage to specify their balance-of-payments target in a consistent manner – and few actually do – only $N - 1$ of them would need to assign a policy instrument to the target in order for all of them to achieve their individual objective, the balance of payments for the residual country again being taken care of by the global accounting identity. From a global perspective this implies that there remains an additional degree of freedom within the system insofar as one country can safely afford to reassign its policy instrument away from the balance of payments towards some other policy objective.[4] Just what this additional objective should be and whose instrument should be directed towards it is, of course, a difficult question. A number of possible responses, however, are outlined in section 9.4.

These illustrations highlight how interdependence between nations will serve to transmit policy effects around the world. Based upon this, Cooper (1984, 1985) offers three reasons why coordination is likely to provide a superior outcome to that obtained when policy is set independently:

1. where policy is set independently, greater interdependence will result in each country's balance of payments being influenced by an increasing number of disturbances.[5] This, Cooper argues, is likely to divert the objective of policy away from domestic targets towards restoration of the external account;
2. even if domestic considerations remain the prime objective, policy performance is still likely to deteriorate because the speed with which the domestic authorities can achieve these objectives declines as interdependence increases.
3. Cooper notes that the likelihood of retaliatory action becomes stronger as interdependence increases and, as is well-known, retaliation can lead to situations where all countries are worse off.

The alternative scenario that Cooper suggests requires that some element of centralised decision-making occur between countries. This has a dual purpose. Perhaps most importantly, by providing a forum through which policy conflict may be resolved, centralised decision-making effectively places an upper limit on the extent to which adverse policy repercussions can occur. In addition coordination provides a means whereby the burden of adjustment can be assessed and more equitably distributed between nations, thereby reducing the likelihood that nations will resort to retaliatory policy action.

Concern with the adverse effects of policy conflict arising from inconsistent objectives and the appropriate assignment of policy instruments in the international economy motivated much of the early work on policy coordination. Building upon work originally undertaken by Mundell (1968), for example, Swoboda and Dornbusch (1973) found it useful to distinguish between the coordination of objectives from those arrangements involving a coordination in the use of instruments. Their essential point can be easily seen with the aid of Figures 9.1 and 9.2.

Here the schedules Y^*_a and Y_b that are compatible with the continuation of international balance in each country. For simplicity, each schedule is drawn independent of the level of output in the other country. Finally, the schedule *TT* is the locus of points showing combinations of Y_a and Y_b that will preserve balance-of-payments equilibrium between the two countries. With capital flows given in the model, this schedule will be upward-sloping reflecting the fact that an increase in Y_a will adversely affect the balance of payments for the home country and require that Y_b be increased for overall balance-of-payments equilibrium to be restored.

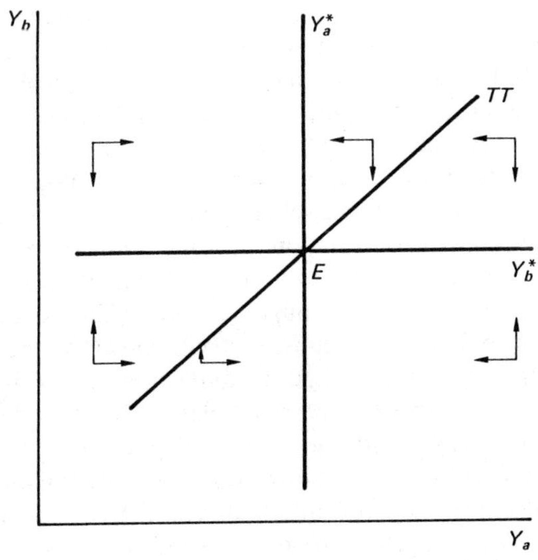

FIGURE 9.1 Target and instrument conflict

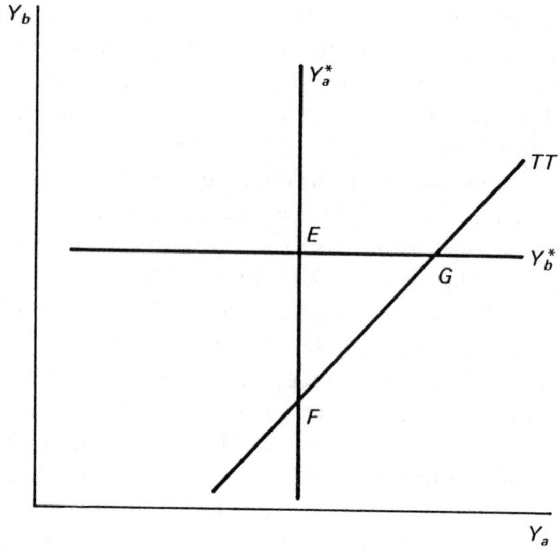

FIGURE 9.2 Target and instrument conflict

Within this framework it is comparatively straightforward to determine the nature of the policy problem that each country might face. At points above and to the left of *TT*, for example, country *A* (*B*) experiences a balance-of-payments surplus (deficit); at points below *TT* it experiences a deficit (surplus). At points below Y^*_a (Y^*_b), country *A* (*B*) experiences less than full employment; at points above they experience inflation. Where all policy objectives are consistent, the scheules intersect at a single point, *E* in Figure 9.1. In this situation coordination between the two countries is only desirable insofar as it will enable each country to attain its respective target through an appropriate use of demand-management policy. Such an assignment, shown by the arrows in the diagram, might occur when the authorities direct their expenditure policies towards the internal balance. Jointly achieving this will simultaneously satisfy the balance of payments.

Additional problems arise, however, if the internal and external balance schedules do not intersect uniquely. The outcome is shown in Figure 9.2. Here the region *EFG* corresponds to a zone of policy conflict within which no possible assignment of policy instruments will reconcile the objectives of the two countries. In the absence of additional instruments being available the only recourse would be for the governments concerned to revise the policy objectives in a mutually agreeable manner.[6]

Although useful in many respects, the preceding analysis suffers from a number of limitations, the most important of which are its failure to provide any role for optimising behaviour on the part of the authorities or any indication of the way that policy-makers will trade-off their performance on one objective against their performance elsewhere in the economy. As a result, recent analysis has tended to emphasise an alternative, strategic approach to the policy problem in the interdependent world.

The original work in this area, conducted by Hamada (1976), examines the potential gains accruing to countries which may choose whether or not to cooperate with one another. Hamada's approach is to cast the problem in the form of a stylised game played by nations, in which each country manipulates the value of its own policy instruments in order to maximise its own welfare. Welfare itself is clearly defined in terms of the policy objectives for each country. The approach is illustrated in Figures 9.3 and 9.4 for the case of a two-country game.

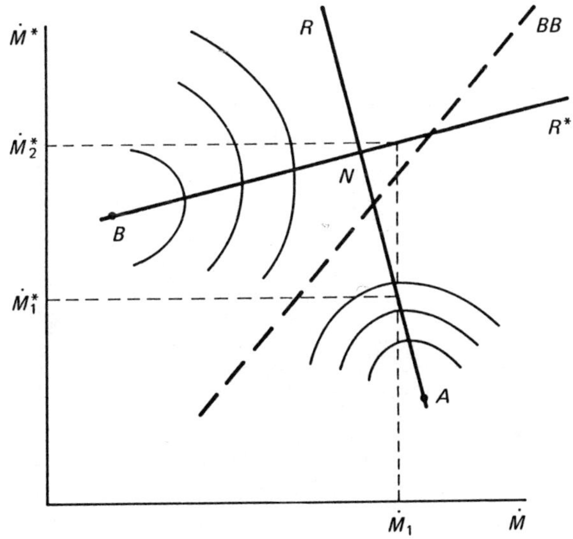

FIGURE 9.3 The gains from cooperation and leadership

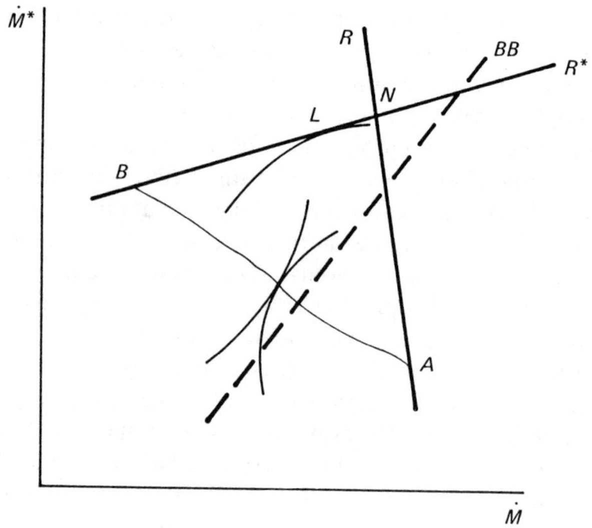

FIGURE 9.4 The gains from cooperation and leadership

Here the policy instruments of the two countries are expressed in terms of their respective monetary growth rates, M and M^*. The exchange rate is assumed fixed. The authorities' preferences – represented by indifference curves defined in terms of the underlying policy objectives for, say, unemployment, inflation and the balance of payments – are shown as the set of concentric schedules centred on points A and B. These positions are assumed to coincide with the bliss points on the social-welfare function for country I and II respectively. Movements away from these positions, in any direction, will therefore correspond to lower levels of welfare for the country concerned, as perceived by their respective governments.

From this we may easily derive the policy-reaction functions, R and R^* for the two countries. These functions show the optimal policy setting for each country on the assumption that the policy stance for the other country will remain unchanged. For the home country this is constructed as the locus of points representing the set of horizontal tangency positions on the home country's utility map; for the foreign country the reaction function is drawn as the locus of vertical tangency positions. For any given level of monetary expansion by the foreign(home) country, the location of the reaction function will correspond to the highest level of welfare attainable by the home(foreign) country. Finally, the schedule *BB* represents the combinations of M and M^* that are consistent with balance-of-payments equilibrium between the two countries. Positions above and to the left of this schedule correspond to a situation of payments surplus for country I; positions below and the right represent a balance-of-payments deficit.

Consider first a situation where the two countries act independently, each setting the value of its own instrument in order to maximise welfare on the assumption that policy in the other country will remain unchanged. The solution would be the non-cooperative, or Nash equilibrium, N, shown in Figure 9.3. The result may be obtained in an iterative manner. Suppose that foreign monetary growth is $\dot{M}^*_1$. Given this the highest level of welfare for the home country will be found at position E_1 and the optimal growth for domestic monetary aggregates will be $\dot{M}_1$. However, faced with domestic monetary growth $\dot{M}_1$, will act in an analogous manner and respond by choosing a new value for monetary growth, $\dot{M}^*_2$, that maximises welfare at E_2 the whole process continuing until it converges upon point N.

Figure 9.4 can be used in order to illustrate two other outcomes to the policy game. The first corresponds to the cooperative or Pareto-efficient solution which is found at points along the contract curve *AB*. The second corresponds to a leadership solution whereby one country sets the value of its own policy instrument in order to obtain a welfare-maximising position on the other country's reaction function. With the home country as leader such a solution would occur at L.

A comparison of these results highlights three important considerations:

1. within a static, one-priced framework, non-cooperative behaviour is sub-optimal with no single country being able to improve the situation for itself by means of an isolated change in policy. Moreover, if the countries involved have a preference for a temporary balance-of-payments surplus, the resulting non-cooperative solution will exhibit a recessionary bias;[7]
2. the leadership solution for the model is usually favourable to the leader but unfavourable for the follower and, as a result,

the game would collapse as neither country would be willing to play in the role of follower;

3. it is clear from Figure 9.4 that cooperation does not necessarily imply an expansionary bias.[8] Instead the precise nature of the optimal cooperative solution will depend upon three factors: the objectives of the policy-makers; the nature of the disturbances affecting the system and, finally, the nature of the transmission mechanism within the international economy. Each of these factors is considered in greater detail below.

Differences in the objectives between countries affect the particular policy actions that nations undertake but leave unchanged the basic principle that there are gains from coordination. Within Europe, for example, Germany may be more inflation-adverse than, say, Italy, but both countries can produce lower inflation rates by cooperating than they would by pursuing policy actions independently. In a similar fashion, the type of cooperative response will also depend upon the nature of the disturbances that affect the system; disturbances that involve a common inflationary or deflationary shock calling for a uniform response, a switch in demand between the coordinating countries requiring an asymmetric response.

In certain respects it is tempting to believe that the general principle of gains from coordination will remain robust independent of the nature of transmission mechanism. Certainly such a view would seem to accord with the results of early work in this area. For example, Corden and Turnovsky (1983) and Corden (1985), in a critical appraisal of the locomotive principle note the importance of appropriate policy choice if expansion in one country is to expand employment and improve the current account for the rest of the world.[9] The point is easily demonstrated. In the Mundellian model, for instance, it is well-known that a fiscal expansion undertaken by a large country operating a flexible exchange rate in a world where capital flows are at least slightly mobile, will stimulate output both at home and abroad. A corresponding monetary expansion, however, will only succeed in raising output at home at the expense of output in the rest of the world. Choice of policy instrument in this case would therefore be critical. Alternatively, differences in economic structure may result in policy effects being transmitted asymmetrically between countries. Argy and Salop (1983) provide one possible example of this whereby differences in the degree of real-wage resistance between countries leads to a situation in which expansion in the home country lowers output in the partner, whilst expansion in the partner stimulates output at home. If the objectives of policy were output and inflation, the cooperative equilibrium in this case would be one in which the home country undertakes contractionary policy whilst the partner expands relative to the non-cooperative solution.[10]

Underlying these arguments, however, is the presumption that the true nature of the transmission mechanism is both known and agreed upon by the coordinating authorities. In fact this is usually far from the truth, and policy-makers are typically uncertain about the nature of the transmission mechanism and frequently disagree about the likely effects of a policies. Where such uncertainty exists the possibility for immiserising cooperation occurs. This point is made by Frankel and Rockett (1988) who examine the effects of policy agreements struck by the USA and Europe where each policy-maker believes in a different model, which may in turn differ from the true model of the international economy.[11] The result is that cooperation around the wrong model may lead to a solution inferior to that produced by decentralised action based upon the same (but incorrect) view of the world.

However, several objections have been made to the Frankel and Rockett analysis. Ghosh and Masson (1988) in particular criticise the approach on the grounds that it implies a considerable degree of irrationality on the part of policy-makers who fail to recognise the effects of model uncertainty. They argue that the appropriate response would be for policy-makers to adopt a portfolio approach to model selection instead. The results from all models then become pertinent and should therefore be taken into account, each being weighted by some non-zero probability that reflects the likelihood of its forecast being the correct one. The result of this approach is to reverse the earlier findings of Frankel and Rockett. Far from precluding policy coordination, model uncertainty may in fact provide an even stronger incentive for countries to cooperate.

9.3 POLICY COORDINATION IN A DYNAMIC FRAMEWORK

A major limitation of the preceding discussion is that coordination is assumed to take place only within a static, single-period framework where policy decisions become immediately effective. Recognising that the full effect of policy may only appear with a delay and that policy decisions themselves are made period after period complicates the analysis considerably, particularly once we allow an explicit role for forward-looking expectations in the model. In this situation there is no longer any guarantee that the cooperative solution will be superior to the non-cooperative. The superiority of the cooperative outcome depends upon the notion of reputation for the policy authorities and the sustainability of any cooperative agreement.[12]

The essential problem is that, in the dynamic framework, government policies, optimally derived at an initial date become suboptimal with the passage of time even though no relevant new information has become available. In effect having previously convinced the private sector that it will conduct the optimal precommitted policy, the government no longer regards itself as being bound by this belief. Such time-inconsistencies therefore provide an incentive for the authorities to renege on earlier policy commitments in subsequent periods and forward-looking agents anticipate this. Thus time-inconsistent policies lack credibility. The only credible policy in this case will be the time-consistent one and this is typically suboptimal. Within this framework the *ex ante* optimal policy is sustained by a government's concern for its reputation established on the basis of its ability to honour policy commitments.

Applying these ideas to the policy coordination problem led Rogoff (1985) to conclude that cooperation in the absence of reputation may be counter-productive.[13] The rationale for this is quite straightforward. The monetary authorities in Rogoff's analysis determine policy on the basis of an objective function expressed in terms of employment and inflation. Once money wage contracts are set there is an incentive for the authorities to renege on previous policy commitments to exploit the output gains accruing to an inflation surprise in the model. However, this incentive is greatest in the cooperative equilibrium because here the inflation–output trade-off is largest. With cooperation a monetary expansion by both countries avoids the problem of an exchange-rate depreciation that would follow consequent to either country undertaking the policy independently. The time-consistent path of money wages and inflation in the model reflects this, being higher under the cooperative solution than they would be if each country acted independently.

Whether reputational considerations can overcome this problem and sustain the optimal policy in the model depends critically upon how agents react to the discovery of a broken commitment. Here the general approach adopted by Barro and Gordon (1983) is informative. In a closed economy, the authorities retain credibility if they produce the expected inflation rate this period; failure to do so, however, is punished by the private sector amending its belief about the future course of the inflation rate in subsequent periods. The temptation for the authorities to renege on policy commitments must therefore be balanced against the discounted cost of punishment delivered in the next period.

For coordination these reputational considerations are important in two respects: first, they influence the behaviour of the coordinating authorities with respect to one another; second, they influence the behaviour of the authorities with respect to the private sector. In the absence of any legally binding institutional arrangements, reputation is the only factor that induces one country to honour the commitments it has made to another. Here a credible Barro–Gordon-style threat might, for example, take the form of one country reverting to a non-cooperative strategy next period if its partner reneges on policy commitments.[14] Oudiz and Sachs (1985), find that time-consistent trajectories can result in situations where such a threat is introduced since now the authorities must balance the anticipated benefits of reneging upon the earlier policy commitment against the potential costs of non-cooperative behaviour by the partner-country in the next period. Introducing reputational considerations with respect to the private sector complicates matters considerably more. Reneging on a policy commitment will now mean that policy-makers face a twin threat: non-cooperation from the partner; a revised belief about the future course of policy by the private sector. Currie and Levine (1989) show that, under certain conditions, both forms of threat may help to sustain the optimal policy, particularly where the punishment interval is long. They suggest, however, that the success of such reputational equilibria is likely to be more problematic in the case of a threat by the private sector than it is if the threat originates from the partner-country.[15]

9.4 EMPIRICAL EVIDENCE

Although the theoretical literature generally supports the notion of gains from coordination, the empirical evidence largely adduced in its support suggests that these gains may be quite small in practice. The evidence in question is based almost entirely upon the results of simulation experiments conducted upon large-scale macroeconomic models of the world economy. These models incorporate the salient features of the major industrial nations (or trading blocs) together with the main channels for economic interdependence operating between them. Within such a framework, the gains from cooperation are usually identified with the difference between simulations where policy in each country is first set independently and then set on the assumption that governments cooperate. An additional twist introduced in recent years is that policy in either regime may be determined within an optimising framework which allows the comparison to be made between the Nash equilibrium and the cooperative, Pareto-equilibrium.[16]

A useful example in this respect is the analysis of Oudiz and Sachs (1984) which examined the behaviour of the G-3 nations, Germany, Japan and the USA. For each country a policy trade-off was estimated on the basis of their experience with respect to inflation, output and the current account of the balance of payments. The results appeared consistent with anecdotal evidence regarding their behaviour: Germany attached a high priority to the control of inflation, and Japan placed a high weight upon movements of the current account. These trade-offs were subsequently used in order to calculate what would have occurred for the period 1984–6 had the three countries pursued coordinated policies.

The results of the exercise did not imply particularly significant gains from coordination. In the case of Germany and the USA the benefits were estimated as approximately 0.2 per cent of GNP whilst those for Japan were only slightly larger at almost 0.7 per cent. Moreover, the coordinated response implied by the study appeared very counter-intuitive with expansionary monetary and fiscal policies being undertaken by the USA and contractionary policies operating in Germany and Japan, the exact opposite of what was actually being advocated at the time.

Similar results have subsequently been reported in several other studies. Oudiz (1985), for example, examines the benefits of coordination between the EMS countries and finds that the gains may only amount to 1 per cent of GNP, whilst Hughes-Hallett (1987), Canzoneri and Minford (1989) and Currie, Levine and Vidalis (1987) report gains that are only slightly larger in studies based upon the performance of the USA, the EC and Japan and the OECD respectively.[17] In the latter study the effect of reputation was also explicitly addressed and the interesting result emerges that the gains from coordination are enhanced where governments acquire reputation by not reneging upon earlier policy commitments.

A number of important qualifications ought to be noted when assessing this evidence. First, the results are only as good as the models within which they are produced. Here particular attention is given to the major role played by the exchange rate in the international transmission mechanism and the difficulty that is commonly experienced in estimating robust specifications for this variable. Clearly misspecification in this area of the model is likely to produce serious consequences for the overall assessment of policy performance within the models and, in particular, for the sign and size of the policy-multipliers they report.[18]

The applicability of the empirical evidence may also be questioned in a second respect. Here the fundamental problem relates to the basic design of the policy experiment conducted on the models. For many of the studies this experiment involves a comparison of economic performance generated by a non-cooperative equilibrium where domestic policy is set optimally by independent nations, and a cooperative solution where policy is determined on the basis of joint welfare-maximisation across nations. How relevant the comparison between these 'optimal' solutions is for real-world-policy formulation is, of course, unclear particularly when it is recognised that the empirical evidence referred to is also contingent upon the assumption that both governments and private agents have access to complete information about the economic system within which they operate.

The possibility that economic agents do not possess complete information was, of course, mentioned in section 9.2 where, following Ghosh and Masson (1988), it was noted that governments who recognise the presence of model uncertainty may do better by coordinating around the 'average' model. Results broadly consistent with this are also implied by Hughes-Hallett (1989) though, rather than suggesting a convergence on the average model, Hughes-Hallett argues that the preferred solution would be obtained where it involves negotiation about what the correct model actually is.[19] However, this produces a somewhat paradoxical result in that the key to reducing risk is for countries to agree upon the model and then proceed to set policy in a non-cooperative manner. Whilst the precise source of this paradox is unclear it does appear to derive in part from the fact that model agreement removes much of the downside risk even though it fails to capture all of the upside gains. This suggests that an exchange of information between central authorities regarding the way in which they see the economy working may initially provide far greater returns than full-blown coordination itself.

In addition to providing evidence over the question of model uncertainty, the study by Hughes-Hallett is also useful in highlighting the potential importance of shared targets for policy coordination. This is best illustrated under the assumption of complete information where the gains from coordination estimated by Hughes-Hallett as accruing to the USA and the rest of the OECD are worth the equivalent of about 3–5 per cent and 4–6 per cent extra GNP growth per annum. The explanation for these gains is found to lie with the fact that the objective function specified by Hughes-Hallett contains the desired path of the exchange rate and this creates the potential for a very direct conflict of interest between policy-makers that can be resolved through coordination. However, even here it is shown that simply agreeing upon a consistent target for the variable is not enough, but it is also crucial to agree the precise path that the shared target should follow. Contingent upon adopting the right path, however, it would appear that targeting the exchange rate alone will provide a significant portion of the gains that would otherwise only occur through a coordination effort across the complete range of policy instruments.[20]

Naturally the possibility that coordination around an exchange-rate target might provide a substitute for complete policy coordination is interesting in the light of the discussion in recent years concerning proposals for international monetary reform. Most notable is the fact that, without fail, all the authors concerned with international monetary reform have suggested fixity of the exchange rates as an integral component of any new regime.[21] Williamson (1985), for example, suggests that the desirability of exchange-rate fixity stems from the fact that variation in real exchange rates forces costly industry shut-downs and start-ups that could have been avoided by greater stability. Others, notably Laskar (1986) and Kenen (1987), have noted that formal analysis of coordinated solutions indicate a public good role for the exchange rate in that the exchange rate exhibits less variability in the coordinated solution than it does in the uncoordinate equilibrium.

9.5 CONCLUSION

Recent developments in the area of international policy coordination have been largely motivated by the increased attention that the subject has received from policy-makers. Initially promoted during the 1980s by a concern that sudden realignment of the dollar might lead to a sharp deterioration in international economic performance, coordination appeared to offer a practical framework for resolving policy conflict. Early theoretical work by Hamada and others suggested that coordination, by internalising the spill-over effects associated with independent policy action, would yield benefits for participating nations.

This view has been subject to reappraisal in recent years and notable modifications based upon an explicit recognition of the potential limitations imposed by the assumption of perfect information and a static, one-period optimisation, have been proposed. A number of important policy implications emerge. First, where imperfect information occurs, particularly in the form of model uncertainty, the need for the policy authorities to coordinate their views of how the world works appears to be almost as important, if not more important than the coordination of economic policy itself. This suggests that considerable benefit could accrue from an exchange of information between nations regarding the international economic transmission mechanism, an arrangement which is already well-institutionalised between central banks. Because an exchange of information falls well short of formal coordination and does not entail any attendant loss of sovereignty, it is possibly an easier objective to achieve than full-blown cooperation itself. Impediments to coordination also appear within a dynamic framework where the possibility of time-inconsistency due to an incentive to renege upon earlier policy commitments implies that coordination can lead to a worse outcome than non-cooperation. In the absence of any legally binding institutional framework, the ability of the policy authorities to establish a reputation for policy commitment in this situation is crucial if coordination is to enhance economic welfare.

Turning now to the empirical evidence, the majority of results available suggests that the benefits acruing to coordination will be small. Despite a variety of mitigating qualifications that might be attached to this evidence, the finding is nevertheless highly significant and certainly suggests that movement toards full-blown coordination across a range of policy instruments may be somewhat premature. The evidence is more favourable with respect to the support it gives to coordination efforts that emphasise the role of shared targets, notably the exchange rate. However, even here it would appear that the simple agreement to coordinate is not enough; the trajectory that the shared target follows is likely to prove at least as important for the final outcome as the agreement to cooperate itself. It remains to be seen, therefore, whether policy coordination has the potential to generate any significant gains in economic welfare.

Notes

CHAPTER 1

1. Friedman (1986).
2. See McKinnon (1979, ch.11) and Tew (1977, ch.15).

CHAPTER 3

1. This chapter is derived from Chant (1987). I am indebted to the Bank of Canada for the opportunity to carry out this study under ideal conditions. At the Bank, Charles Freedman, Clyde Goodlet, Paul Jenkins, John Murray and Gordon Thiessen gave valued support through their encouragement and comments. In addition, Keith Acheson, Tom Courchene, John McManus, Jim Pesando, and Henri-Paul Rousseau made helpful comments. Finally, the editors of this volume, Kevin Dowd and Mervyn Lewis, made many suggestions that improved the chapter. The views in this chapter are those of the author; no responsibility for them should be attributed to the Bank of Canada.
2. As Lewis (1989) points out these transformation services can be characterised as a form of insurance. For example, financial institutions that borrow short and lend long offer suppliers of funds insurance against the possibility that they will need the funds prior to the maturity of the borrower's investment.
3. Recent data from the UK can be used to illustrate the point. At the end of 1987, sight deposits were only 30 per cent of the total sterling deposits of non-bank customers of retail and wholesale banks. These

figures overstate the importance of chequeable deposits because sight is not synonomous with chequeable deposits for the non-retail banks. On the other hand, short-term deposits are a major source of funds. Deposits maturing in 7 days or less account for 61 per cent of total deposits for retail and wholesale banks combined and 84 per cent of deposits for retail banks alone. See Lewis and Davis (1987) Tables 4.1 and 4.2.

4. Advances accounted for over 55 per cent of the sterling assets of banks in the UK at the end of 1987.
5. The absence of transactions costs and enforcement costs means that households are able to sell claims against future income in order to finance current consumption. Indeed this model can be extended to include uncertainty about the future by the device of introducing 'contigent claims' that entitle their holders to payments in the event of a specified state at given time in the future. In practice, a full set of contingent claims will be limited by the ability to specify the state adequately. A complete set of these contingent claims is possible in the simple economy presented here because of the lack of any enforcement or transactions costs.
6. If individuals were risk-neutral they would choose to hold only one asset. Even though the outcome would be uncertain, the probability of gaining e above the expected return would offset exactly the cost to investors of the prospect of losing e.
7. This simple diversification model forms the basis of explanations of indirect finance advanced by Klein (1973) and Kane and Buser (1979). Klein argues that costs of diversification is a necessary condition for the emergence of intermediaries (p.930) and notes that 'an economic incentive is provided for the pooling of funds and financial intermediaries are the logical instrument for such pooling arrangements'. Kane and Buser (1979) study the degree of diversification among security issues held by US commercial banks. The costs of diversification that they identify include 'differences between odd-lot and round-lot trading fees, asset indivisibilities . . . administrative – costs associated with selecting evaluating managing and continually keeping – track of a large number of securities . . . and information risk' (p.23).
8. A parallel should be noted between this explanation and the model of simple diversification. In each case the investor can improve on the possibilities available to him in isolation by using a financial institution. In one case he avoids the risk inherent in his investment opportunities, whereas in the other he avoids the risk inherent in his consumption needs. For further discussion of financial institutions and insurance against risk, see Lewis (1989).

9. The assumption of heterogeneity in attitudes towards risk has been criticised by Klein (1983):

   > One should be hesitant to accept risk aversion explanations for contractual terms because these explanations are logically equivalent to relying on tastes to explain behavior (p.370).

   Gordon (1974) has shown that differences in apparent tastes for risk can arise from differences in resource endowments, even with identical preferences. In his explanation for implicit labour contracts he assumes that workers are more risk-averse than employers because their human capital is not as easily marketable as other capital and hence they are less diversified.
10. Diversification does not offer any benefit because the presence of purely social risk, and the implied absence of private risk, means that all assets must share the same uncertainties.
11. Search costs differ from verification costs in terms of the transferability of the information gained. Information from the search can be easily transferred because once an investment is found its location can be revealed to other benefits because it is assumed that an individual cannot transfer the results of a verification to another person in a convincing way. The other individual must verify the quality of the investment for himself.
12. This wealth could take the form of the banker's reputation. Depositors would realise that the banker is staking the value of his bank as a going concern as a safeguard for their interests. See Klein (1973).
13. This section applies the analysis of Cheung (1983), Fama and Jensen (1983), Jensen and Mackling (1976) and Klein (1983) to the explanation of financial institutions. A major contribution to the topic is Diamond (1984).
14. Fama and Jensen (1983) discuss the variety of forms that this monitoring may take.
15. This point and its implications for intermediation was suggested to me by Kevin Dowd and Mervyn Lewis.
16. The banks, as lenders, would still have to monitor the activities of these firms. The point is that these firms prefer to borrow from intermediaries rather than issue marketable securities because use of an intermediary permits a tighter control over the flow of information.
17. See, for example, Tobin (1982) and Hart and Jaffee (1974).

CHAPTER 5

1. For an amusing look at some differences in analytical 'styles' between economists and financial economists, see Summers (1985).
2. A more detailed discussion of what has happened to sources of corporate debt funding during the 1980s appears in Crabbe *et al.* (199).
3. See, for example, Meyers (1990). The counter-argument is that the Federal Reserve influences the economy through changes in the stock of money, not through changes in the supply of credit. In this latter view, then, the relative share of bank lending in credit markets is irrelevant.
4. They also may have contributed to a new era of international regulatory and policy coordination; however, this topic is not specifically addressed in this chapter.
5. The actual decline in velocity occurs in late 1982. Consequently, some analysts have argued that financial innovation could not be responsible for it because the nationwide introduction of NOW accounts occurred so much earlier.
6. While this shift was partially a matter of convenience, it was encouraged by the pricing of NOW accounts; frequently, banks required large minimum or average NOW balances before they would reduce or waive service charges on these accounts. See Carraro and Thornton (1986) for a discussion of these requirements and some rough estimates of the costs of holding NOW account relative to demand deposits.
7. See Tatom (1990) and the references cited there.
8. See Gilbert (1986) for a detailed discussion of Regulation Q and for a complete list of the steps involved in its phase-out.
9. The assumption that the demand for $M1$ is homogeneous of degree one in real income is not necessary for the general argument that follows. It is only necessary that the demand for real $M1$ and saving are homogeneous of *different* degrees.
10. In this case, there is simply a shift from demand deposits and, perhaps, currency into NOW accounts and the demand for real $M1$ is presumed to remain unchanged. However, other reasons why the demand for real $M1$ might be affected indirectly are discussed in the text.
11. Whether the interest elasticity of $M1^*$ velocity will rise or fall is unclear; the gradual phasing out, and eventual elimination, of Regulation Q ceilings might actually reduce the observed interest elasticity of these balances if depository institutions alter their deposit rates quickly in response to changes in general money market rates.

12. This discussion draws heavily on Thornton (1983b).
13. While the previous discussion limited these factors only to y and i, other important factors would be included in a more general analysis.
14. For example, if potential output grows at 2.5 per cent and the desired rate of inflation is zero per cent, the desired path for nominal GNP growth would then be 2.5 per cent.
15. If the time-series of the natural log of velocity measured quarterly is correctly described as being a random walk, the quarter-to-quarter growth rate of velocity is completely unpredictable.
16. Indeed, a variant of this argument is the standard one used to 'show' that interest rates are a better intermediate target than money because hitting some target interest rate implied a more stable level of velocity. The validity of this argument hinges critically on the monetary authority's ability to control the 'real' interest rate.
17. Furthermore, it could affect the amount of time needed to achieve some desired path, *ceteris paribus*.
18. Other changes that occurred under the Monetary Control Act of 1980 may have enhanced the Federal Reserve's ability to control *M*1. See Garfinkel and Thornton (1989).
19. For a discussion of the Fed's decision to de-emphasise *M*1 in conducting monetary policy, see Thornton (1983a). For recent discussions of the continuing effect of financial innovation on the conduct of monetary policy, see Kohn (1989) and Greenspan (1990).
20. A number of analyses have noted the increase in *M*1 velocity's interest elasticity. Some early ones include Hetzel (1987), Trehan and Walsh (1987) and Rasche (1987); among the latest is Tatom (1990). Also, see Stone and Thornton (1987) for a discussion of other explanations of the decline in *M*1 velocity.
21. This prediction is conditional on depository institutions not altering the rates they pay on NOW accounts quickly and completely enough in response to changes in market interest rates, which appears to be what has actually occurred.
22. If these studies are correct, the validity of the financial innovation hypothesis may turn out to have been based on yet another occurrence of the well-known *post hoc, ergo propter hoc* fallacy.
23. While this evidence must be interpreted cautiously because it abstracts from the growth of demand deposits, it is interesting to note that demand deposits declined by \$29.2 billion in the first two quarters of 1981 and other chequeable deposits increased by \$39.8 billion. Hence, nearly three-quarters of the increase in other chequeable deposits was offset by a decline in demand deposits. Demand deposits declined continuously through the third quarter of 1982, declining by an additional \$8.2 billion. Over this same period,

other chequeable deposits rose by $24.3 billion. Consequently, only about a third of the rise in other chequeable deposits during this nine-quarter period was offset by a decline in demand deposits.

24. Tatom (1990) attempts to link changes in velocity and some other variables directly to a particular measure of financial innovation, the ratio of other chequeable deposits to total chequeable deposits, and obtains mixed results. He finds that the currency deposit ratio is related to his financial innovation measure in a statistically significant way, but velocity and some other measures are not. Tatom's analysis, however, is based on his particular measure of financial innovation and, hence, subject to the criticism noted above.
25. This does not mean, however, that such changes are unrelated to monetary policy. The rise in the *k*-ratio in the first two quarters of 1989, for example, is the result of restrictive monetary policy that reduced the growth of total chequeable deposits relative to currency, despite the rather sharp decline in the market interest rates. See, Garfinkel and Thornton (1990) for further discussion of the importance of the observed change in the behaviour of the *k*-ratio for monetary policy.

CHAPTER 6

1. The author is Vice President and Associate Director of Research at the Federal Reserve Bank of Dallas. The views expressed in this chapter are his alone and should not be construed as representing the official position of any part of the Federal Reserve System. I would like to especially thank Kevin Dowd, Mervyn Lewis, George Kaufman, and Robert Clair for comments on earlier drafts of this paper.
2. In terms of job creation, the US economy has surely been the envy of the world. No other major country – not even Japan – came close in this regard. From the end of 1982 through the close of 1988, US civilian employment expanded 15 per cent while Japanese employment grew to only 6.6 per cent. This growth translates into an average annual gain of over 2.5 million jobs in the USA compared with approximately 615 000 jobs in Japan. (The figures represent the *net* gains in employment. See the *Handbook of Labor Statistics*, US Department of Labor, Bureau of Labor Statistics, August 1989.)
3. The 'South-west Plan' was a misnomer. Many of the more notorious insolvent thrifts were domiciled in Texas. The problem of insolvent depository institutions is national, however, not regional, in scope (Short and Gunther, 1988).

4. It is true that the Chairman of the Federal Home Loan Banking System, M. Danny Wall, got the amount of money that he requested – whether intentional initially – by a factor of roughly ten times. It is fairly clear, however, that until recently, Congress as a whole had refused to face up to the realities of the thrift problems. In a real sense, Mr Wall got the job because he promised to contain the situation. The *political* crisis came when Mr Wall realising that containment was impossible, came clean publicly and admitted the dimensions of the problem were much greater than he had heretofore acknowledged.
5. From this point on, when I use the term 'bank' (with no modifier) I will mean any depository institution. In the American context, this covers commercial banks, savings and loan associations, savings banks and credit unions. Each type of banking organisation is covered by a legally separate deposit insurance agency. All the agencies are effectively backed by the full faith and credit of the US government.
6. Most developed countries have now some system of deposit insurance. Most are of recent vintage compared to that in the USA. Further, in no other country has the deposit insurance system played the same role as it has in the USA.
7. 'Casual observation indicates that [households and companies] are very much aware of what money market fund balance sheets are, much more aware than of what bank balance sheets are. Nor is it accidental that funds and banks differ so in their balance sheets' (Kareken, 1981, p.4). Money-market funds are mutual funds holding a portfolio of short-term liquid assets.

   Note that the argument does not asume that investors never make errors or even that their analysis is complete or even adequate. It merely asserts that depository creditors of banks are less knowledgeable about their bank deposits than about other investments. This is a conundrum that must be explained.
8. Banking regulators do not specify exactly which banks are too large to fail. At the time the doctrine was publicly announced by the Comptroller of the Currency, 'at least' the top 11 banks were included. Banking analysts generally believe that at least the top 20 banks are presently included.
9. For an excellent summary of the regulatory actions in the early 1980s, see Barth, *et al*. The authors already saw the cost of policy procrastination: 'Not closing these [insolvent] institutions most likely increases the eventual cost to the FSLIC, as the institutions try to overcome their problems through riskier activities. Therefore, delay is costly.' To put things in perspective, if thrift problems had been

resolved in 1985 – the year that article was written – the cost would probably have been in the order of one-tenth what it will be now.

10. See the studies by the FDIC and FHLBB cited in the references.
11. A political decision was made to hand over the problem of managing the thrift problem to the FDIC, even though FSLIC is the insurer of record.
12. Both Dowd (1989) and England (1988) are conspicuous exceptions. Each envisions a world of competitive banking without deposit insurance. As will be seen in what follows, there is no presumption that private deposit insurance is not a viable product. To be viable, however, premiums would have to be risk-sensitive.
13. In the USA, many banks are part of a holding company. Some activities not permissible for commercial banks are permissible for the parent company. The concept is that the non-bank activities, some of which are viewed as inherently more risky than banking, be conducted outside the bank itself. The bank would then be isolated from deleterious effects of the non-banking activities. Indeed, the Federal Reserve System believes these should be 'a source of strength' for the banking activities of the holding company.
14. It should be noted that Litan has backed away from his original proposal. He is a co-author of Benston *et al.* (1989) which represents a more centrist position in the public-policy debate.
15. White, and Rolnick and Weber followed in the intellectual footsteps of Rockoff (1974). This seminal work was largely neglected, however, except by economic historians. The debate over free banking has now gained broad attention in the economics profession.
16. White (1984, p.1) defines free banking as 'the system under which there are no political restrictions on the business of issuing currency convertible into full-bodied coin'.
17. Jordan (1989) does offer a rather explicit transition proposal to a free banking system that builds on the existing structure of Federal Reserve Banks. On the face of it, the proposal appears economically feasible but politically improbable. Also, see Dowd (1989).
18. Also validated is the classical conclusion that, without a limitation on the quantity of bank liabilities, there is no anchor for nominal values in the economy (O'Driscoll, 1985, pp.6–7).

CHAPTER 7

1. These developments are discussed in Lewis and Davis (1987).
2. Button and Swann (1989).

3. Breyer and MacAvoy (1987).
4. See Posner (1974), Peltzman (1976) and Keeler (1984).
5. Pincus and Withers (1983), p. 55.
6. For example, Fama (1985) provides an analysis of where the burden of reserve requirement 'taxes' upon banks falls, which illustrates some of the complexities involved.
7. The US experience is examined by Kane (1984).
8. Morgan Guarantee Trust Co. of New York, *World Financial Markets*, December 1986.
9. Federal Reserve Board Staff (1979).
10. The rate r_K may also be interpreted as including the yield on deposits with non-bank financial institutions.
11. See Kasriel (1985), Mayes and Hunn (1987) and van Hoose (1988).
12. See Artis and Lewis (1991). Note that a degree of credit rationing is endemic in direct lending for the information-asymmetry/adverse-selection reasons outlined in Stiglitz and Weiss (1981).
13. Sir John Hicks (1969, ch.6).
14. Friedman (1980). He in fact favoured an alternative approach, that of monetary-base control, which he described as equivalent to 'control of the output of motor cars by controlling the availability of a basic raw material, say steel, to manufacturers – a precise analogy to controlling the availability of base money to banks and others'.
15. Whether financial intermediaries need to be distinguished from other private economic agents (i.e. whether the indirect *v.* direct financing distinction matters) for macroeconomic policy purposes in such a new system is a question we leave to others to answer.
16. Alternatively, as McCallum (1986) demonstrates, a policy reaction function in which the monetary aggregate is adjusted in response to deviations of market interest rates from their target value, will suffice.

CHAPTER 8

1. The credibility hypothesis was first discussed at length by Fellner (1976, 1979). Cukierman (1985), Fischer (1986) and Rogoff (1987a) review various aspects of the recent literature. For a more comprehensive evaluation, the reader should consult Blackburn and Christensen (1989), from which the current chapter draws heavily.
2. Begg (1982) remains indispensible as an introduction to rational expectations theory.
3. One of the more popular treatments of game theory is Friedman (1977).

4. A note of caution needs to be injected here. Given that agents are atomistic, the notion of a private-sector strategy is vacuous. Only if agents could somehow collude would it be posible for them to formulate a coordinated plan of action but this is precluded by assumption. The private sector does not have a strategy: what it does have is a rational expectations formation mechanism and it is this that accounts for the game elements in policy design.
5. In fact, Phelps (1967) and Phelps and Pollack (1968) had anticipated this result somewhat earlier. It was Kydland and Prescott (1977) however, who drew widespread attention to it.
6. This type of game possesses a definite hierarchial structure, with some players being more dominant than others in the sense of being able to impose their own decisions on the decisions taken by their rivals. It is natural to think of the government as a dominant player, recognising the influence of its own actions on the actions of others. The private sector, by contrast, is appropriately seen in a more passive role: each agent, being individually weak, takes as given the behaviour of everyone else.
7. In a Nash game, all players are assumed to have the same status. Each one chooses his own course of action, taking as given the actions of others. In a Nash equilibrium, each player's strategy is optimal regardless of the strategies played by others.
8. The government may prefer some inflation because of the revenue from seignorage. Similarly, another benefit of surprise inflation is that it acts as a capital levy on nominally denominated public debt and so reduces the need for more distortionary methods of taxation. A qualification to this might arise in the presence of transaction costs where higher inflation forces agents to economise on money holdings (see, for example, Kimbrough, 1986).
9. The reader may wish to think of this problem in terms of time-varying demand and supply elasticities. As soon as agents set nominal wages conditional on their inflationary expectations, the supply of labour becomes perfectly elastic. Employment, therefore, becomes demand-determined which the government can exploit by inflating away real wages. Similar considerations apply to the case of dynamically inconsistent optimal taxation (see, for example, Calvo, 1978; Fischer, 1980; Kydland and Prescott, 1980). One example of this is when a government, in seeking to raise revenue, is tempted to engineer a surprise deflation of the real value of its debt. Another is when agents run the risk of accumulating capital which the government is inclined to tax unexpectedly away. In general, time inconsistency arises whenever the elasticities of tax bases respond to government announcements; the government is then able to impose

an *ex-post* levy and avoid the excess burden associated with other (non-lump sum) methods of taxation.

10. See, for example, Alesina and Tabellini (1985). The presence of distortions is also what lies behind the time-inconsistency problem in dynamic optimal taxation (see note 8). If the government had access to non-distorting taxes, the problem would vanish.
11. See, for example, Sargent (1981). The argument being made here is the familiar one concerning the incompatibility of pursuing independent monetary and exchange-rate policies. Lucas and Stokey (1983) and Persson, Persson and Svensson (1987) give examples of partial commitment in dynamic optimal taxation problems.
12. This is discussed more fully in Section 8.4.
13. The use of the term threat here is a little misleading because agents cannot coordinate on a joint plan of action. They can, however, lose faith in the government should it behave badly and this is what might stop bad behaviour in the first place.
14. The reader may also wish to note that, under full information, the Folk-Theorem is applicable only in infinitely repeated games. This is because, with a finite horizon, the government will always inflate in the final period since there is no punishment for doing so. Agents, however, will understand this and raise their expectations in this period also. Hence, the incentive to inflate moves back to the penultimate period which agents also understand. And so on and so forth until the one-shot Nash equilibrium obtains for all stages. A similar argument has been used by Hahn (1982) and others to show why money cannot exist under perfect foresight.
15. These events are influenced by a number of factors, notably the government's rate of discount and time-horizon. A decrease (increase) in the former (latter) of these tends to raise the chances of mimicry by making the penalty for inflating heavier.
16. It will be noted that I am avoiding the alternative interpretation whereby governments are distinguished according to their commitment technologies. This is because a government that is committed to a policy is, by definition, unable to manipulate this policy for the purposes of signalling.
17. The added complication arises from the fact that agents run the risk of punishing an honest government and not punishing a dishonest one. It has been suggested that the private sector could establish confidence intervals for monetary policy, observations that lie outside of which trigger the feeling of opportunism. An appropriate choice of confidence interval would ensure that the government would only ever inflate for stabilisation reasons.

18. It is notable that all the analyses in this area rest upon the assumption that policy-makers have quicker access than agents to data on the money supply. In practice, however, this lead in information is trivial, being barely over a week in the US for example.
19. Forerunners of this new literature on political business cycles include Blanchard (1985) and Minford and Peel (1982).
20. This is so in the models of Rogoff (1987b) and Rogoff and Silbert (1988) where electoral budget cycles occur from signalling activity on the part of the incumbent party.
21. Evidence to support this presumption can be found in Alesina and Sachs (1988), Beck (1982a) and Havrilesky (1988).
22. Excellent accounts of this view include Beck (1982b), Clifford (1965), Hetzel (1985) and Woolley (1984).
23. A couple of others worth noting are professional economic advisers and the financial community.
24. In a recent study of twelve industrialised countries, Parkin and Bade (1985) find evidence to support the hypothesis that the less subservian the central bank is to the political administration the lower inflation rates tend to be. This can be used to support the proposal to establish an independent monetary authority as a means of reducing the potential inflationary bias in an economy. Notice also that central bank independence may reduce both the partisan variability and pre-election manipulation of monetary policy.
25. On the relationship between central banks and governments, see Beck (1982b), Clifford (1965), Hetzel (1985), Kane (1980, 1982), Weintraub (1978) and Woolley (1984).
26. See, for example, Acheson and Chant (1972, 1973).
27. See, for example, Acheson and Chant (1973), Brunner (1981), Goodfriend (1986) and Lombra and Moran (1980).
28. The discussion draws on the work of Bryant and Wallace (1980) and Sargent and Wallace (1981).
29. See, for example, Sargent (1981) and Baxter (1984). It is, of course, true that a lack of coherence in macroeconomic policy may reflect merely technical difficulties associated with coordinating the actions of different policy-makers or even bad planning on the part of a single policy-maker. Whatever the reason, the important point to note is that an unforeseeable reversal in fiscal deficits renders any alleged commitment to an anti-inflationary monetary policy susceptible to severe problems of credibility.

CHAPTER 9

1. The term 'non-cooperative' is used in a game-theoretic context whereby each country is assumed to maximise its own welfare independently.
2. More accurately, the sum is equal to the increase in the quantity of outside money in the system.
3. Moreover, this argument can be applied equally well to the exchange rate. In a N-country world there exists only $N-1$ exchange rates and, as such, it is clearly impossible for all countries to experience an appreciation or depreciation simultaneously.
4. This statement requires some qualification. Brainard (1967) has shown that, with the introduction of uncertainty and stochastic disturbances, it is generally advisable to have more instruments available than fewer.
5. Cooper (1985) also argues that the magnitude of such disturbances will increase. However, the basis for this argument appears less clear.
6. One such instrument is, of course, the exchange rate. In the situation described, for example, a depreciation by the home country would shift the *TT* schedule upwards towards position *E*.
7. The possibility of this type of international low-level equilibrium trap is also considered by Johansen (1982).
8. This point is commonly made in the context of the possibility that relaxation of the external constraint with coordination will enable governments to expand to a greater degree than would otherwise be the case.
9. The locomotive principle was adopted by heads of state at the Bonn summit in 1978 as a means of promoting world recovery. In this major economies were to act jointly in order to stimulate world demand whilst avoiding the deterioration on the current account that would otherwise take place.
10. There are, of course, obvious implications of this for the discussion of policy response by countries to various disturbances. In general the nature of the optimal policy response will depend upon both the type of shocks that hit the economies and the channels of the transmission mechanism between them.
11. A similar scenario is examined by Frankel (1988) in the context of a closed economy where the problem of model disagreement occurs between two sets of domestic policy-makers. The obvious example for the UK might be disagreement between the central bank and the Treasury.

12. These issues were first addressed by Kydland and Prescott (1977) and have been applied in the coordination literature by a number of authors, notably Miller and Salmon (1985), Currie and Levine (1985) and Rogoff (1985). The salient features of the analysis are surveyed in Currie and Levine (1989).
13. In addition, Canzoneri and Henderson (1988) also argue the reverse: reputation without cooperation may be counter-productive.
14. Such a threat is clearly credible since, in the non-cooperative equilibrium, each country is operating on its reaction function and therefore acting in an optimal manner.
15. The main problem is that with types of reputational equilibria the length of punishment period is indeterminate. The essential argument for Currie and Levine is, therefore, that the policy-maker in the other country is more able to make a strategic decision on the optimal length of punishment than can an atomistic private sector.
16. Where optimisation is not utilised, coordination typically reduces to a simple case of synchronisation of policy implementation across countries. In this situation the gains from coordination are expressed as the difference between the multiplier effects produced when expansion occurs in one country compared with the results generated when all countries expand simultaneously.
17. Hughes-Hallet (1987), for example, reports gains of 0.5 per cent for the USA per annum and 1.3 per cent for the EC per annum.
18. A policy-multiplier expresses the ratio of the induced change in any particular output variable such as GDP or inflation to a standardised change in a policy instrument. They are used extensively in the analysis of policy effects with macroeconometric models.
19. Hughes-Hallett also considers the effect of uncertainty originating from unanticipated disturbances and misspecification of the partner's objective function. In neither case are these sources found to be particularly significant.
20. Naturally failure to agree upon a consistent path for the exchange rate places us back in the $N-1$ problem – not everybody can enjoy an exchange rate depreciation simultaneously. Attempting to do so will result in what Canzoneri and Henderson (1988) refer to as the waste of instrument power as policy-makers push against one another.
21. For a useful summary of the main proposals the interested reader is directed to Artis (1989).

Bibliography

Acheson, Keith and Chant, John F. (1972), 'The Choice of Monetary Instrument and the Theory of Bureaucracy', *Public Choice*, no 12.

Acheson, and Chant, J. F. (1973) 'Bureaucratic Theory and the Choice of Central Bank Goals', *Journal of Money, Credit, and Banking*, no 5, pp.637–55.

Alesina, Alberto (1987a) 'Macroeconomic Policy in a Two-Party System as a Repeated Game', *Quarterly Journal of Economics*, no 102, pp.651–78.

Alesina, Alberto (1987b) 'Credibility and Policy Convergence in a Two-Party System with Rational Voters', mimeo, NBER.

Alesina, Alberto and Cukierman, Alex (1988) 'The Politics of Ambiguity', NBER Working Paper no 2468.

Alesina, Alberto and Sachs, Jeffery (1988) 'Political Parties and the Business Cycle in the United States, 1948–1984', *Journal of Money, Credit, and Banking*, no 20, p.63–82.

Alesina, Alberto and Spear, Stephen E. (1987) 'An Overlapping Generations Model of Electoral Competition', NBER Working Paper no 2354.

Alesina, Alberto and Tabellini, Guido (1985) 'Rules and Discretion with Non-Coordinated Monetary and Fiscal Policy', mimeo, Harvard University.

Alt, James E., and K. Allec Chrystal (1983) *Political Economics* (Brighton, Wheatsheaf, and Berkeley, University of California Press).

Argy, V. and Salop, J. (1983) 'Price and Output Effects of Monetary and Fiscal Expansion in a Two-Country World under Flexible Exchange Rates', *Oxford Economic Papers*, vol. 35, no 2, pp.228–46.

Arrow, Kenneth J. (1971) *Essays in the Theory of Risk-Bearing* (Chicago, Markham).

Artis, Michael J. (1989) 'International Economic Policy Co-ordination: Theory and Practice', *Oxford Review of Economic Policy*, vol 5, no 3, Autumn, pp.83–93.

Artis, M. J. and Lewis, M. K. (1991) *Money in Britain Monetary Policy, Innovation and Europe* (Oxford, Philip Allan).

Artis, M. J. and Ostry, S. (1986) *International Economic Policy Coordination*, Chatham House Papers 30 (London, Routledge & Kegan Paul for the Royal Institute for International Affairs).

Backus, David and Driffill, E. John (1985) 'Inflation and Reputation' *American Economic Review*, no 75, pp.530–8.

Bagehot, W. (873/1973), *Lombard Street*, (originally published London, 1873; republished London, Kegan, Paul & Co, 1973).

Baillie, R. T., Lippens, R. E. and McMahon, P. (1983) 'Testing Rational Expectations and Efficiency in the Foreign Exchange Market', *Econometrica*, 51, pp.553–63.

Barro, Robert J. (1986) 'Reputation in a Model of Monetary Policy with Incomplete Information', *Journal of Monetary Economics*, no 17 pp.3–20.

Barro, R. J. and Gordon, D. B. (1983a) 'Rules, Discretion and Reputation in a Model of Monetary Policy', *Journal of Monetary Economics*, vol. 12, pp.101–21.

Barro, R. J. and Gordon, D. B. (1983b) 'A Positive Theory of Monetary Policy in a Natural Rate Model', *Journal of Political Economy*, vol. 91, pp.589–610.

Bator, F. (1958) 'The anatomy of market failure', *Quarterly Journal of Economics*, pp.351–79.

Baxter, Marianne (1984) 'The Role of Expectations in Stabilization Policy', *Journal of Monetary Economics*, no 15, pp.343–62.

Bean, C. R. (1983) 'Targeting Nominal Income: An Appraisal', *Economic Journal*, 93, December, pp.806–19.

Beck, Nathaniel (1982a) 'Parties, Administrations and American Macroeconomic Outcomes, *American Political Science Review*, no 26, pp.83–93.

Beck, Nathaniel (1982b) 'Presidential Influence on the Federal Reserve', *American Journal of Political Science*, 1982b, 26, pp.83–93.

Begg, David K. H. (1982) *The Rational Expectations Revolution in Macroeconomics: Theories and Evidence* (Oxford: Philip Allan).

Benston, G. J. and Smith, C. W. (1976) 'A Transaction Cost Approach to the Theory of Financial Intermediaries', *Journal of Finance*, 31, pp. 215–31.

Benston, G. J., *et al.* (1986) *Perspectives on Safe & Sound Banking: Past, Present and Future* (Cambridge, Mass., MIT Press).

Benston, G. J., *et al.* (1989) *Restructuring America's Financial Institutions* (Washington, DC, The Brookings Institution).

Bhagwati, J. (1986) 'Trade in Services and Developing Countries', Discussion Paper no 307 (New York, Columbia University).

Black, Fischer (1970) 'Banking and Interest Rates in a World Without Money: The Effects of Uncontrolled Banking', *Journal of Bank Research*, I (Autumn) pp.8–20.

Blackburn, Keith and Christensen, Michael (1989) 'Monetary Policy and Policy Credibility', *Journal of Economic Literature*, no 27, pp.1–45.

Blanchard, Olivier J. (1985) 'Credibility, Disinflation and Gradualism', *Economic Letters*, no 17, pp. 211–17.

Brainard, W. (1967) 'Uncertainty and the Effectiveness of Policy', *American Economic Review, Papers and Proceedings*, vol. 57, no 2, pp.411–25.

Breyer, S. and MacAvoy, P. W. (1987) 'Regulation and Deregulation', in *New Palgrave Dictionary of Economics* (London, Macmillan).

Brunner, Karl (1981) 'The Art of Central Banking', Centre for Resaerch on Government Policy, Working Paper no 81–6.

Bryant, John and Wallace, Neil (1980) 'A Suggestion for Further Simplifying the Theory of Money', Federal Reserve Bank Minneapolis Staff Report no 62.

Burns, Arthur F. (1988) *The Ongoing Revolution in American Banking* (Washington, DC, American Enterprise Institute for Public Policy Research).

Button, K. and Swann, D. (1989) *The Age of Regulatory Reform* (Oxford, Clarendon Press).

Calvo, Guillermo A (1978) 'On the Time-Consistency of Optimal Policy in a Monetary Economy', *Econometrica*, 46, pp.1411–28.

Cameron, R. (1967) *Banking in the Early Stages of Industrialisation* (Oxford, Oxford University Press).

Canzoneri, Matthew B. (1985) 'Monetary Policy Games and the Role of Private Information', *American Economic Review*, no 75, pp.1056–70.

Canzoneri, M. B. and Grey, J. (1985) 'Monetary Policy Games and the Consequences of Non-Cooperative Behaviour', *International Economic Review*, vol. 26, no 3, pp.542–64.

Canzoneri, M. B. and Henderson, D. (1988) *Strategic Aspects of Macroeconomic Policymaking in Interdependent Economies* (Washington, The Brookings Institution).

Canzoneri, M. B. and Minford, P. (1989) 'Policy Interdependence: Does Strategic Behaviour Pay? An Empirical Investigation Using the Liverpool World Model' in D. R. Hodgman and G. E. Wood (eds) *Macroeconomic Policy and Economic Interdependence* (London, Macmillan).

Capie, F. and Wood, G. E. (eds)(1991) *Unregulated Banking: Chaos or Order?* (London, Macmillan).

Carraro, Kenneth C. and Thornton, Daniel L. (1986) 'The Cost of

Checkable Deposits in the United States', Federal Reserve Bank of St Louis *Review* (April), pp.19–27

Chan, Y. (1983) 'On the Positive Role of Financial Intermediation in Allocation of Venture Capital in a Market with Imperfect Information', *Journal of Finance*, 38, pp.1543–68.

Chant, J. (1987) *Regulation of Financial Institutions – A Functional Analysis*, Bank of Canada Technical Report no 45, 1987.

Cheung, S. N. S. (1983) 'The Contractual Nature of the Firm', *Journal of Law and Economics*, 26, pp.1–21.

Chrystal, K. Alec (1990) *Consumer Debt: Whose Responsibility*? (London, Social Affairs Unit).

Clifford, Jerome A. (1965) *The Independence of the Federal Reserve System* (Philadelphia: University Press).

Cooper, R. N. (1984) 'The Prospects for International Economic Coordination', in Buiter, W. H. and Marston, R. C. (eds) *International Economic Policy Coordination* (Cambridge, Cambridge University Press).

Cooper, R. N. (1985) 'Economic Interdependence and Coordination of Economic Policies', in R. W. Jones and P. B. Kenen (eds), *Handbook of International Economics*, vol. 2 (Amsterdam, North-Holland).

Corden, W. M. (1985) 'On Transmission and Coordination under Flexible Exchange Rates', in W. H. Buiter and R. C. Marston (eds) *International Economic Policy Coordination* (Cambridge, Cambridge University Press).

Corden, W. M. and Turnovsky, S. (1983) 'Negative Transmission of Economic Expansion', *European Economic Review*, vol. 20, pp.289–310.

Crabbe, Leland E., Pickering, Margaret H. and Prowse, Stephen D. (1990) 'Recent Developments in Corporate Finance', *Federal Reserve Bulletin* (August) pp.593–603.

Cukierman, Alex (1985) 'Central Bank Behaviour and Credibility – Some Recent Developments', mimeo, Federal Reserve Bank of St Louis.

Cukierman, Alex and Meltzer, Allan H. (1986a) 'A Theory of Ambiguity, Credibility and Inflation under Discretion and Asymmetric Information', *Econometrica*, no 54, pp.1099–1285.

Cukierman, Alex and Meltzer, Allan H. (1986b) 'A Positive Theory of Disinflationary Policy, the Cost of Democratic Government and the Benefit of a Constitution', mimeo, University of Carnegie-Mellon.

Cukierman, Alex and Meltzer, Allan H. (1986c) 'The Credibility of Monetary Announcements', in Manfred J. M. Neuman (ed.) *Monetary Policy and Uncertainty* (New York: Duicker & Humbolt).

Currie, D. A. and Levine, P. (1985) 'Macroeconomic Policy Design in an Interdependent World' in W. H. Buiter and R. C. Marston (eds)

International Economic Policy Coordination (Cambridge, Cambridge University Press).

Currie, D. A. and Levine, P. (1989) 'The International Coordination of Monetary Policy: A Survey', London Business School, mimeo.

Currie, D. A., Levine, P. and Vidalis, N. (1987) 'Cooperative and Non-cooperative Rules for Monetary and Fiscal Policy in an Empirical Two-Block Model', in R. Bryant and R. Portes (eds) *Global Macroeconomics: Policy Conflict and Cooperation* (London, Macmillan).

Davis, K. T. and Lewis, M. K. (1982) 'Can Monetary Policy Work in a Deregulated Environment?', *Australian Economic Review*, no 1.

Davis, K. T. and Lewis, M. K. (1983) 'Monetary Tactics and Monetary Targets: A Guide to Post-Campbell Monetary Policy', *Economic Papers*, April.

Diamond, D. W. (1984) 'Financial Intermediation and Delegated Monitoring', *Review of Economic Studies*, 51, pp.393–414.

Diamond, D. W. and Dybvig, P. H. (1983) 'Bank Runs, Deposit Insurance, and Liquidity', *Journal of Political Economy*, vol. 91, no 3, pp.401–19.

Dornbusch, Rudiger (1976) 'Expectations and Exchange Rate Dynamics', *Journal of Political Economy*, 84, December, pp.1161–76.

Dow, J. C. R. and Saville, I. D. (1988) *A Critique of Monetary Policy* (Oxford, Oxford University Press).

Dowd, Kevin (1988) *Private Money: The Path to Monetary Stability*, Hobart Paper no 112 (London, The Institute of Economic Affairs).

Dowd, K. (1989) *The State and the Monetary System* (Hemel Hempstead, Herts, Philip Allan, and New York, St Martin's Press).

Downs, Anthony (1957) *An Economic Theory of Democracy* (New York: Harper & Row).

Downs, A. (1961) 'In Defence of Majority Voting', *Journal of Political Economy*, 69, April, pp.192–9.

Driffill, E. John (1987) 'Macroeconomic Policy Games with Incomplete Information: Extensions and Generalizations', mimeo, University of Southampton.

England, Catherine (1988) 'Agency Costs and Unregulated Banks: Could Depositors Protect Themselves?' *Cato Journal*, 7 (Winter) pp.771–97.

Fama, E. (1980) 'Banking in the Theory of Finance', *Journal of Monetary Economics*, vol. 6, no 1, pp.39–57.

Fama, E. (1985) 'What's Different about Banks', *Journal of Monetary Economics*, vol. 15, no 1, January, pp.29–39.

Fama, E. F. and Jensen, M. C. (1983) 'Agency Problems and Residual Claims', *Journal of Law and Economics*, 26, pp.327–49.

Federal Deposit Insurance Corporation (1983) *Deposit Insurance in a Changing Environment* (Washington, DC).

Federal Home Loan Bank Board (1983) *Agenda for Reform* (Washington, DC).

Federal Reserve Board Staff (1979) 'A Discussion Paper Concerning Reserve Requirements on Eurocurrency Deposits', mimeo, April.

Fellner, William (1976) 'Towards a Reconstruction of Macroeconomics – Problems of Theory and Policy', *American Enterprise Institute.*

Fellner, William (1979) 'The Credibility Effect and Rational Expectations: Implications of the Gramlich Study', *Brookings Papers on Economic Activity*, no , pp.57–89.

Fetter, Frank Whitson (1965) *Development of British Monetary Orthodoxy* (Cambridge, Mass: Harvard University Press).

Fischer, Stanley (1980) 'Dynamic Inconsistency, Cooperation and the Benevolent Disembling Government', *Journal of Economic Dynamics and Control*, no 2, pp.93–107.

Fischer, Stanley (1986) 'Time-Consistent Monetary and Fiscal Policy: A Survey', mimeo (Cambridge, Mass., Massachusetts Institute of Technology).

Flannery, Mark J. and Protopapadakis, Aris A. (1985) 'Risk-Sensitive Deposit Insurance: The Pricing of Federal Deposit Insurance', Federal Reserve Bank of Philadelphia, *Business Review* (September/October) pp.45–57.

Fousek, P. G. (1957) *Foreign Central Banking: The Instruments of Monetary Policy* (Federal Reserve Bank of New York).

Frankel, Jeffrey A. (1979) 'On the Mark: A Theory of Floating Exchange Rates Based upon Real Interest Differentials', *American Economic Review*, December, pp.601–22.

Frankel, J. A. (1988) 'The Implications of Conflicting Models for Coordination between Monetary and Fiscal Policy-makers', in R. Bryant *et al.* (eds) *Empirical Macroeconomics for Interdependent Economies* (Washington, The Brookings Institution).

Frankel, J. A. and Rockett, K. E. (1988) 'International Macroeconomic Coordination when Policy Makers Do Not Agree on the True Model', *American Economic Review*, vol. 78, pp.318–40.

Friedman, B. M. (1975) 'Targets, Instruments, and Indicators of Monetary Policy', *Journal of Monetary Economics*, 1, October, pp.443–73.

Friedman, James W. (1977) *'Oligopoly and the Theory of Games'* (Amsterdam: North-Holland).

Friedman, Milton (1953) 'The Case For Flexible Exchange Rates' in *Essays in Positive Economics*, University of Chicago Press.

Friedman, M. (1980) 'Memorandum on Monetary Policy', in Treasury and Civil Service Committee, *Memoranda on Monetary Policy*, Series 1979–80 (London, HMSO).

Friedman, M. (1986) 'The Resource Cost of Irredeemable Paper Money', *Journal of Political Economy*, vol. 94, no 3, pp.642–7.

Friedman, M. A. (1968) 'The Role of Monetary Policy', *American Economic Review*, vol. 58, no 1 (March).
Friedman, M. A. and Schwartz, A. J. (1963) *A Monetary History of the United States 1867–1960* (Princeton, Princeton University Press).
Garcia, Gillian (1988) 'The FSLIC is "Broke" in More Ways Than One', *Cato Journal*, 7 (Winter) pp.727–41.
Garfinkel, Michelle R. and Thornton, Daniel L. (1989) 'The Link Between M1 and the Monetary Base in the 1980s', Federal Reserve Bank of St. Louis *Review* (September/October) pp.35–52.
Garfinkel, M. R. and Thornton, Daniel, L. (1990) 'The Monetary Base and the Money Multiplier: A Critical Appraisal', unpublished manuscript.
Ghosh, A. R. and Masson, P. R. 'International Policy Coordination in a World with Model Uncertainty', *IMF Staff Papers*, vol. 35, no 2, pp.230–59.
Gilbert, R. Alton (1986) 'Requiem for Regulation Q: What It Did and Why It Passed Away', Federal Reserve Bank of St Louis *Review* (February) pp.22–37.
Goodfriend, Marvin (1986) 'Monetary Mystique: Secrecy and Central Banking', *Journal of Monetary Economics*, no 17, pp.63–92.
Goodhart, C. A. E. (1988) *The Evolution of Central Banks* (Cambridge, Mass., MIT Press).
Goodhart, C. A. E. (1989) 'The Conduct of Monetary Policy'. *Economic Journal*, vol. 99, no 396, (June).
Goodhart, C. A. E. (1990) 'Are Central Banks Necessary?' in *Unregulated Banking: Chaos or Order?* Capie, F. and Wood, G. E. (eds) (London, Macmillan).
Gordon, D. F. (1974) 'A Neo-Classical Theory of Keynesian Unemployment', *Economic Inquiry*, 12, pp.431–59.
Greenfield, R. L. and Yeager, L. B. (1983) 'A *laissez-faire* approach to Monetary Stability', *Journal of Money, Credit and Banking*, vol. 15, no 3 (August).
Greenspan, Alan (1990) '1990 Monetary Policy Objectives', Testimony of the Chairman of the Federal Reserve System before Congress, 20 February 1990.
Gurley, J. G. and Shaw, E. S. (1960) *Money in a Theory of Finance* (Washington, Brookings Institution).
Hahn, Frank (1982) *Money and Inflation* (Oxford: Basil Blackwell).
Hall, R. E. (1986) 'Optimal Monetary Institutions and Policy', ch. 5 in C. Campbell and W. Dougan (eds) *Alternative Monetary Regimes* (Baltimore, Johns Hopkins University Press).
Hamada, K. (1974) 'Alternative Exchange Rate Systems and the Interdependence of Monetary Policies', in R. Z. Aliber (ed.) *National Monet-*

ary Policies and the International Financial System (Chicago, University of Chicago Press).

Hamada, K. (1976) 'A Strategic Analysis of Monetary Interdependence', *Journal of Political Economy*, vol. 84, pp. 677–700.

Hamada, K. (1979) 'Macroeconomic Strategy and Coordination under Alternative Exchange Rates', in R. Dornbusch and J. A. Frankel (eds) *International Monetary Interdependence* (Cambridge, Mass., MIT Press).

Hamada, K. (1985) *The Political Economy of International Monetary Interdependence* (Cambridge, Mass., MIT Press).

Havrilesky, Thomas (1988) 'A Partisan Theory of Fiscal and Monetary Regimes', *Journal of Money, Credit and Banking*, no 20, pp.83–101.

Hayek, F. A. (1976) *Denationalization of Money* (London: Institute of Economic Affairs).

Hetzel, Robert, L. (1985) 'The Formulation of Monetary Policy', mimeo, Federal Reserve Bank of Richmond.

Hetzel, Robert L. (1987) 'Will Recent High Growth Rates of Money Revive Inflation?' *Contemporary Policy Issues* (January) pp.41–53.

Hicks, J. R. (1969) *A Theory of Economic History* (Oxford, Clarendon Press).

Hodgman, D. R. (1963) *Commercial Bank Loan and Investment Policy* (Champaign, University of Illinois).

Hughes-Hallett, A. J. (1987) 'The Impact of Interdependence on Economic Policy Design: The Case of the US, EEC and Japan', *Economic Modelling*, vol. 10, pp.377–96.

Hughes-Hallett, A. J. (1989) 'What are the Risks in Coordinating Economic Policies Internationally', in R. MacDonald and M. P. Taylor (eds) *Exchange Rates and Open Economy Macroeconomics* (Oxford, Blackwell).

Jensen, M. and Meckling W. (1976) 'Theory of the Firm: Managerial Behavior, Agency Costs and Ownership Structure', *Journal of Financial Economics*, 3, pp.305–60.

Johansen, C. (1982) 'A Note on the Possibility of an International Equilibrium with Low Levels of Economic Activity', *Journal of International Economics*, vol. 13, pp.257–65.

Jordan, Jerry L. (1989) 'The Future of Price Stability in a Fiat Money World', *Cato Journal*, 9 (Fall) pp.471–86.

Kane, Edward J. (1980) 'Politics and Fed. Policy Making: The More Things Change, the More they Remain the Same', *Journal of Monetary Economics*, no 6, pp.199–212.

Kane, E. J. (1982) 'External Pressure and the Operation of the Fed', in Raymond E. Lombra and Willard E. Witt (eds) *Political Economy of*

International and Domestic Monetary Relations, (Iowa State University Press).

Kane, E. J. (1984) 'Technology and Regulatory Forces in the Developing Fusion of Financial Services Competition', *Journal of Finance*, vol. 39, no 3, pp.759–71.

Kane, Edward J. (1985) *The Gathering Crisis in Federal Deposit Insurance* (Cambridge, Mass., MIT Press).

Kane, E. J. (1989) *The S&L Insurance Mess: How Did it Happen?* (Washington, DC, The Urban Institute).

Kane, E. J. and Buser, S. A. (1979) 'Portfolio Diversification at Commercial Banks', *Journal of Finance*, 34, pp.19–34.

Kareken, John H. (1981) 'Deregulating Commercial Banks: The Watchword Should be Caution', Federal Reserve Bank of Minneapolis, *Quarterly Review* (Spring/Summer).

Kareken, J. H. (1984) 'Bank Regulation and Effectiveness of Open Market Operations', *Brookings Papers on Economic Activity*, no 2.

Kasriel, P. L. (1985) 'Is Deposit Rate Deregulation an RX for *M*1?' *Economic Perspectives*, Federal Reserve Bank of Chicago, September/October, pp.6–17.

Kaufman, Henry (1986) *Interest Rates, the Markets, and the New Financial World* (New York, Times Books).

Kay, J. and Vickers, J. (1988) 'Regulatory Reform in Britain', *Economic Policy*, October.

Keeler, T. E. (1984) 'Theories of Regulation and the Deregulation Movement', *Public Choice*, no 44, pp.103–45.

Kenen, P. B. (1983) 'Exchange Rates and Policy Coordination', *Brookings Discussion Papers in International Economics*, no 61.

Kimbrough, Kent, P. (1986) 'Inflation, Employment and Welfare in the Presence of Transactions Costs', *Journal of Money, Credit, and Banking*, no 18, pp.127–40.

Klein, B. (1983) 'Contracting Costs and Residual Claims: The Separation of Ownership and Control', *Journal of Law and Economics*, 26, pp.367–74.

Klein, M. A. (1973) 'The Economics of Security Divisibility and Financial Intermediation', *Journal of Finance*, 28, pp.923–31.

Klemkosky, Robert C. (1989) 'The 1980s: An Evolutionary Decade for the Financial System', *Business Horizons*, 32 (November–December) pp.2–13.

Kohn, Donald L. (1989) 'Policy Targets and Operating Procedures in the 1990s', in *Monetary Policy Issues in the 1990s*, A Symposium Sponsored by the Federal Reserve Bank of Kansas City.

Kupiec, Paul H. (1990 'Financial Liberalization and International Trends in Stock, Corporate Bond and Foreign Exchange Volatilities', Federal Reserve Board Finance and Economics Discussion Series no 131 (July).

Kydland, F. and Prescott, E. (1977) 'Rules rather than Discretion: The Inconsistency of Opimal Plans', *Journal of Political Economy*, vol. 85, pp.473–93.

Kydland, Finn and Prescott, Edward C. (1980) 'Dynamic Optimal Taxation, Rational Expectations and Optimal Control Theory', *Journal of Economic Dynamics and Control*, vol 2, pp.79–91.

Laskar, D. (1986) 'International Cooperation and Exchange Rate Stabilization', *Journal of International Economics*, vol. 21, pp.151–64.

Leland, H. E. and Pyle, D. H. (1977) 'Information Asymmetries, Financial Structure, and Financial Intermediation', *Journal of Finance*, 32, pp. 371–87.

Levi, Maurice D. (1990) *International Finance: The Markets and Financial Management of Multinational Business* (New York, McGraw Hill), 2nd edn.

Levich, Richard M. (1989) 'Is the Foreign Exchange Market Efficient?,' *Oxford Review of Economic Policy*, vol. 5, no 3, Autumn, pp.40–60.

Lewis, M. K. (1990) 'Banking as Insurance' in E. M. P. Gardener, *The Future of Financial Systems and Services: Essays in Honour of J. R. S. Revell* (London, Macmillan).

Lewis, M. K. (1990) 'Liquidity' in J. Creedy, *Foundations of Economic Thought* (Oxford, Basil Blackwell).

Lewis, M. K. and Davis, K. T. (1987) *Domestic and International Banking* (Oxford, Philip Allan and Cambridge, Mass., MIT Press).

Litan, Robert E. (1986) 'Taking the Dangers Out of Bank Deregulation'. *The Brookings Review* (Fall) pp.3–12.

Litan, R. E. (1987) 'What Should Banks Do?' (Washington, DC, Brookings Institution).

Litan, R. E. (1988) 'Reuniting Investment and Commercial Banking', *Cato Journal*, vol. 7 (Winter) pp.803–21.

Lombra, Raymond E. and Moran, Michael (1980) 'Policy Advice and Policy-Making at the Federal Reserve', *Carnegie-Rocherster Conference Series on Public Policy*, no 13, pp.9–68.

Lucas, Robert E. (1976) 'Econometric Policy Evaluation: a Critique', *Carnegie-Rochester Conference Series on Public Policy*, no 1, pp.19–46.

Lucas, Robert E. and Stokey, Nancy L. (1983) 'Optimal Fiscal and Monetary Policy in an Economy Without Capital', *Journal of Monetary Economics*, no 12, pp.55–93.

Lutz, Vera C. (1936) *The Rationale of Central Banking*, (London: P. S. King).

McCallum, B. E. (1986) 'Some Issues concerning Interest Rate Pegging, Price Level Determinancy, and the Real Bills Doctrine', *Journal of Monetary Economics*, vol. 17, no 1, January.

McKinnon, R. I. (1979) *Money in International Exchange: The Convertible Currency System* (New York, Oxford University Press).

McKinnon, R. I. (1984) 'An International Standard for Monetary Stabilization', in *Policy Analyses in International Ecomics*, no 8, (Washington, DC: Institute for International Ecomics).

McKinnon, R. I. (1988) 'Monetary and Exchange Rate Policies for International Financial Stability: A Proposal', *Journal of Economic Perspectives*, vol. 2, no 1, pp.83–106.

Mayes, D. G. and Hunn, N. (1987) 'The Macroeconomic Effects of Financial Deregulation', NEDO, EWP 26.

Meese, R. A., and Rogoff, K. (1983) 'Empirical Exchange Rate Models of the Seventies: Do They Fit Out of Sample?' *Journal of International Economics*, 14, pp.3–24.

Meltzer, A. H. (1988) *Carnegie–Rochester Conference Series on Public Policy*, no 29, pp.3–10 (Amsterdam, North-Holland).

Meyers, William (1990 'How America Is Losing Control Over Interest Rates', *Institutional Investor* (April) pp.49–54.

Miller, M. H. and Salmon, M. (1985) 'Policy Coordination and Dynamic Games', in W. H. Buiter and R. C. Marston (eds) *International Economic Policy Coordination* (Cambridge, Cambridge University Press).

Miller, M. H. and Williamson, J. (1988) 'The International Monetary System: An Analysis of Alternative Regimes', *European Economic Review*, vol. 32, pp.1031–54.

Mills, Terence C. (1989) 'The Time Series Relationship Between UK Equity, Dividend and Gilt-Edged Stock Indices', City University Business School, Midland Montagu Centre for Financial Markets, working paper no 11, November.

Minford, A., Patrick L. and Peel, David A. (1982) 'Political Theory of the Business Cycle', *European Economic Review*, no 17, pp.253–70.

Mundell, R. A. (1968) *International Economics* (New York, Macmillan).

Nordhaus, William (1975) 'The Political Business Cycle', *Review of Economic Studies*, no 42, pp.169–90.

O'Driscoll, G. P., Jr. (1985) 'Money in a Deregulated Financial System', Federal Reserve Bank of Dallas, *Economic Review* (May) pp.1–12.

O'Driscoll, G. P. (1986) 'Deregulation and Monetary Reform', Federal Reserve Bank of Dallas, *Economic Review* (July 1986) pp.19–31.

O'Driscoll, G. P., Jr (1988a) 'Deposit Insurance in Theory and Practice', *Cato Journal*, 7 (Winter) pp.661–75.

O'Driscoll, G. P. (1988b) 'Bank Failures: The Deposit Insurance Connection', *Contemporary Policy Issues*, 6 (April) pp.1–12.

Oudiz, G. (1985) 'European Policy Coordination: An Evaluation', *Recherches Economiques de Louvain*, vol. 51, pp.301–9.

Oudiz, G. and Sachs, J. (1984) 'Macroeconomic Policy Coordination Among the Industrial Economies', *Brookings Papers on Economic Activity*, vol. 1, pp.1–64.

Oudiz, G. and Sachs, J. (1985) 'International Policy Coordination in Dynamic Macroeconomic Models', in W. H. Buiter and R. C. Marston (eds) *International Economic Policy Coordination* (Cambridge, Cambridge University Press).

Parkin, Michael and Bade, Robin (1985) 'Central Bank Laws and Monetary Policy', mimeo, University of Western Ontario.

Patinkin, D. (1961) 'Financial Intermediaries and the Logical Structure of Monetary Theory', *American Economic Review*, reprinted in his *Studies in Monetary Economics* (New York, Harper & Row).

Persson, Mats, Persson, Torsten and Svensson, Lars (1987) 'Time Consistency of Monetary and Fiscal Policy', *Econometrica*, no 55, pp.1419–32.

Phelps, Edmund S. (1967) 'Phillips Curves, Expectations of Inflation and Optimal Employment Over Time', *Economica*, no 34, pp. 254–81.

Phelps, E. S. (1972) *Inflation Policy and Unemployment Theory: The Cost–Benefit Approach to Monetary Planning* (London, Macmillan).

Phelps, Edmund and Pollack, Robert A. (1968) 'Second Best National Saving and Game Equilibrium Growth' *Review of Economic Studies*, no 2, pp.185–99.

Pincus, J. J. and Withers, G. A. (1983) 'Economics of Regulation', in F. H. Gruen (ed.) *Surveys of Australian Economics*, vol. 3 (Sydney, Allen & Unwin).

Posner, R. A. (1974) 'Theories of Economic Regulation', *Bell Journal of Economics and Management Science*, no 5, pp.335–58.

Rasche, Robert H. (1987) 'M1 Velocity and Money Demand Functions: Do Stable Relationships Exist? in Karl Brunner and Allan H. Meltzer (eds) *Empirical Studies of Velocity, Real Exchange Rates, Unemployment and Productivity* (North Holland, Carnegie-Rochester Series on Public Policy) (Autumn) pp.9–88.

Rockoff, Hugh (1974) 'The Free Banking Era: A Re-examination', *Journal of Money, Credit, and Banking*, 6 (May) pp.141–67.

Rogoff, K. (1985) 'Can International Monetary Policy Coordination be Counter-productive?', *Journal of International Economics*, vol. 18, pp.199–217.

Rogoff, Kenneth (1985) 'The Optimal Degree of Commitment to an Intermediate Monetary Target', *Quarterly Journal of Economics*, no 100, pp.1169–89.

Rogoff, Kenneth (1987a) 'Reputational Constraints on Monetary Policy', *Carnegie-Rochester Conference Series on Public Policy*, no 26, pp.141–82.

Rogoff, Kenneth (1987b) 'Equilibrium Political Budget Cycles', NBER Working Paper no 2428.

Rogoff, Kenneth and Silbert, Anne (1988) 'Equilibrium Business Cycles', *Review of Economic Studies*, no 55, pp.1–16.

Rolnick, Arthur J. and Weber, Warren E. (1982) 'Free Banking, Wildcat Banking and Shinplasters', Federal Reserve Bank of Minneapolis, *Quarterly Review*, (Fall) pp.10–19.

Rolnick, A. J. and Weber, W. E. (1983) 'New Evidence on the Free Banking Era', *American Economic Review*, 73 (December) pp.1080–91.

Rolnick, A. J. and Weber, W. E. (1984) 'The Causes of Free Bank Failures: A Detailed Examination', *Journal of Monetary Economics*, 14 (October) pp.267–91.

Rolnick, A. J. and Weber, W. E. (1986) 'Inherent Instability in Banking: The Free Banking Experience', *Cato Journal*, 5 (Winter) pp.877–90.

Santomero, A. M. (1984) 'Modelling the Banking Firm: A Survey', *Journal of Money, Credit and Banking*, 16, pp.576–602.

Santoni, Gary J. (1988) 'The October Crash: Some Evidence on the Cascade Theory', Federal Reserve Bank of St Louis, *Review*, May/June, pp.18–33.

Sargent, Thomas J. (1981) 'The Ends of Four Big Inflations', NBER Working Paper.

Sargent, T. J. (1981) *Rational Expectations and Inflation* (New York, Harper & Row).

Sargent, Thomas and Wallace, Neil (1981) 'Some Unpleasant Monetarist Arithmetic', *Federal Reserve Bank of Minneapolis Quarterly Review*, no 5, pp.1–17.

Sayers, R. S. (1967) *Modern Banking* (Oxford, Clarendon Press) 7th edn.

Selgin, G. A. (1988) *The Theory of Free Banking: Monetary Supply under Competitive Note Issue* (Totowa, N. J., Rowman, Littlefield).

Shadow Financial Regulatory Committee (1989); Messrs Aspinwall, Benston *et al*, 'An Outline of a Program for Deposit Insurance and Regulatory Reform', Statement no. 41, (mimeo, 13 February).

Shiller, Robert J. (1981) 'Do Stock Prices Move Too Much to be Justified by Subsequent Changes in Dividends?' *American Economic Review*, 71 pp.421–36.

Short, Eugenie D. (1987) 'Bank Problems and Financial Safety Nets', Federal Reserve Bank of Dallas, *Economic Review* (March) pp.17–28.

Short, Eugenie D. and Gunther, Jeffery W. (1988) *The Texas Thrift Situation: Implications for the Texas Financial Industry* (Dallas: Federal Reserve Bank of Dallas).

Short, Eugenie D and O'Driscoll, Gerald P. Jr. (1983) 'Deregulation and Deposit Insurance', Federal Reserve Bank of Dallas, *Economic Review*, (September).

Silber, William, L. (1983) 'The Process of Financial Innovation', *American Economic Review*, 73 (May) p.91.

Startz, Richard (1979) 'Implicit Interest on Demand Deposits', *Journal of MacroEconomics*, October, pp.515–34.

Stigler, G. J. (1964) 'Public Regulation of the Securities Market', *Journal of Business*, reprinted in G. J. Stigler, *The Citizen and the State: Essays on Regulation* (Chicago: University of Chicago Press).

Stigler, G. J. (19710 'The Theory of Economic Regulation' *Bell Journal of Economics and Management*, Spring no 2(1) pp.1–21.

Stigler, G. J. and Friedland, C. (1962) 'What can Regulators Regulate? The Case of Electricity', *Journal of Law and Economics*, October; reprinted in G. J. Stigler, *The Citizen and the State: Essays on Regulation* (Chicago: University of Chicago Press).

Stiglitz, J. E. (1985) 'Credit Markets and the Control of Capital', *Journal of Money, Credit, and Banking*, no 17, pp.133–52.

Stiglitz, J. E. and Weiss, A. (1981) 'Credit Rationing in Markets with Imperfect Information', *American Economic Review*, no 71, pp.393–410.

Stone, Courteney C. and Thornton, Daniel L. (1987) 'Solving the 1980s' Velocity Puzzle: A Progress Report', Federal Reserve Bank of St Louis *Review* (August/September) pp.5–23.

Summers, Lawrence H. (1985) 'On Economics and Finance', *Journal of Finance*; 40 (July) pp.633–6.

Swoboda, A. K. and Dornbusch, R. (1973) 'International Adjustment, Macroeconomic Policy and Monetary Equilibrium in a Two-Country Model of Income Determination', in M. B. Connolly and A. K. Swoboda (eds) *International Trade and Money* (London, Allen & Unwin).

Tatom, John (1990) 'The Effects of Financial Innovations on Checkable Deposits, M1 and M2', Federal Reserve Bank of St Louis *Review* (July/August) pp.37–57.

Tew, B. (1977) *Evolution of the International Monetary System, 1945–1977* (London, Hutchinson).

Thornton, Daniel L. (1983a) 'The FOMC in 1982: De-emphasizing M1', Federal Reserve Bank of St Louis *Review* (June/July) pp.26–35.

Thornton, Daniel L. (1983b) 'Why Does Velocity Matter?' Federal Reserve Bank of St Louis *Review* (December) pp.5–13.

Timberlake, R. H. Jr (1978) *The Origins of Central Banking in the United States* (Cambridge, Mass., Harvard University Press).

Timberlake, R. H. Jr. (1984) 'The Central Banking Role of Clearing-house Associations', *Journal of Money, Credit and Banking*, vol. 16, no 1 (February).

Tobin, J. (1958) 'Liquidity Preference as Behaviour Towards Risk', *Review of Economic Studies*, 25, pp.65–86.

Tobin, J. (1982) 'A Commercial Banking Firm: A Simple Model', *Scandinavian Journal of Economics*, 84, pp.495–530.

Tobin, J. (1963) 'Commercial Banks as Creators of Money', in D. Carson (ed.) *Banking and Monetary Studies*, reprinted in J. Tobin, *Essays in*

Economics, vol. 1, *Macroeconomics* (Amsterdam, North Holland, 1971).

Tobin, J. (1969) 'A General Equilibrium Approach to Monetary Theory' *Journal of Money, Credit and Banking*, February.

Tobin, James (1970) 'A Proposal for International Monetary Reform' *Eastern Economic Journal*, 4, pp.153–9.

Trehan, Bharat and Walsh, Carl E. (1987) 'Portfolio Substitution and Recent M1 Behavior', *Contemporary Policy Issues* (January) pp.54–63.

Triffin, R. (1960) *Gold and the Dollar Crisis* (New York, Yale University Press).

Turnovsky, S. and d'Orey, V. (1986) 'Monetary Policies in Interdependent Economies with Stochastic Disturbances: A Strategic Approach', *Economic Journal*, vol. 96, pp.696–721.

Van Hoose, D. D. (1988) 'Floating Rate Loan Contracts and Monetary Policy', *Finance and Economics Discussion Series'*, no 13 (Washington, DC, Federal Reserve Board).

Van Horne, James C. (1985) 'Of Financial Innovations and Excesses', *Journal of Finance*, 40 (July) pp.621–31.

Vickers, John (1986) 'Signalling in a Model of Monetary Policy with Incomplete Information', *Oxford Economic Papers*, no 38, pp.443–55.

Wallace, N. (1983) 'A 'Legal Restrictions' Theory of the Demand for "Money" and the Role of Monetary Policy', *Federal Reserve Bank of Minneapolis Quarterly Review*, vol. 7, no 1 (Winter).

Weintraub, Robert (1978) 'Congressional Supervision of Monetary Policy', *Journal of Monetary Economics*, no 4, pp.341–62.

Wenninger, John (1984) 'Financial Innovation in the United States', in Bank for International Settlements, *Financial Innovations and Monetary Policy* (Basle: BIS) pp.260–70.

White, Lawrence H. (1984) *Free Banking in Britain, Theory, Experience, and Debate, 1800–1845* (New York and Cambridge, Cambridge University Press).

White, Lawrence H. (1986) 'Regulatory Sources of Instability in Banking', *Cato Journal* 5 (Winter) pp.891–97.

Williamson, J. (1985) 'The Exchange Rate System', *Policy Analyses in International Economics*, no 5, Institute for International Economics.

Woolley, John (1984) *Monetary Politics – the Federal Reserve and the Politics of Monetary Policy* (Cambridge: Cambridge Uniersity Press).

Yeager, L. B. (1985) 'Deregulation and Monetary Reform', *American Economic Review*, vol. 75, papers and Proceedings (May).

Author Index

Subject Index